The Child's Mind

What is the child's mind? How does it work? And what should parents and teachers know about it to help them in their daily interaction with children?

This book is a fascinating, non-technical introduction to the mental life of the child. Written in a simple, accessible way for those without an academic background in philosophy, the book explores and explains key elements of the child's mind without overwhelming the reader with complicated theories. Some of the areas discussed are:

- How children learn concepts
- The acquisition of beliefs, skills, knowledge and understanding
- The place of memory
- Can we teach thinking skills?
- What is intelligence?
- Imagination and creativity
- The development of emotion.

Throughout the book, connexions are made with ideas about home life, education and the school curriculum. Teachers, student teachers and parents will all find this book an intriguing journey into the mind of the child.

John White is Professor of Philosophy of Education at the Institute of Education, University of London. He has written several books on the learner's mind, educational aims and the school curriculum.

The Child's Mind

John White

London and New York

First published 2002
by RoutledgeFalmer
11 New Fetter Lane, London EC4P 4EE

Simultaneously published in the USA and Canada
by RoutledgeFalmer
29 West 35th Street, New York, NY 10001

RoutledgeFalmer is an imprint of the Taylor & Francis Group

© 2002 John White

Typeset in Bembo by Steven Gardiner Ltd, Cambridge
Printed and bound in Great Britain by St Edmundsbury Press,
Bury St Edmunds, Suffolk

British Library Cataloguing in Publication Data
A catalogue record for this book is available from the British
Library

Library of Congress Cataloging in Publication Data
A catalog record for this book has been requested

ISBN 0-415-24783-7

Contents

Acknowledgements

I am grateful to the many students of the Institute of Education, University of London, who over the years have helped me to refine my ideas on the mind and its place in education. I would also like to thank the Institute itself for the endless stimulation it has provided on all educational matters in the time I have been a member of it.

Only one place rivals it in my affections. This is Birkbeck College, also part of London University. Like the Institute, its lights have always shone brightly in the evening – as an intellectual home for teachers and other day-time workers on undergraduate and other courses.

Birkbeck gave me an education. I thought I was going to get one earlier at Oxford University, but that left me in a wilderness. Birkbeck was wonderful. Tutors with ideas, fellow-students keen to thrash them through. It was a world away from Oxford.

It was at Birkbeck that I began to find out about the mind. First, from Richard Peters, who ran the joint honours course in Philosophy and Psychology, for which I had enrolled. A brilliant teacher, he carved out silences, which he was careful not to interrupt, for us to wrestle invisibly with some bewilderingly difficult question he had put to us.

I am at least as indebted to David Hamlyn, in his case for introducing us to the philosophy of mind in a systematic and lucid way, undermining misconceptions, revealing interconnexions, taking us down with him into the depths.

More immediately, I am very grateful to Anna Clarkson, my editor at Routledge/Falmer, for her steadfast support in the writing of this book.

Turning to the latter, parts of Chapter 5 have appeared in White, J. (1998) *Do Howard Gardner's Multiple Intelligences Add Up?* London: Institute of Education.

Introduction

One day last summer I was enjoying a pub lunch on a terrace over-looking Lathkill Dale in Derbyshire. I soon realised that most of the other diners were primary school teachers. They were on some kind of in-service training day. From what I overheard, one or two of them would have liked to spend the afternoon wandering about in the sunshine. But at two o'clock they all dutifully went back inside the inn for the next session. As I was leaving, I passed the open door of the room where they were meeting. On the overhead there was a diagram of brain cells. The lecturer was saying 'So that's what learning is', pointing to a link between two cells. 'Learning is what happens when there is transmission through the synapse.'

Would the teachers have spent the afternoon more profitably walking through Lathkill Dale? I do not know. Did they go home knowing more about what it is for children to learn something? How helpful to their daily work was the lesson on neurophysiology?

The sad thing is that they all must have had a fair idea of what learning is already. How could they not have, seeing they spend their days trying to get children to learn things? Probably their grasp of the topic was not very systematic or well-grounded theoretically. It arose from the specific features of their experience. But given they wanted to know more, what was the best way forward? Did finding out facts about the brain throw light on what they were already unreflectively aware of?

I doubt it. Studying synapses may help us to know what is physiologically necessary for learning to occur, but teachers do not normally need to know this for their job. What happens in the brain when children learn is different from what learning *is*.

There is another way of helping teachers – including parents – to deepen their understanding. Hence this book.

The question 'How does the mind work?' can be taken in more than one sense. Steven Pinker's (1997) lively book of this title seeks to explain why it is that we have mental images, feel disgust, want to have children. He looks for the *underlying mechanisms* that produce these things. He finds them chiefly in brain activity seen in computational terms, but also, more broadly, in an evolutionary account of why we human animals come to have the mental life we do.

This book also looks at how the mind – more specifically, the child's mind – works, but more directly. Pinker is more at home among the *causes* of mental phenomena than among the phenomena themselves and their interrelationships. We all know that our mental life seems to fall into different areas: thought, memory, sensation, emotion, desire and so on. Most, if not all, of these are central to the task of bringing up and teaching children. How far should understanding something about how *these* work be part of the equipment of every teacher and parent?

Knowing how the child's mind works in this sense is understanding more about what emotion, belief, imagination, etc. *are*; the complex and manifold connexions between them; the nature, more globally, of the mind of which they all form a part.

There are philosophical books written about these matters that explore them for their own sake. This book is more practically committed. It has in view, first and last, the needs of parents and teachers. Each of its chapters seeks to throw light not only on some aspect of the child's mind, but also on educational applications. Just as Chapter 2, for instance, goes from an account of what concepts are to matters of how children acquire them, Chapter 9 takes us from the nature of emotion in general to the opportunities for emotional education that this examination suggests. A fuller account of this is to be found in the chapter-by-chapter account of the book at the end of this introduction.

The book also connects with matters of current educational debate. Suppose as a teacher you want to make up your own mind about the fashionable notions of 'thinking skills' and 'creative development' promoted by the government. You would also like to know where you stand on issues of intelligence and the IQ that are always bobbing up in educational circles and in the media. You are aware that psychologists are now writing about 'emotional intelligence', claiming that EQ is as important for schools as IQ. You have just come back from an INSET day and feel vaguely uneasy, without knowing why, about the message that learning is all a matter of changes in brain states.

To answer a question left hanging a while back: teachers and parents can be excellent at their job without feeling the need to go further into issues like those mentioned in the last few paragraphs. But some find the questions troublesome and would like to get clearer about them.

If you are among them, you may want to know 'how the mind works' in the sense that you are looking for a fuller understanding of the phenomena just mentioned and interconnexions between them. Will a study of neurophysiology or computer models of the brain help you sort out your ideas here? You are just not sure. All you know is that if you are to do your job properly you have somehow got to get things clearer.

Psychology is the science of the mind, but your experience of it may have been disappointing. It may have come into your teacher education course and you may have read the odd work or article since then. Book titles and chapter headings have looked promising enough: the infant mind, teaching thinking, motivating classroom learning, multiple intelligences, creativity and learning. . . . But however absorbing particular topics have been, somehow these books have never quite delivered the goods – at least not the goods *you* want. They have given you theories – Piaget's, Skinner's, Bruner's. They have described experiments, looked at brain mechanisms, described cases, presented diagrams. But – for you at least – it has never all quite come together. You have had bits and pieces of the story, but not the whole picture. You have been given isolated symbols of main roads, farm tracks, woodland, power-lines, windmills – when what you have needed all along is a *map*.

That is what this book aims to provide – a map of the child's mind and its main features, showing how they are interrelated with each other. It concentrates on what is particularly likely to interest parents and teachers. Minds are the raw material of the educator. They are what teachers and parents work on and shape, just as the sculptor works on and shapes blocks of marble. (I realise this simile should not be pushed too far.) If it helps sculptors to know the general properties of marble, it helps educators to know what minds are, how they work and how their different parts fit together. This knowledge, like the sculptor's, makes them less likely to make a wrong move. More positively, it guides them, often unconsciously, in their day-to-day work of child-rearing and teaching.

Maps do not give you a detailed knowledge of a terrain. This book will not tell you everything you need to know about children's minds. What it *will* give you is a framework. It describes the essential features of any child's mind and why it is impossible to understand one part of the mind without understanding other parts.

How does it do it? The method will best be revealed by the book itself as we work through different features of the child's mind. The only point to make here is this. Before we ever come to psychology or philosophy we each already have inchoate ideas of what minds, including children's minds, are like and must be like. The ideas are as often as not dim ones, deeply hidden in the thought-structures we have about minds and bodies, thinking, knowledge, memories, mental images, the self. There is a job to be done in bringing these inchoate ideas into the light, helping us to clarify them, disentangle them from less reliable notions with which they may have got caught up.

In time-honoured pedagogical fashion, then, this book begins from what you already know. It picks up from the pre-philosophical understanding of how children's minds work just mentioned and engages you in elementary philosophical clarification. Bit by bit, it builds up a more complete, more precise picture. It does not present you with a wide array of new facts (although factual matters do come into the picture – for example, to do with similarities between human beings and other animals). Like all philosophy, this book aims to give deeper insights into what is half-known already – to make the way you conceptualise mental phenomena more systematic and interconnected. In this way, as well as being a practical guide in the upbringing of children, it may also serve as a vehicle of self-knowledge.

I have just described the book as a practical guide, but I do not want to claim too much. The book does not set out to give you tips on what to do in specific situations. The chapter on motivation, for instance, does not dispense detailed advice about how to switch on an unswitched-on class. The practicality of the book lies farther back, in helping you to bring to bear on all your work an improved understanding of the delicate piece of equipment at its centre.

Some investigations are about what the world *is* like; others, about what it would be *good* for it to be like. The questions this book tackles fall into the first category. It maps what a part of the world is like – the territory of children's minds. But a number of the topics under discussion raise ethical issues, too. What aspects of the child's imagination should be encouraged, and why? All of them, some of them? In which ways? Should schools teach general thinking skills? Should parents and teachers rely exclusively on intrinsic motivation?

My strategy in the book has been to welcome these ethical questions, even though they do not fall under the philosophy of mind, the branch of philosophy to which the book belongs. Occasionally I pursue these questions at some length. More often I simply indicate that I am about to pass the frontier from one philosophical territory into another and rein the argument hard back. My intention has been, as far as possible, to keep the lines as clear as possible. The book is basically an essay in the philosophy of mind as applied to children's education. It abuts onto issues about what we *should* be doing in upbringing and schooling. Many of these lead back to fundamental questions about what the aims of education should be in general. There is a whole other literature about these ethical matters. If you wish to follow it up, you will find occasional references to it in the sections on Further reading at the end of each chapter.

Mention of the Further reading sections leads me to the book's style. My aim has been to introduce readers new to the subject to philosophical perspectives on the child's mind in a readable and immediate way. I would like them to see the importance of the issues discussed for their own interactions with children. To this end I have kept the text free of footnotes and to a large extent free of references to those arguments from other philosophers on which much of the work relies. Considerations of accessibility and readability have won out, in other words, over normal academic conventions.

If you want to go further into the philosophy of mind in general – that is, without necessarily applying this to education – you will find the first part of the Further reading sections at the end of each chapter helpful. I have also usually included a later paragraph within these Further reading sections on work in the applied field of philosophy of education. This includes some now-classic texts in the area as well as recent writings.

Alternatively, you may have your sights trained on studies in psychology rather than philosophy – either as a teacher or parent, or as an A level student of psychology. If so, you will find in this book a map of the mind's main features that you will be hard pressed to discover in the psychological literature. It has always been amazing to me that academic psychology, as the scientific investigation of the mind, so often leaves one without an overall picture of what the mind and its main areas are. This book seeks, among other things, to make up for that shortfall.

I turn now to a chapter-by-chapter account of the book.

Chapter 1 looks at the big picture – at the child's mind in general as distinct from its more specific areas. Is the mind the same as the soul, or as the spirit? Is it to be identified with the intellect – as so much of what takes place within the school curriculum would seem to suggest? How do we go about finding out what sorts of things minds are? What are their distinguishing features? Is consciousness the key? If so, what about the Unconscious? Do only human beings have minds, or do other animals have them as well? The chapter claims that not all the features of the child's mind are of interest to educators, only those which – unlike, say, headaches – can be altered through learning. It goes into more depth on what these educationally-relevant aspects of the mind involve. Concepts and concept-learning come centrally into the picture at this point. These are briefly introduced here, anticipating a fuller treatment of them in Chapter 2.

Before leaving Chapter 1, a word about how it links up with the Appendix. This is called 'More about minds'. One of the great mysteries about our mental life is how it is connected with our physicality. Mind–body issues have exercised philosophers from Plato and Aristotle through to the present day. Today's specialists in the philosophy of mind tend, in fact, to focus on mind–body questions almost exclusively. It is not surprising that discussions in this area have become increasingly complex and technical in recent years. The present book, which has grown out of experience of working with teachers, moves in a different direction. It is built around the claim that, intrinsically fascinating and important though this more technical material is, it has less immediately to offer parents and teachers (and some of those beginning basic courses in psychology or philosophy) than a more comprehensive survey of the mind, its main areas and their place in education. At the same time, a brief introduction to work in the mind–body field would seem helpful. Hence the Appendix. I say more about it below.

Chapter 2 goes further than Chapter 1 into the nature of concepts and their acquisition. What are concepts? Are they ideas in our heads? Do they depend on the use of language? If they do, does that mean that non-human animals cannot possess them? The chapter uses a wide-angle lens to include a kind of conceptualisation of which dogs, cats and other species are capable, arguing that this also plays a vital part in human life, not least in upbringing. Language-dependent concepts are treated as a separate topic and their main features spelt out. There is a digression in this first part of the chapter on the currently fashionable notion of philosophy for children.

The second part of the chapter looks at how concepts are learned – if indeed they *are* learned as distinct from being part of children's genetic constitution as innate ideas. Do children acquire a concept like blue by abstracting the common feature of the blue things they experience, as some versions of 'learning by discovery' have claimed? How far can children acquire concepts on their own? How important in concept learning are children's social relationships? Must children be deliberately inducted into the world of concepts?

Chapter 3 builds on both its predecessors. Its main topic is believing and its role in children's lives. As we grow up, our minds become stocked with countless interconnecting beliefs, some false, probably most true. Collectively they make up, in the words of the chapter title, 'maps by which we steer'. Part of the process of education is about guiding children away from false beliefs towards the true ones that lie at the root of *knowledge*. (But if we put all our eggs in the Truth basket, does this not rule out encouraging children's flights of fancy or their enjoyment of fiction?) After a brief introduction to the various main types of knowledge and their relation to teaching and learning, the chapter concludes with a section on memory and its place in education. In the days when faculty psychology was strong, memory-training, often of rote-learnt items, was a standard part of education. Does it still have a place?

Chapter 4 examines a way of looking at the mind that modern educators have always found attractive. It sees the mind as analogous to a biological entity – a plant seed, perhaps, or a fertilised animal egg. Just as the apple pip, given the right conditions, develops by stages into a mature Worcester Pearmain, so the child's mind unfolds by stages into maturer and maturer forms. This picture goes with a certain view of upbringing and schooling, one which leaves as much as possible to the guidance of nature. But how acceptable is this way of seeing the child's mind? Can the biological analogy survive criticisms brought against it? If social shaping is as important in concept-formation as Chapter 2 may indicate, is it more of a hindrance than a help to children's learning for them to be brought up on developmentalist lines?

Psychologists as well as philosophers are students of the mind. How do the two disciplines differ in their approach? One example of this comes in Chapter 5. This looks at the nature of intelligence. What is the relationship between a child's intelligence and his or her IQ? Is intelligence a biological phenomenon, implanted in children innately? Or is it the product of social shaping? Psychologists have made claims on either side of this argument. Some have turned away from IQ-related accounts to write, as Howard Gardner does, about 'multiple intelligences'. Part of the philosopher's remit is to examine the logical credentials of these various psychological approaches. Another part is to examine more directly how the notion of intelligence is to be understood, and how it is to be connected with other mental phenomena and ideas about upbringing discussed in this book.

Chapter 6, on thinking, has obvious links with the chapter on intelligence and also draws on conclusions established in earlier chapters. Increasingly, parents as well as teachers want children not just to learn facts but also to think for themselves. In England and Wales government policy has recently reflected this by building the teaching of general thinking skills into the National Curriculum. But what is thinking? How can we get a grip on such an intangible phenomenon? Is the belief that there are general thinking skills well-founded? Or is it the product of another of those recurring enthusiasms in educational circles that seem to open all sorts of doors but in fact lead up gumtrees? This chapter goes into these issues. In doing so, it warns against assuming that thinking is just one sort of thing. It can take several very different forms, all of which should have a place in the education – perhaps with very different priorities from those most current today.

Chapter 7 grows out of Chapter 6 in that when children are exercising their imagination they are engaged in a kind of thinking. Once again, when people ask themselves the question 'What is the imagination?' they are often at a loss to know how to go on. They come up against that frustrating sense of bewilderment that affects us all when we try to get a grip on the abstract, slippery terms we use in describing our mental life – 'belief', 'concept', 'consciousness', 'thought', 'feeling'. This chapter tries to show how to get over this bewilderment as far as 'imagination' is concerned. It shows how a huge, ungraspable issue can be broken down into a number of smaller, more manageable issues. It argues, in fact, that there is not one concept of the imagination, but at least three, all of which are vitally important in developing the child's mind. Children not only see pictures in their minds, they also learn to put themselves in other people's places or are encouraged to hypothesise about physical events in science or social events in history. What, finally, about creativity? Educators have perennially found this an attractive notion. What role does it have in children's learning?

How to motivate children in their learning is a question always high on teachers' – and parents' – agendas. Chapter 8 does not set out to give specific practical tips on this, but it *does* aim at providing a sketch-map of the topic that picks out its educationally important features.

Children are active creatures. Understanding their motivations needs to be set in the wider context of an understanding of human agency itself. The earlier part of this chapter looks at the roles of desires and beliefs in children's behaviour and how these may be shaped in educationally significant directions. The later part goes into different kinds of motivation − intrinsic, purely instrumental, and part-whole − on which teachers and parents can rely. It also looks at motivation as a topic in its own right in the *content* of children's education. This has to do with their growing self-knowledge and understanding of other people.

The child's emotional life is the topic of Chapter 9. What *kind* of phenomenon is anger, or pride, or fear? When children feel these things, are they like, say, feelings of thirst that appear to take place inside them and to be unobservable to outsiders? If so, what can educators do about them beyond encouraging the children in traditional British fashion to 'keep a stiff upper lip'? This chapter argues for a different way of looking at the emotions, focussing on the *thoughts* embodied in them and the ways these can be developed − and challenged − through education. It also explores what teachers and parents can do in other directions − in shaping the expression of emotions and their role in behaviour and the formation of character. The chapter concludes with a section on the education of love.

The concluding Chapter 10 leaves behind specific areas of mental life and looks, more globally, at the whole child. A child is a person, a self. But what *is* this self that thinks, feels pain and desires things? Can it be discovered by introspection? Is it identifiable with the mind or soul? Or with the body? Or with the items in our stream of consciousness? Again, could the self be equated with the subject of experience − the 'I' that comes into expressions like 'I feel hungry' or 'I think I know the way'? The last part of the chapter charts several stages in the development of the self from birth to late childhood. What part in this is played by the child's mastery of personal pronouns − and by the self-awareness which then becomes possible on the back of this mastery?

Some readers may wish to begin the book with this last chapter, precisely because it does raise global questions about the whole child. Those who do so may find it best then to go back to Chapter 1 and work through the chapters in order. Other readers may prefer to begin directly with Chapter 1 and then work through the book in the same way. It will have been clear from this summary that later chapters build on the conclusions of early ones, so reading the chapters in the order presented is perhaps the best way of building up a systematic picture of the mind and its sub-divisions.

The book ends with the Appendix, already flagged, called 'More about minds'. This takes up the issue, briefly mentioned in Chapter 1, of how the mind is related to the body and more particularly to the brain. It moves away from the more directly educationally applicable material of the main body of the book into what has become the central preoccupation of philosophers of mind. The late twentieth century saw a number of attempts to challenge the picture bequeathed to us by Descartes in the seventeenth century of the mental and the physical as two separate metaphysical realms. Descartes's view that minds and bodies causally interact at a point in the brain has been replaced by a variety of physicalist theories, each claiming in different ways that there is no separate realm of mental phenomena over and above the physical. Not all contemporary philosophers believe in physicalism, however, some holding that it cannot account, for instance, for what our experience feels like to us when we are in pain. It is not surprising that philosophers should spend so long crossing swords on this issue, because it is fundamentally about the nature of reality in general and whether it is, or is not, wholly physical. The chapter is an introduction to some of the most prominent of the recent theories. It is also a reminder that the further we proceed along these metaphysically central highways, the more likely we are to leave direct educational relevance behind.

Chapter 1

What is the child's mind?

Two perspectives

What is the child's mind?

There are two ways of looking at this. An ancient belief is that human beings are essentially immortal souls. In this earthly life we are embodied. Our bodies are unlike those of other animals. Our soul animates them. In this life it enables us to keep our animal nature under the proper control of reason. When we die, our body decays but mental functions somehow live on. Not all of them, no doubt. Some may be too bound up with the body and perish when it dies: toothache, the sense of smell, butterflies in the stomach that come with fear. But beyond the grosser phenomena are subtler, more refined, less obviously bodily-dependent features of our mentality – perhaps our capacity for abstract thought, for contemplation, for holding to our beliefs, for remembering things. When we die, it may be only the higher part of our mind that lives on. On some views it is this superior, reflective part of us that we call the soul. It is what we really *are*.

Many today reject all this. They would say there is no scientific basis for it. There is no evidence that we survive death. Perhaps the very notion that we can is meaningless. We need to start with what we know and not with a theological fairy story. What we know is that human beings are a species of animal. Like other species, we have evolved from other forms of life. Our minds are not entities distinct from our bodies and outliving them. Our mental life is continuous with that of other animals. Some of these are capable of intelligent action, feelings of fear and pain, abilities to see, hear and smell. Peculiarly human attributes such as the capacity for abstract and creative thought can only be understood in the light of this broader biological background.

Eighty years ago the educationalist Fred Clarke (1923, p. 2) wrote 'the ultimate reason for teaching Long Division to little Johnny is that he is an immortal soul'. You find few such pronouncements in today's more secular society. Yet the ancient view lives on in more subtle, sometimes unnoticed, ways.

Among other things, it affects ideas about education. As mentioned, it holds that if the soul – or mind – can outlive the body, these must be separable phenomena. The essential attributes of this enduring mind have least to do with the physical. Physical pains, sense-perception, desires for food, drink, sex make no sense in the absence of bodies. But thinking, at least *some* thinking, is different. The more detached from their bodily concerns children's thinking is, the closer it is to their essential nature.

We see the shadow of this traditional outlook – which goes back ultimately to Plato, via Descartes – in the prestige we attach to abstract thinking. It appears in the pride of place given to mathematics in the school curriculum. And in the belief that intelligence is best displayed through performance at the abstract tasks used to measure IQ.

True, the school curriculum typically contains other disciplines than mathematics and mathematically-related subjects like science. It also includes one's native language, foreign languages, history, geography, art, music, physical education. Even so, there is something of a pecking order among these in many educational systems. The more intellectual subjects – those more concerned with the acquisition of knowledge – are the most important, then the arts and physical education. It is as though the most abstract studies such as mathematics are put at the top of the pile while those below them get graded according to how close they are to this abstract ideal.

Some work I recently did on the school curriculum for a national British agency illustrates this well. I was looking at the match between the new aims for the school curriculum and specific requirements for all twelve National Curriculum subjects. I presented my report in *alphabetical* order of subjects. Art and Design came first, followed by Citizenship and then Design and Technology. This seemed the obvious way of doing things. I thought nothing of it

But this struck the agency officials with whom I was dealing as *most surprising*. They had taken it as read I would follow the standard order the government followed in all its documentation:

English, Mathematics, Science, Design and Technology, Information and Communication Technology, History, Geography,

Modern Foreign Languages, Art and Design, Music, Physical Education, Citizenship.

Buried in this is an official hierarchy of importance among curriculum activities, a hierarchy that broadly – admittedly not entirely – reflects the traditional priority given to the abstract and theoretical.

When we say colloquially of a child that 'she has a good mind', do we refer to her prowess in the gym or ability to draw or to play the clarinet? Hardly. We mean her intellectual abilities in knowledge-oriented disciplines like mathematics, science, history, languages. It is her powers of theoretical thinking that are at issue. The arts come lower in our estimation because they are associated not so much with the rational pursuit of truth as with the pleasures of the senses, with emotion and imagination.

The curriculum also contains physical education. The very name reflects a sharp division between mind and body. PE generally comes below intellectual activities in the school's pecking order, a healthy body being seen as a prerequisite for a healthy mind. *Mens sana in corpore sano*. More muscular variants in the English public school tradition have given bodily activities, in the form of team games, more status. But even so the basic idea here has been to tame the body, keep it exercised, healthily tire it out and control its sexual tumescences so that the mind can operate more freely.

I have emphasised the tendency of our culture – originally often for religious reasons – to divide mind from body and to rate the former higher than the latter. There is also a sociological side to this. The pecking order has traditionally run, too, through types of school. Abstract and other intellectual activities have been most closely associated with élite education in grammar and private schools and in the universities. Mass schooling has in the past traditionally had the more utilitarian aim of fitting people for a life of predominantly *physical* labour.

'He's not an academic' – the words of a successful, self-made owner of a conservatory firm. He was telling me about his son, who had just joined him in the business and would take over one day. 'Why should he be?' I felt like replying.

Problems with the traditional conception

Can children's minds and bodies be separated in the way the traditional conception requires?

For secular thinkers, the Platonic–Cartesian association between minds and souls which persist after the death of the body is obviously troublesome. For those who accept some version of evolution theory, so is the absolute divide between human beings and other animals. Is it really true that dogs and cats and chimpanzees have no mental life?

There are problems, too, in the assumption that minds are some kind of enduring entity or substance. We are familiar enough with physical entities, with chairs and tables, stones and stars. We think of them as occupying a certain volume of space, as having dimensions of length and breadth, a certain weight, and so on. But what kind of entity would a mind be like? It does not seem to be a spatial thing. Could it be an entity which exists in time but not in space?

Just because the word 'mind' is a noun, we should not jump to the conclusion that it picks out substantial things in the way that other nouns – 'planet', 'shirt', 'sea cucumber' – pick them out. We also use nouns like 'stupidity', 'indignation', or 'pride' but do not imagine that somewhere in the world there are entities to which these words refer. We understand them as abstract terms formed from the corresponding adjectives, 'stupid', 'indignant', 'proud'. Might we get further in thinking about minds if we started with the adjective 'mental'?

If we did, rather than asking 'what is the mind?' we could now ask 'what are mental phenomena?' While we had problems in giving an account of what kind of entity a mind could be, we would face no such difficulties – at least initially – in listing mental attributes.

Different people's lists will differ, but the following items will appear in many of them: thinking, remembering, feeling, wanting, deciding, being afraid, reasoning, seeing things and hearing things, imagining, intelligence, motivation. We could then ask 'what do items like these have in common in virtue of which we call them "mental"?'

One thing is for sure. The list shows immediately that associating the child's mind with rational thought or with the intellect is on the wrong track. We will not find the common factor *there*.

Take seeing things. Sophie looks round the room and sees a radiator, a door, a bookcase, a lamp. Did she have to *think anything out* in doing this? If the room had been very dark, she might have had to work out whether that dim shape was a lamp, whether that other one was indeed a vase. Thinking would certainly have come in at that point. But as things are, in good light, she simply looks round the room and sees things. There is nothing to decipher or reason through here. The whole process is immediate and unproblematic.

Take wanting. Jacob is thirsty and wants a drink. Or he is at school, it is 3.30 and he wants to go home. Desires like these are rarely based on reasoning things through. Sometimes they may be. I am hungry and want to eat. Shall I finish off the packet of salami in the fridge? Shall I go out for fish and chips? Shall I ring up for a Four Seasons? In the end, having reviewed a few pros and cons, I settle on the pizza. That is what I come to want. But while a desire like this is the product of reasoning, not all our wants are like this. Sometimes desires just happen to us, even sweep over us. We are insulted and we want to strike back; sexually roused and want satisfaction of a different sort; tired and want to sleep. In none of these cases need thinking come into the picture.

Take pain – a toothache, say. When my tooth plays up I can have all sorts of thoughts about it: 'What should I do?' 'Shall I try the emergency dentist?' 'What about crushing aspirin against it?' But the thinking that I do is not itself the toothache. The toothache comes – and I think about it. Sometimes, indeed, a toothache may come and I do not think about it at all, I just *feel* it in all its intensity.

These counterexamples – sense-perception, wanting, pain – help to undermine the association of the mental with rational thought. Minds are more inclusive.

If so, what stamps a mental phenomenon as *mental*? In virtue of what do we call seeing and hearing, problem-solving, wanting to play the Lottery, feeling a headache, all aspects of mind?

Before we turn to that, a comment on the educational upshot of all this. If we accept that mental phenomena are not restricted to intellectual matters, which path shall we take?

One way is to preserve the traditional link between education and the intellect and say that only certain types of mental phenomena – those to do with truth-seeking, reasoning and reflecting – are of interest to educators.

Another is to abandon this traditional link and say that education has to do with the development of other aspects of the child's mind than the intellectual. In this book, as should become clearer as the rest of the argument unrolls, I shall be taking the second of these paths.

This, incidentally, is a point at which this book diverges from another work with a similar title, which has now deservedly become a classic text: Margaret Donaldson's (1978) *Children's Minds*. This is a psychological, rather than a philosophical, piece of work. Its main focus is a critique of a Piagetian approach to children's thinking. It does not set out to provide, as this book does, a comprehensive look at the child's mind and its interrelated features. Donaldson takes 'mind' in the narrower, intellectual, sense and her book largely about children's reasoning abilities and their acquisition of basic skills. Unlike this book, it does not discuss the educational significance of the imagination, the emotions, or motivation.

Conscious and unconscious mind

If rational thinking is not the hallmark of children's minds, what is? We seem to need a broader category of the mental that includes not only thinking but also things like seeing, wanting, feeling pain.

What about 'consciousness'? When I look round the room and see that purple-leaved plant whose name I can never remember, my consciousness is directed onto it. Seeing something is a way of being conscious or aware of it. Similarly, when I have a pain in my knee, I have a conscious experience of an unpleasant kind. My consciousness can thus take different forms. As I type these words, I *see* them coming up on my computer screen. In the background I *hear* traffic noise from the main road. At the same time, and more focally, I am *thinking out* the argument I am constructing. More peripherally again, I feel a slight *ache* in my right leg; and experience a correspondingly slight *anxiety* about whether anything is amiss with it. All the italicised words are different forms my consciousness may take.

Among the educationally interesting features of consciousness is the distinction, just indicated, between focal and peripheral awareness. There is no sharp division, only a difference in degree. Teaching, understood as an activity intended to bring about learning, usually requires the learner to *concentrate on*, or *pay attention to* some subject-matter, to make it the object of his or her focal awareness. One of the difficulties of teaching is that what the teacher wants to be focal is sometimes only of peripheral concern to the pupil – distracted as she is by the deadbeat wasp that is dragging itself along the window-ledge. One of its satisfactions can be when what was focal – using the pedal properly when learning the piano – becomes automatic, pushed out towards the very edge of the learner's awareness.

Shall we say, then, that what holds all the different kinds of mental phenomena together as *mental* is that they are all forms of consciousness, whether focal or peripheral? If we do, though, what about *unconscious* phenomena, or, if we like to put it this way, the Unconscious Mind?

We have to be careful here, not least with the capitalised version. It is too easy to slip back into 'entity thinking'. Some of Freud's formulations have not been helpful. He sometimes leads us to think of the Unconscious as a sort of mysterious *place*, a hidden cellar, or perhaps a subterranean stream, beneath the level on which conscious experiences take place. But this is not the only way of interpreting what he has to say about the unconscious mind. On the alternative view, Freud is dealing with more complex versions of something with which we are familiar enough in our ordinary lives and from fiction.

A student half-listening to a lecture realises with embarrassment that all the doodles he has been making on the margin of his note-pad are of penis-shaped objects. There had been a sexual interest behind what he was doing, of which he was unaware. Unconscious wishes or desires like this are everyday occurrences. Freud's achievement was to extend the explanatory schemes we rely on in such cases to account for the more deeply buried repressions and self-deceptions associated with neuroses.

Freudian psychology aside, there's a much more basic way in which mental phenomena can be unconscious. As we shall soon see, this opens up a topic of key importance for teachers and learners.

Take believing. Think of the everyday, unremarkable beliefs we have about our lives and the world we live in. I believe that I live in North London, I am overweight, there are too many cars on the road these days. In writing this last sentence my mind was focused on these three beliefs. They were the object of my conscious attention. Usually, of course, I do not have occasion to dwell on them in this way. Yet even when I am not aware of them, I still believe these things. I continue to hold these beliefs as part of what I understand about my life and my world. They stay with me all the time – even, presumably, when I am asleep.

All our states of believing something are unconscious mental phenomena in the sense that they continue to exist even when they are not brought to consciousness. I shall use the word *continuants* to describe continuing features of mind such as believing.

Contrast believing with catching sight of a familiar face, working out a maths problem, feeling a stab of toothache. Here our consciousness is currently in operation. These are conscious events happening now, not more permanent states of mind. I shall call these mental *occurrences*. Other examples are: felt wants, e.g. for food when hungry; felt emotions, e.g. feeling terrified by an insect crawling over my arm; having unbidden mental images of blackberries after an August expedition to the local woods.

States of believing are not the only type of continuant. As well as wants or desires currently experienced – such as for food when hungry – we have longer-standing desires of which we are only intermittently aware – for peace on Earth, for the prosperity of our family. As well as an occurrent fear of spiders, there are more enduring versions of fear in the shape of being afraid for several months we may lose our job or our new partner.

Think, too, of the *skill* that children may have in riding a bicycle, in carpentry, in doing jigsaws, in solving algebraic equations. They can possess a skill like this when not exercising it. Louise knows how to ride a bicycle at this moment, even though she is not actually doing so. Even when she is asleep, it is still a truth about her that she has this know-how. Skills are like beliefs in this respect.

A final type of continuant is found in traits of character or personal qualities – good or bad. Take a young person who is kind, independent-minded, incorruptible, morally courageous. She may be a kind person without engaging in kind actions at the moment. When she is actively kind, she is no doubt conscious of all sorts of things – the other person's situation, what she might do to help him. At other times, she is still a kind person even though such conscious events are not occurring.

Continuants, occurrences and the essence of teaching

Mental phenomena divide into two kinds: occurrences and continuants. This raises a problem for any attempt at defining the child's mind in terms of forms of consciousness. Occurrent phenomena – hearing the phone ring, feeling hot, reminiscing about a holiday – are all conscious states; but continuants – believing that ice is cold, being proud of one's country, knowing how to play *Monopoly* – are not.

This book concentrates on educational issues. That means I shall not look at the detailed attempts made by philosophers of mind to solve this problem. Suffice it to say here that any suggestion that our mental life could be *always* continuant and *never* occurrent – always dormant but never active – is hard to credit.

Educationally speaking, continuants are of great importance.

• Parents and teachers help to equip children with webs of inter-connecting beliefs about all sorts of things – themselves, their social world, the natural world, moral behaviour, the arts, politics.

- They teach them skills – physical skills involved in playing games or making things, and mental skills like knowing how to plan out their time or test historical claims against evidence.
- They develop desirable personal qualities in children like friendliness or confidence and try to suppress unwanted ones like bad-temperedness or maliciousness.

Intertwined with all three kinds of continuant are enduring desires and emotions. Parents and teachers try to build up desirable forms of these – a love of music, the desire to help others in distress – and minimise fears of cats or delight in others' misfortunes.

These various species of continuant make up the content of education. Teachers and parents want children to acquire appropriate rather than inappropriate beliefs, skills, desires, emotions and personal qualities. They form the *enduring mental equipment* they want children to possess.

Distinctions between types of continuant are reflected in the very language of education. Think of the general types of thing children learn.

- They *learn that* something is the case – that daffodils bloom in the spring, that Mars is a planet. These beliefs constitute items of *knowledge*, in that all of them are both true and well-founded. Sometimes, however, the beliefs children acquire are not true and cannot constitute knowledge – as when children in some cultures are brought up to believe that the Earth is the centre of the universe, or that men are intrinsically superior to women.
- As well as propositional learning, or learning that . . ., children also *learn how to* do something – talk, swim, play the recorder, do mental arithmetic.
- In the course of their moral education they *learn to* be tolerant, truthful, respectful of others. In the aesthetic area they *learn to* love – be lovers of – music and poetry.

What is true of learning is also true of teaching: a mother can teach her daughter *that* she must not play in the road, *how to* make rice pudding, *to* be considerate.

These various types of continuant are best conceived as equipment. They are not only the desired end-products of teaching, but also the basis from which parents and teachers begin their work. Teaching is a matter of modifying existing beliefs, skills and personal qualities (including desires and feelings) in the direction of more adequate beliefs, skills and qualities.

How do parents and teachers do this? Only by engaging the *non-continuant*, that is, the *occurrent* features of the child's mind.

Teaching, including parenting, directs the learner's – usually, but not always, focal – consciousness onto certain objects rather than others. Children are encouraged to look at things, listen to things, use their imagination, think through problems, try to remember things, feel moral or aesthetic emotions, try their hand at some new physical activity.

The points made in the last three paragraphs are of crucial importance and will recur, in different forms, throughout this book. Teaching, and education more generally, can only be understood in terms of this distinction between mental occurrences and mental continuants.

Putting children's experience – in the shape of what they see, hear, feel, think about – at the heart of the parent's or teacher's job is surely correct. These mental occurrences happen in the *present*. Continuants add both *past* and *future* considerations.

In stimulating children to think, feel, imagine, be physically active, educators draw on the mental equipment they already possess – their 'knowledge-that', their skills, their enduring desires, feelings and dispositions of character. In turning to the past in this way, teachers also have an eye on the future. For a large part of their purpose lies in improving learners' mental equipment. Teachers of science want to deepen pupils' understanding of atomic structure; sports teachers want young tennis players to hone their net skills.

So there is a temporal patterning in education: from continuants via occurrences to continuants. The patterning is subtler than it may look. It would be too simple to claim that learning within any particular area – mathematics, say – is wholly a function of a movement through the following three stages, with the third stage as the teacher's goal:

1   A child has mathematical equipment (in the shape of knowledge, skills, attitudes towards the subject) at level X;
2   The teacher draws on this equipment to get the child to think in a new area;
3   The child comes to have more advanced mathematical equipment at level Y.

For one thing, at stage 2 teachers may draw on *other* equipment than that described in stage 1. A mathematics teacher, for instance, may use her pupils' interest in sports or music as a hook. Equally, it would be wrong to see a teacher's goals wholly in terms of stage 3. Part of what teachers aim at is that their pupils should have enjoyable experiences – in the present. They want them to take an intrinsic delight in the thinking, looking, imagining which come into stage 2. True, there is a continuant element in this aim. Teachers want children's delight in mathematical thinking or listening to poetry to become enduring. It is part of what they mean when they say they want children to come to love their subject. Even so, the teacher's aim is present- as well as future-orientated.

Objects that may or may not exist

Another feature of the child's mind cuts across the distinction between occurrent and continuant phenomena. Like the latter, it is key to all forms of education.

I mentioned just now the role of the parent or teacher in directing the pupil's consciousness onto certain *objects* rather than others. Let us look more closely at what kinds of thing these objects might be.

A child looks at and sees *a drop of pondwater* under a microscope; thinks about *a problem in geometry*; listens to *a story*; tries to remember *the past participle of 'avoir'*. The italicised phrases are all objects of consciousness in some form: looking, seeing, thinking, listening, trying to recall. These examples show that objects of consciousness are not always *material* objects. An 'object' in this context is what one's mind is directed towards.

Objects come into a child's mental life in other ways. She may be afraid *of the dark*. As she listens to *The Ancient Mariner*, she may have mental images of *sea-snakes, torrid heat, unbearable thirst*. She may want to *become an engineer*.

Continuants, too, can be object-directed. In building up children's stock of beliefs, parents and teachers want them to believe *that bullying is wrong* or *that gases expand when heated*. They also want them to come to know how to *tie up their shoelaces* or *access the Internet*.

For area after area of children's mental life, we just cannot make sense of it unless we think of it as object-directed. Children cannot look without looking *at something*. They cannot just be proud without being proud *of something*. They cannot believe without believing *that something is the case*. So, too, for all the other examples.

We will see in a moment just how important this object-directedness is in education. On the way to that, here is another – equally significant – feature of it.

Joan of Arc heard voices, but they were imaginary ones. Novelists think about fictional situations. Some people may believe, falsely, that trees can talk. A peculiar feature of the objects we are discussing is that they *need not* match reality. Of course, more often than not they *do* match it. Most of the things we hear are sounds that actually exist, not products of our imagination. Most of our beliefs are true rather than false. Even so, it remains true that the objects of our beliefs and perceptions *may* in some cases fail to fit the facts.

The objects in question are called *intentional objects*. They are the objects towards which our minds are directed when we see, think, love, imagine, remember, believe, want and so on. Examples of intentional objects are in the italicised phrases above.

A defining feature of an intentional object is that it *may or may not exist*. Children can hear pneumatic drills in the street – or voices in their heads. If they are thinking about something, this could be something that exists – like the ice cream van – or does not exist – like a land of fairies. They can be afraid of the unleashed alsatian they sometimes meet in the fields, or of the demons they know are peering at them from all sides of the room. They can have a visual experience of the computer screen they are now facing, or of their imaginary friend. They can recall embarrassing events which really happened – and personal triumphs which they have deceived themselves into believing.

It is the same with at least some continuants. Children can believe what is true – that the Moon is thousands of miles away – or what is false – that it is populated by intelligent creatures. They can be fearful, in a habitual way, of their teacher; or of poltergeists. Adolescents can want to lose weight, or to live for ever.

How do intentional objects come into the educator's job? Part of this has to do with directing children away from unreality and towards reality. Parents want their children not to be afraid of the dark, or of ghosts. They do not want to eradicate fear in them altogether, for it makes sense to be afraid of what is really fear-worthy – suspicious strangers, unleashed dogs.

Similarly with beliefs. If a child has got the wrong end of the stick about what 'rabbit' means and thinks that cats are rabbits, he must be corrected. School teachers want pupils to have true, not false, beliefs about the structure of matter or the rise of totalitarianism.

Pains, educators and health care professionals

Is it a defining characteristic of *every* feature of the child's mind that it is object-directed, that is, directed onto intentional objects?

There is a problem. It lies in the experience of pain or other sensations like itchiness or the experience of being tickled.

Let us talk about pains. If Sophie is suffering toothache, is her mind *directed onto something* – as her fear of the wasp that has just landed on the table is directed on to the wasp?

Apparently not. Toothache is certainly a conscious state if anything is. But it does not seem to be *directed* consciousness. We do not feel pain *at* anything or *about* anything or *for* anything: we just feel it, full stop. If so, this is surely a counterexample to the thesis that all consciousness is consciousness *of something*.

Or is it? Someone may object that it is simply not true that pain is never directed. We can have mental pains. We can be pained by an insult. Here the object of our distressed state is a demeaning remark – or rather what we take to be one.

But we are talking about physical pains like toothache, not mental pains. Mental pains are really emotional states – states of anguish, anxiety, grief, sadness and so on. Physical pains are importantly different from them in lacking this element of directedness.

. . . But do they lack it? After all, the objector may continue, we talk of *feeling* pain, e.g. toothache. Does this not point to a distinction between a mental state – the feeling – and the object of that mental state – the pain, the toothache? On this view the toothache itself comes out as the intentional object of the feeling.

I do not think this further objection will do. We really cannot divide off 'feeling' from 'a toothache' as if these were separable phenomena. There is only one thing here. If we liked, we might call it a 'toothachy feeling'.

The objector is not finished yet. Is not the object of Sophie's experience when she feels toothache *the decayed tooth*? After all, when she is afraid of the wasp on the table, the object of her fear is identical with what has caused her fear, i.e. the wasp. Why should we not say the same with regard to the toothache?

In reply I would say that the decayed tooth is certainly the *cause* of the toothache, but that does not make it its *object*. Cause and intentional object are logically different things. If I hope for a Green victory at the next election, the victory can scarcely have *caused* my hoping – given it may never happen – even though it *is* its object.

Not all states of consciousness involve consciousness of some object. Pains are one counterexample, experiences of feeling warm or being tickled are others. More generally, *sensations* do not take intentional objects. This makes sensations exceptional among types of mental phenomena, since all the others, at least all the others we discussed above, are object-directed.

The child's mind contains two radically different kinds of phenomena:

• Things like thinking, recalling, seeing, feeling fear and other emotions, desiring or intending, which do require intentional objects;
• Things like pains and other sensations, which do not.

This has consequences for how education is related to the child's mind. Everyone will agree that education has to do with the development of the mind. Probably everyone will also agree that it has nothing to do with the development of pains, tickles and other sensations. It is indeed odd, once we think about it, to talk about the development of pains and tickles at all. How can a headache be developed?

Parents and teachers are uncontroversially in the business of developing children's beliefs, skills, desires, judgements, emotions. They transmit them and/or extend them, deepen them, refine them. But there is no way they can do such things to headaches or feelings of giddiness. True, they can do *something* about a child's headache: they can give him or her an aspirin. They can in this way *change* the mental state the child is in, but not all change involves *learning*. When they give the child the aspirin, they are acting not as educators but are on the same patch as health care workers.

The medical profession and the education profession are both agents of mental change in their clients. The dividing line that runs through the mind – between intentional or object-related phenomena on the one hand and sensations on the other – helps to demarcate one profession from the other. If we leave mental health out of the reckoning for the moment, doctors and nurses concerned with physical health are interested, among other things, in alleviating or preventing painful sensations. Parents and teachers are interested in developing various types of intentional phenomena.

Is this generalisation too crude? Nurses will tell you that they do not see patients simply as bodies: they treat them as persons, help them to overcome their fears, respect their rights as autonomous agents, encourage them to adopt healthier life-styles. Likewise, it is not as if teachers and parents have *no* interest in the non-intentional part of the mind. Physical education teachers are pleased when their pupils say how great they feel when they work-out or practise diving. Bringing about pleasurable sensations associated with exercise is part of their job. Similarly, literature teachers reading a Poe tale to their class would feel a certain inadequacy if there were no goose-pimplings or frissons around.

Perhaps the generalisation does indeed need filing away at the edges, but at least as far as educators go it is reliable enough. Buzzes of pleasure are not, *on their own*, the target of the gym instructor. They are part of something larger – learning how to get better at vaulting and doing back somersaults. Shivers induced by ghost stories belong to a more comprehensive emotional experience. Educators have no professional interest in bringing about or modifying sensations in themselves.

Other professions or occupations *do* have this aim. Medics want to reduce pains, torturers to intensify them, prostitutes to induce pleasurable sensations, big-dipper operators and 'sensationalist' movie-makers feelings of a more stomach-churning and nail-biting variety. Sadistic Dickensian schoolmasters enjoy beating children, but their affinities are more with the torturer than the educator. The latter's business is with the non-sensational part of the mind.

Why is this? Why do sensations lie outside the educator's remit?

Education, concepts and object-related mind

The answer leads us into the heart of education.

Educators deal with object-related aspects of mind. Recall the examples introduced earlier, about children looking at *a drop of pondwater* under a microscope; thinking about *a problem in geometry*; listening to *a story*; trying to remember *the past participle of 'avoir'*; being afraid *of the dark*; having mental images of *sea-snakes*; wanting to *become an engineer*; believing *that bullying is wrong* or *that gases expand when heated*.

In each of these cases the child's mind is directed onto an object. In describing these objects I have used a variety of *concepts* – <u>drop</u>, <u>pondwater</u>, <u>problem</u>, <u>story</u>, <u>sea-snakes</u>, <u>bullying</u>, <u>wrong</u>, <u>expand</u>.

Some of these may not be the concepts that the children themselves would use in describing their experiences. It is their perspective that I want to emphasise here. Perhaps the child with the microscope says, more vaguely, that she is looking at *things swimming around*.

The crucial point is that the child must conceptualise what she is looking at or thinking about in *some* way. The objects of her attention cannot be *bare*, as it were. They come already clothed in whatever concepts she is capable of applying to them.

Take a child who sees mountains and faces in a cloudscape. Her visual awareness is object-directed. But we cannot say anything about the object of her awareness except in terms of how she characterises this. She sees what she is looking at *as* mountains or faces.

Putting things like this means that the child must possess the concepts of *mountain* and *face*. If she were too young to have learnt them, she would not be able to see clouds in that way. Later on she may see <u>grotesque</u> faces in the clouds, but as yet this way of seeing things is not open to her because she has not yet acquired the concept <u>grotesque</u>.

The same is true of other intentional phenomena. The child has to conceptualise objects in some way. She has, say, a certain belief. She believes that *ice melts in the sun*, or that *birthday parties are fun*. Again, if she were too young to have the concepts <u>ice</u>, <u>melt</u>, <u>sun</u>, <u>birthday</u>, <u>party</u>, <u>fun</u>, she could not believe these things.

I can now say more about the dividing line in the child's mind between intentional phenomena and sensations. The former, being object-directed, require the child (as perceiver, believer, imaginer) to conceptualise the object in some way. Sensations, lacking objects, do not depend on the child's use of concepts.

I must fill out this last point briefly.

Children can and do have the concepts <u>pain</u> and <u>headache</u>. But I am not talking of that here, but of whether, when they are experiencing, say, a headache, this experience *requires* the application of any concepts on their part. While they are suffering the headache they *may* be thinking 'I wish this would go'. Concepts certainly come in at this point. But they come in with the thinking, not with the pain as such. Thinking can accompany pain, but is not to be identified with it. Pain itself is a non-concept-involving form of consciousness.

We have reached the root of the question why education is not to do with pains and other sensations. Concept-involving mental phenomena can be developed into new forms precisely because they are concept-involving. Headaches may be *changed*, by pills or other means, but they cannot be *developed*.

To put it another way. Children can acquire, on the basis of the emotions, desires, thoughts, skills and personal qualities they have now, more complex and refined versions of these phenomena. But they cannot acquire more complex and refined versions of the stomach ache they have now. Stomach aches lie outside the ambit of learning and education.

Education has to do with the development of mind. Not of every type of mental phenomenon, because some types – sensations – are not developable. It has to do with the development of those types which depend on intentional objects and so on concept-application.

The last few pages have had a lot to say about sensations. In the rest of the book I will now refocus. I will leave behind toothache and butterflies in the tummy and concentrate on the educable aspects of the child's mind. 'Mind' henceforth will be taken to mean 'concept-involving mind'.

I argued earlier that we can think of education as a process by which continuants such as beliefs, skills and personal qualities are developed into more adequate versions of the same things. This happens by educators' focusing on occurrent features of the child's mind, such as his or her conscious thought-processes, judgements, perceptions, desires and emotional reactions.

Since all these phenomena – occurrent and continuant – require the subject's use of concepts, it is evident how large a part of the parent's or teacher's task has to do with changing the way children conceptualise things. The movement is from less adequate to more adequate conceptualisation.

What counts as 'more adequate' is a big topic in its own right. It has to do with the proper aims of education. A complete account of education would have to include a discussion of its aims. This would lead into ethical and political realms which lie beyond this book's remit – although connexions will be made with them at many points.

How can education alter the way children conceive things? Belief is a good starting point. Young children have all sorts of beliefs about the world around them, about themselves, about other people. Sometimes, for whatever reason, the beliefs they have are false. They think they are ugly although other people find them attractive; or that there is a ghost in their bedroom; or that black people are dirty. One task of education is *where necessary* to ensure that children remain in touch with reality.

I say 'where necessary' because developing children's imagination is important too, and this often means transcending reality (see Chapter 7). Remember Charles Dickens's abhorrence of Mr Gradgrind's system of education in *Hard Times*, with its exclusive attachment to facts and repudiation of all fancifulness.

This qualification aside, reality is obviously important. Children cannot be left with false beliefs like those suggested. Their parents and teachers have a responsibility to teach them what is true. The belief that there is a ghost in the bedroom has to be replaced by the belief that there is no ghost in the bedroom. *How* this is done brings in the child's occurrent experiences. Parents may ask the child where the ghost is, or why he thinks there is one. They are encouraging him to think more focally about the proposition 'there is a ghost in the room' and about whether there are grounds for it. All this depends on the use of concepts.

Educators' responsibilities are not confined to the replacing of false beliefs by true ones. Equally important is the building of new true beliefs on true beliefs which the child already has. Given that the child knows what flowers are, she is in a position to differentiate between pansies and roses, carnations and delphiniums. Again, the learning process is a shift from one belief structure to another – in this case a more determinate one.

In both cases – the replacement of false beliefs and the extension of true ones – the child is coming to acquire *knowledge*. He not only comes to have the kinds of belief I have described, but also comes to hold these beliefs on appropriate evidence (see Chapter 3).

I showed earlier how intentional objects and concept-application go together. It is easy to see how concepts enter into the examples of belief-development just given. Clearly, the child who believes that *there is a ghost around her bed* must have the concepts expressed in this thought. New concepts may or may not be introduced by the parent-teacher. Possibly in this case the belief can be tested and rejected simply by reliance on concepts the child possesses already. In the other kind of case, however, to do with the extension of belief-structures into more determinate forms, new concepts – carnation, daffodil, etc. – *do* come into the picture.

I have concentrated on the acquisition of beliefs to illustrate how the notions of intentionality and concept-application come into the process whereby one continuant is replaced by a more adequate one via engaging pupils in some kind of occurrent mental activity. This is only one kind of illustration. The learning of skills and the acquisition of desirable personal qualities could be spelt out in the same way.

Conclusion

I have been using the word 'concept' without explaining what I mean by it. But it is time for a fuller account. I will be providing this in Chapter 2.

First, though, to tie up a few loose ends on the wider topic of the child's mind. I began the chapter by contrasting a religious with a biological conception. The religious view sees human souls as eternal. At least a part of our mental life – including its more abstract powers of thought – outlives the death of the body. Non-human animals have no souls. This contrasts with the biological view which stresses the continuity between human and non-human life, and sees human minds as an evolutionary development from those of other species.

It should be clear by now that my sympathies, like those of many of us, are with the biological approach. Most of us find no difficulty in ascribing some form of mental life to at least some of the 'higher' animals. We are happy enough to say that cats and dogs can see, hear, smell things, feel pain, perhaps also feel emotions like fear. When we get on to oysters and beetles we may not know what to think. But at least with mammals close to ourselves the idea that they, like us, are capable of some forms of consciousness seems to fit the facts.

As will be seen in the next chapter, the continuities between non-human and human mental life are important educationally, not least in the upbringing of the very youngest children. But there is an unresolved problem about the minds of other animals.

Most of us would say that cats, dogs and monkeys can feel pain. No object-directedness is at work here, no use of concepts. But what about seeing, hearing, smelling? If, as is likely, we are willing to attribute these to them, does it not follow that cats, dogs and monkeys, just like us, *are capable of using concepts*? Is not the same true if we allow that they can feel afraid or angry?

Why should this constitute a problem? Because, I suggest, of the connexion we typically make between possessing concepts and possessing language. If a child sees clouds as *mountains*, to use one of our earlier examples, we assume she must understand the word 'mountain' (or its equivalent in other languages) in order to have this concept. What, then, should we say about our cats and dogs? That if they are capable of concept-involving things like seeing and hearing, they must in some sense possess their own language? Or that, since they *do not* have language, their mental life must be limited to sensations? Chapter 2 will help to throw light on this issue.

This book concludes with an Appendix called 'More about minds'. It picks up from this first chapter. If you feel that there are key questions about the mind that have not yet been addressed – not least about the relationship between the mind and the body – you may find this Appendix helpful.

Summary and key points

Historically there have been two contrasting ways of thinking about the mind: as an entity separable from the body; and as a biological phenomenon inseparable from it. The former view, which comes to us from Plato, via Descartes, has often associated the mind with abstract thinking. Echoes of this are seen in educational systems today in the priorities attached to different curriculum subjects.

Mental phenomena are of many sorts, not all of which involve reasoning. Are they all forms of consciousness? If so, what shall we say about unconscious phenomena?

Among the latter are continuants. Together with mental occurrences, they constitute the child's mind's two great sub-divisions. They are central in understanding the nature of learning, teaching and educating.

Another key sub-division of the child's mind is into intentional and non-intentional phenomena. The former, but not the latter, are object-related and thereby concept-involving. Education, unlike health care, is concerned only with intentional aspects of the child's mind, since only these are capable of being developed or cultivated. The modification of children's beliefs is discussed as one example of this.

Further reading

For brief alphabetical entries on most of the topics in this book, see Honderich, T., (ed.) (1995) *The Oxford Companion to Philosophy* Oxford: Oxford University Press. For more specialised and usually longer entries, see Guttenplan, S. (ed.) (1994) *A Companion to the Philosophy of Mind* Oxford: Blackwell.

The classic modern view of the mind as an entity distinct from the body is found in Descartes, R., *Meditations*, 1, 2, 6 and *Passions of the Soul*. For an accessible brief commentary, see Blackburn, S., (1999) *Think*, Oxford: Oxford University Press, chs 1, 2. The close association between the mind or soul (as an immortal entity) and abstract thinking goes back to Plato's dialogues, especially *Phaedo* and *Republic*. The educational theory embedded in the latter (Books 6 and 7) has influenced many later accounts of education and its aims. See also Further reading for Chapter 2. On mental phenomena in general, see McGinn, C., (1982) *The Character of Mind* Oxford: Oxford University Press, ch. 1; and Kenny, A., (1989) *The Metaphysics of Mind* Oxford:

Oxford University Press, chs 1, 2. An excellent short philosophical discussion of similarities in mental life between human and non-human animals is MacIntyre, A., (1999) *Dependent Rational Animals* London: Duckworth, chs 1–7. Readings on relationships between minds, brains and bodies are found at the end of the Appendix.

Chapter 2

Concepts and concept learning

What are concepts?

Developing children's minds means working with and modifying the concepts they already possess. This is true of their perceptions, beliefs, abilities, intelligence, imagination, desires and emotions. In every area concepts are pivotal.

But what *are* they? When I ask my students to brainstorm on this for a few minutes, the replies dashed down on the flipchart always include two items: 'ideas in one's head' and 'connexion with language'. We can start with the former.

Ideas in one's head?

If asked for examples of concepts, some students typically come up with things like <u>gravity</u>, <u>democracy</u>, <u>mind</u>, <u>evolution</u>. But we can also have much more mundane concepts: <u>tea-leaves</u>, <u>slug pellets</u>, <u>paper-clips</u>. Although it may be the case that the *word* 'concept' is usually used only in higher-flown, theory-related contexts, this does not mean it lacks application to lower-flown, everyday reality. There is a concept <u>pencil</u>, just as there is a concept <u>pullover</u>, even though we have little occasion to refer to either.

However ordinary or extraordinary the concept, what is it to say that it is an idea in the mind? One thing is sure. It cannot be part of the furniture of some inner psychic chamber. There is no such chamber.

Part of the temptation to see things this way comes from the Lockeian thought that concepts have their source in children's experience of the world. On this view, they come to acquire the concept <u>blue</u> from the blue things they see; <u>tree</u> from their experience of trees. Somehow their repeated experience of blue things forms in their mind an idea of blueness, in which all the *other* features of blue things – the zip and the plastic on a blue purse, the metalwork and shininess of a blue Volkswagen – have been sifted away. Only what is common to them remains. This abstracted – or abstract – idea is their concept blue.

Where is language in all this? Where is the *word* 'blue'? On the view in question concepts are bare bits of mind stuff, as yet linguistically unclothed. Maybe they are mental images – like the experience of blueness in the mind's eye. Whatever they are like, they enable children to engage in mental operations private to themselves – thinking things out, perceiving the world around them, contemplating, recollecting, deciding to do something. It is only when they want to pass on their ideas to others that words and language come into the picture. Only then do children stick the labels 'blue' or 'hurts' on to their private experiences of these things.

This way of thinking about concepts has been important education-ally – as we shall see. Despite this, it is scarcely convincing. If the mind is not a place, concepts cannot be entities within it made out of mental raw material.

This is not to say that concepts are *not* in children's minds, only that they are not in their minds in *this* way. How else could they be?

Not – usually – as a current object of consciousness. Children do not often, if ever, have concepts before their minds in the way they have Harry Potter before their minds when reading his latest adventure.

Unless, perhaps, they happen to be doing philosophy. If they are, they will be reflecting on concepts like morality, space, truth, knowledge, God. Some precocious boys and girls may indeed be thinking about the concept of concept – just as I am doing now. But this is a pretty rarified kind of activity.

Or is it? I cannot resist tilting at the fashionable belief that all young children are little philosophers in the making. We are told that were it not for the repressions of formal education they would go on and on puzzling over questions like 'What is time?' and 'Why be moral?' Sunday papers are suckers for stories about five-year-old Socrateses. In the teeth of their readers' incredulity they forthrightly back pioneer classes on philosophy in the reception class.

Philosophy for children is getting to be big business. Conferences, textbooks, courses, academic societies. Some primary schools – the ones featured in the supplements – build it into their curriculum. (Why are these schools so often in the most deprived areas?)

As a philosopher myself, you might expect me to welcome all this razzmatazz. But as a philosopher my professional interest is in questioning received ideas. So it is with this one. I am all in favour of very young children being encouraged to ask questions and seek out answers. But not all questions are philosophical ones.

And even where a question *does* have philosophical potential, like 'Where does space end?', it is not simply *asking* such a question that makes a young child into a philosopher. It is the hard thought that comes *next* that counts – the dwelling on paradoxes, making interconnexions with related issues, becoming acquainted with others' writings on the topic. Tots, to my knowledge, do not typically go in for *this*.

Most of the odd beings who have found themselves drawn into philosophy tend to begin leaning that way around their early teens – a few earlier, many later. Articles on the nursery Nietzsche and pre-school Presocratics belong with TV glitz shows like *The Brainiest Kid in Britain* or such classic texts of education for creativity as *The Goldmine Between Your Ears*.

But I must bring the argument back to concepts. I was beginning to explain the true sense in which concepts are *in our minds*.

Take superglue. The concept of <u>superglue</u> is one most of us possess, many children included. We possess it even when we are not thinking about the stuff. For years, ever since I first came across it as a crockery mender, I have possessed this concept. I have had it whether mending crockery or chairlegs or not mending anything. I have had it through-out my waking hours and throughout my sleep.

The concept <u>superglue</u> has been in my mind in the same way as my ability to use a typewriter has been in my mind – not as an occurrent phenomenon but as a continuant. Possessing a concept is more like possessing a skill than owning an object.

Language can mislead here. We talk about the concepts of <u>democracy</u>, of <u>superglue</u>, of <u>butterfly</u>. Three very different things. But what kind of thing are they? Are they mental? Are they in the mind? . . . Before we know what is happening, we find ourselves on the track of some kind of elusive entity. But why assume we are dealing with entities?

It is best not to get fixated on the question 'What is a concept?' The question 'What is it to *have a concept?*' is much more fruitful. It is also much easier to answer. If a child has the concept <u>butterfly</u>, she can do all sorts of things she could not do before she had it. She can recognise butterflies. She can understand references to butterflies in what she reads or hears. She can talk about butterflies, find out more about them, think about them, sketch pictures of them from memory. We are talking about new *abilities* that she possesses.

Concepts and language

If having a concept is having certain abilities or skills, what about the second staple of my brainstorming sessions: the connexion between concepts and language?

Concepts are plainly not the same as words. The concept <u>butterfly</u> is expressed in the English language by the word 'butterfly', in German by 'Schmetterling', and in French by 'papillon'. Concepts, as it were, lie behind words. They are the ideas that words express.

Does this mean, then, that concepts are *separable* phenomena from words?

Beware the red light ahead. There is a danger we will find ourselves back inside the picture of the mind as a private space stocked with free-floating ideas.

It is more reasonable to think of having a concept of, say, <u>butterfly</u>, as *knowing how to use the word* 'butterfly' in English (or 'Schmetterling' in German, etc.). (See the reference to Geach in Further reading below.) This ties in with the discussion of abilities and continuants in the last section. If a child knows how to use the word 'butterfly', she has the capabilities mentioned there: to recognise butterflies, to understand what people say about them, to talk about them herself.

Does this mean that concepts *cannot be separated* from language? If so, this has wider implications for the way we think about minds. If, as was argued in the last chapter, virtually the whole of our mental life – barring sensations – involves the use of concepts, then it equally involves the use of language. Developing a child's mind becomes on this view a matter of developing his or her linguistic abilities.

Governments put great weight on programmes of universal literacy. From the perspective on concept possession that we are currently considering, we can well see why. Literacy enlarges a child's linguistic capabilities. In so doing, it not only gives him or her useful skills, which in turn can be the basis for more sophisticated and specialised abilities later. It also has a larger role in developing the young mind as a whole. If imagination, emotion, thinking, and perception all depend on having concepts, and having concepts is a matter of knowing how to use language, the mental life of illiterates is likely to be narrowly confined.

There is a huge amount of truth in this. Basic literacy is indeed central to developing children's minds. But there is still a problem. We have been assuming that concepts *must* be understood linguistically. But should we be?

Are there examples of concept-possession not dependent on language? The clearest-cut cases, if they exist, would be of creatures who do not possess language at all and yet operate with concepts. Non-human animals like cats, dogs and birds do not use language. Could any of these be conceptualisers?

All this brings us straight back to the problem raised at the end of the last chapter, about animal minds. If cats and dogs can see, hear, feel afraid of things, then according to the argument there, they must be capable of some kind of conceptualising. Could they do this without language?

Rats, cats and catfood

If a cat can see its catfood and be afraid of dogs, is it not then a concept-user? But if it is, what does it mean to say that it is? My having the concept butterfly, I suggested above, involves having certain skills or forms of know-how – to recognise butterflies, speak about them, and so on. If the cat's seeing its catfood brings conceptual ability with it, does it have similar skills?

It has none which require language. It cannot talk about catfood or understand what other people say about it.

Can it at least *recognise* its catfood? This looks like a starter. Zeus is fed twice a day. When his Science Diet pellets are put in a bowl, he immediately goes over to it and begins crunching them up. It looks as if he recognises something with which he is already familiar via his senses of smell and sight. If so, we are dealing with a type of recognition not dependent on language.

How, if at all, might concepts come into this story?

Rats can be trained to discriminate between triangles and other shapes, through being rewarded with food when they jump from their jumping stand at triangles but not circles or squares. Whether a triangle is large or small, coloured or plain, right-angled or not right-angled, placed above or below, the rats produce the same response in each case. Does this point to some language-independent recognition of triangles? If so, how, if at all, might concepts be involved?

One thing is pretty certain. The rats do not acquire the concept triangle as *we* understand this. They do not recognise the triangles *as triangles*, where built into this are all the logical connotations that the term 'triangle' has for us. We understand that triangles are geometrical figures with three straight sides and three angles. The concepts number and mathematics are embedded in the concept. Rats, like human babies, lack this kind of understanding, which only comes with induction into the discipline of mathematics.

Similarly, Zeus cannot see or smell his catfood *as catfood*, as we understand this. We bring to our concept catfood our awareness that cats are animals of a certain sort – mammals, domestic pets – as well as our understanding of food as a basic necessity for survival. Zeus knows nothing of all this.

Our concepts triangle and catfood depend on our possessing a symbolic system within which these concepts can be related to others logically connected with them. But although rats and cats do not possess this, and cannot therefore recognise triangles or catfood *as* these things, it does not follow that they cannot recognise them *as anything*. Why does the rat respond only to triangles? Presumably because such responses generate a food reward whereas responses to non–triangles do not.

If so, can we not say that rats recognise triangles not as triangles, but as something like *leading-to-food*? Of course, they do not have the concepts conduciveness and food that we do, since for us these notions are language-dependent. But the differential responses that they make to various shapes strongly suggest that they perceive triangles in some way as signs of food. Similar points can be made about Zeus and the catfood.

What has any of this to do with concepts? Suppose I have the concept paperclip. This means, among other things, that I can recognise all sorts of particular paperclips as *the same* in some way, in this case as paperclips. I can do this whether the paperclips are coloured or plain, large or small, rusty or bright. Something of this is true of our rats and cats. Rats recognise all sorts of different triangles as in some way *the same*, in their case as leading-to-food and satisfaction. Zeus reacts in the same way to portions of Science Diet pellets, Kit-e-Kat, Whiskas: he sees or smells them all as (something like) leading-to-satisfaction.

These animals, like us, can classify different phenomena together as the same. They cannot do this in anything like a *reflective* way, as human beings can learn to do. Having words for things enables us to *say* what binds together all sorts of different teacups (or toenails or trumpets) as the same. Even so, at a pre-reflective, pre-linguistic level, animals like these have the ability to see/smell/hear items $a, b, c, d, e \ldots$ all as X. We share this ability with them. (See references to Hamlyn, ch. 6 and Price in Further reading below.)

The recognitional ability the rats and cats possess is connected not only with perception but also with action. The rat not only recognises triangles as signs of food to come, but also, in doing so, reacts in the appropriate manner to get the food. The same is true of Zeus and the catfood. We are talking not only about a sign *of* something (e.g. food or satisfaction to come), but also of a sign *for* something, i.e. for some action in response.

This, then, is an argument for saying that conceptualising does not necessarily require language. It is implicit in the ability to recognise different phenomena as the same in some respect, and that is an ability found in the sign cognition of language-less animals. Educationally, as we shall see, this is an important conclusion.

Can blind people have colour concepts?

Can a person blind from birth possess a colour concept like red? How could this be possible, since redness is a visible quality? But suppose she says things like 'Are you wearing your red dress today?' or 'Have we left the envelope for the Red Cross?' How are we to understand her use of the word? What kind of grasp of the concept could she possibly have if she cannot see colours?

She uses the word 'red' grammatically. She does not say things like 'Won't you red in?' She uses it as an adjective rather than a verb. She understands it as describing some property of something rather than, say, an activity. She understands it, moreover, as a certain sort of property, as something spread across the surface of things such as dresses and crosses. She also grasps that it is a property others can see but she cannot.

All this gives her a considerable understanding of the concept, overlapping significantly with the understanding of it that sighted people have. What she lacks is experience of redness. This means that her concept is not identical to sighted people's. Yet it is the same concept in many respects.

What she cannot do with her concept is *recognise* red things. As we saw with our rats and cats, the ability to recognise instances is one thing that characterises concept possession. But the blind person does have *other* kinds of ability. She can understand what others say when they use the word 'red'; and she can use the word appropriately herself.

The two aspects of concept-possession

The blind person and the triangle-recognising rat each possess concepts, but in different ways. Let us start with the language user. A child's possessing a concept in this case is a matter of knowing how to use a word correctly and appropriately. This has many aspects: it includes the ability to recognise instances, to use the word properly in speech or writing, to understand others' use of it. Underlying all this is an understanding, not always explicit, of the role of the word in the language, i.e. of its grammatical features as a describing word, a naming word, a conjunction, etc., and of logical links that its associated concept has with other concepts (<u>red</u> is a <u>colour</u>, a <u>colour</u> is a <u>property</u> of things). The example of the blind woman has revealed these deeper levels of understanding. It has also shown how they can be detached from the ability to recognise instances, given that she has the former understanding without the latter ability.

Can children recognise instances without understanding how a relevant word functions? Normally, these go together. If an older child can recognise red things as red, he must have some understanding – again, this does not have to be explicit – of the logical features of the concept <u>red</u>. But what about a toddler who can use the word 'cup' in a rudimentary way? She can pick out cups and not confuse them with plates or tumblers, but does her correct use of 'cup' bring with it an understanding of the role of this word in the language, of its grammar and logical connexions? This surely seems too sophisticated for an eighteen-month-old child.

Remember, though, that the understanding in question can be implicit. Understanding is also a matter of degree, rather than something you either have or do not have. If the toddler can use the word 'cup' more or less correctly in some contexts, she at least has some understanding that cups are (substantial) things (rather than properties of things), and is likely to know something of the sort of thing a cup is. She knows that it belongs to the class of things used for eating and drinking. None of this, as I say, is explicitly grasped, and what grasp there is is less firm and sophisticated than an adult would have; but even so the child must have some embryonic understanding of the concept.

So, when dealing with concepts expressed in language, it is hard to see how the ability to recognise instances could fail to be accompanied by at least some implicit understanding of the role of concepts in the language. But the cats and rats are different. They have a primitive recognitional ability, even though they are language-less.

Origins of human conceptualising

This suggests a possible biological basis for human conceptualising. An ancient tradition has it that only human beings have concepts, non-human animals do not: there is an absolute divide. But this ignores common features connecting the two. Like other human abilities and reactions, conceptual ability has its roots in what we call our 'animal' nature. Sign-cognition is the basis on which more complicated, language-dependent, forms of conceptualising are built.

Sign-cognition is 'tied' to the perceptual situation in which an animal finds itself. Human beings, relying on the conceptual apparatus they acquire through language, are capable of 'autonomous' thinking. Children can think about things in the absence of perceptual triggers – about the fall of the Roman Empire or about their absent father. The rat's ability to recognise triangles is actualised only in the presence of triangles. Not only this. Since it sees triangles as signs of food, it has to be in a receptive state for this – hungry rather than just fed.

The biological benefit of (tied) sign-cognition is obvious. It enables animals to pick out features of their environment that help them attain innate goals such as eating, mating, escaping from danger. Many philosophers have argued the primacy of practical reasoning over theoretical reasoning in human life. If they are right, this may have deep biological roots in the sign-cognitive abilities of species from which we have evolved.

It would be wrong to leave the impression that sign-cognition is confined to non-humans and that for human beings the only form of conceptualising is linguistically dependent. Sign-cognition plays an important part in human life, too – not least in human education.

If we were capable only of language-dependent concepts, conceptual learning could not begin before young children had an entrée into language. Admittedly, it is hard to say when this might be: although infants do not produce words until around the end of the first year of life, they are exposed to others' language from the cradle onwards. They may thus acquire some degree of *understanding* of language before they can utter words themselves. A non-speaking infant of, say, a year old, may be able, if asked, to put coloured plastic balls appropriately into the coloured slots of a plastic tray. But the further we move back to the very earliest months and weeks of life the less plausible it is that any understanding of language is present.

Yet babies are not *mindless* in these early months. As well as the pains and other sensations they feel, they have sensory experience, are capable of action like feeding from the breast, and of reactions to familiar or strange people or surroundings. Sign-cognition is already present in seeing and smelling the breast, or the mother more generally, as leading-to-food. It is present in perceiving the mother and other people around her as leading-to-pleasure-and-comfort (or in unfortunate cases as leading-to-pain-and-unhappiness). If this is right, concept-acquisition begins in the cradle – a point that cannot be stressed too much in any programme of parental education. We will come back to this when discussing concept-learning below.

If concepts only appeared in a child's life when language appeared, how could language learning begin? Children hear language spoken before they can speak it themselves. They hear statements and questions and commands, and the words embedded in these. What do they hear these *as*?

Not as carrying the linguistic freight with which we fully-fledged language users hear them, for the children themselves are only on the threshold. We must assume they hear them as signs, just like other perceptible features of their surroundings – the breast or bottle, rattles, their mother's face, smiles, laughter. They are surrounded by language, as they are surrounded by all these other things. The 'Who's a beautiful boy?' comments and other affectionate remarks are heard as presages of comfort and delight. Later, when parents begin to focus attention on specific words, these, too, must at first be signifiers. 'It's Daddy!' 'Where's Teddy?' 'Pussy'. The child latches on to them because they are connected with the desires already present in her growing desire-structure: for food, comfort, social attachment, amusement, play, the satisfaction of curiosity.

Sign-cognition in human life is not restricted to infancy. It is not as though we begin life like little animals of other species functioning at sign-cognition level, and then, once language arrives, move into a different cognitive gear and leave more primitive operations behind us. Many of our most sophisticated activities depend on sign-cognition. Take this example of a skilled marksman shooting at a snipe:

> In spite of, or even because of the creature's zig-zag flight, he can estimate very accurately where it will be a fraction of a second after he has pressed the trigger. This estimating is a form of sign-cognition. The visible course of the bird's flight during a certain half second is an inductive sign of where it will be in the next half second. And the signified movement is highly specified as to direction and velocity. The marksman shows his excellent

'judgement', as we say, in directing his gun in just this direction and pressing the trigger at just this moment. But his good judgement does not manifest itself by what philosophers call an 'act of judging', that is, by asserting a proposition in words, not even in private and imaged words. His 'act of judging', if we must call it by that name, is wholly pre-verbal.

(Price 1953, p. 101)

There are plenty of less recherché examples of our reliance on sign-cognition. We see dark clouds and think of rain; we notice a dark look on someone's face and wonder how we have offended them; we hear the doorbell ringing and guess we have a visitor. Our unreflective responses to 'body language' are another example. Children learn to see and respond to their surroundings in this way from an early age. As much as verbal learning, it is a vital part of their education.

We have mainly concentrated, in both the human and non-human examples, on forms of sign-cognition orientated towards the *future*: we see *x* and expect *y* to follow. But the example of the dark look reminds us that signs can also be signs of what has happened, or might have happened, in the past. Similarly, a detective can see the imprint of a shoe as a sign of an intruder in the garden; and an archaeologist, a differently coloured patch of excavated earth as an indication of earlier settlement. There can also be signs of what is happening contemporaneously: the wincing and teeth-gritting of the leader in a stage in the Tour de France show us the pain he must be feeling and his determination to overcome it; the sound of an engine and swish of wheels behind me as I write tell me a car is passing in the road.

Concept-learning in PE and other subjects

Sign-cognition is important in physical education and sports training. Few children outside the landed gentry are trained in shooting snipe as part of their education, but many learn to play games like football or tennis. In doing so they learn appropriate responses to events they see on pitch or court. They see these as indications of something about to happen – the leg-movements of the opposing striker as pointing to a back pass, the flight of the ball across the net as a sign of its landing at such and such an angle. Knowing such expectations, too, skilled footballers or tennis players can bluff their opponents into thinking that something will happen when it will not. Concept-learning is as much a part of the PE lesson as it is of the mathematics class. We will come back to this.

Learning to cook is another example. Part of the art of cookery – and this applies to everyday versions as well as cordon bleu – is being able to see something being prepared – a sauce, sausages, soup – as finally ready, or ready for another operation. The omelette maker sees the consistency of the egg mixture in the pan as a sign that in another few seconds it will begin to turn leathery and so needs turning out.

There are many places where perception of signs and suitable responses to them come into classroom work – especially in manual or bodily activities such as technology, PE, home economics, practical parts of science. All these activities require, to be performed well, a finely honed intelligence. (For more on this, see Chapter 5.)

In the pecking order of curriculum subjects most of these come rather low. Intellectual activities, which do not depend so much on sign-cognition, tend to take precedence. How far is this, too, a consequence of the ancient prejudice in favour of the peculiarly human and the exclusion from the realm of the mental of whatever we have in common with other animals?

The difference language makes

Sign-cognition plays a vital part in human life and some of its more specialised activities. Its role in concept learning should not be ignored. That said, the larger part of this has to do with concepts in the more restricted sense, to do with understanding words (or other symbols) and being able to operate with them. Concept-possession, I suggested above, is a kind of skill. If a child has the concept <u>mountain bike</u>, he knows how to use the words 'mountain bike' appropriately. He can produce the words himself in speech or writing in appropriate contexts. He can understand others when they use them. He can recognise mountain bikes when he sees them.

Underlying these abilities is a deeper, usually implicit, under-standing, as we saw earlier, of the logical connexions between <u>mountain bike</u> and related concepts such as <u>wheel</u> and <u>gear</u> and many others. This includes a grammatical understanding of the role of the concept within our system of concepts in general, i.e. of <u>mountain bike</u> as having a referential rather than adverbial use.

Implicit in these abilities and types of understanding is a grasp of the principle whereby different phenomena are to be grouped together as falling under the concept. Mountain bikes can be of different materials, colours and sizes, but what all of them have in common is that they are wheeled vehicles powered by the rider and rideable off-road.

Not that concepts can always be tightly defined in terms of other concepts. Precision differs from concept to concept. The account just given of <u>mountain bike</u> was not intended as an exact definition, and an exact definition might in any case be impossible. Unlike, say, the precise definitions that can be given of some mathematical or scientific concepts – of <u>hexagon</u>, or perhaps <u>electron</u>.

Concepts expressible in language are not only about tangible things like mountain bikes. They are about colours and other properties of things, persons, actions and the way we perform them, relationships between things, logical connexions like 'if x then y' and 'either a or b'. Grammatically, the words expressing them get classified into nouns, adjectives, pronouns, verbs, adverbs, prepositions, conjunctions. Traditionalists about education are on firm ground in underscoring the importance of grammar in the cultivation of the mind. Children have to be able to use concepts of these different sorts as if this were second nature to them. *How* they come to do this is another matter. Traditionalists may be treading softer terrain in calling for the return of old-fashioned grammar lessons.

Concepts are expressible not only in *verbal* language. Newspapers reported in the summer of 2001 the achievement of Diana Graham, aged two, who from the age of five months mastered sign language in order to communicate with her deaf mother:

> Diana is now fluent in the complicated art of communication, having learnt some signs to express emotions even before she could talk.
> She now chats to her 36-year-old single mother, Susan, telling her when the phone rings or if someone is knocking at the door of their home in Stanley, Co. Durham.
>
> (*The Times*, 16 August 2001)

Two final points. People sometimes say that children can – and do – have different concepts of say, <u>cat</u>, depending on their experience. One may see all cats as spiteful, another as cuddly.

These associations are subjective and need to be distinguished from the objective, logical connexions which enter into the meaning of the term. Cats are *necessarily* animals or mammals, but they are not necessarily cuddly or spiteful. In the objective sense children can – and do – all have the *same* concept.

Last, a reminder that possessing a concept is not an all-or-nothing business, but a matter of degree. Educationally, this is of central importance. Take the traditional concept of marriage in this country, as a monogamous union between a man and a woman, involving public vows of love and faithfulness. A five-year-old child will not understand all its elements, including its sexual aspects. But neither will she be totally ignorant of what marriage involves. She understands in part what later she will grasp more fully.

Where do concepts come from?

Signs again

Sign-cognition first. Its pervasive presence in human life has been described above. How can it be developed through upbringing and formal education?

It must have an innate basis. Trees and stones are not capable of it. It can only be found in creatures capable of perception and action, creatures who can perceive something as a sign *of* something else and as a sign *for* a certain response.

Given this, the human learner needs repeated experience of things going together so that the connexion between them can be reinforced in his or her mind. This is one reason why a stable environment is key to children's progress in their earliest years.

This repeated experience may happen without or with teaching. A child may hear a certain note in her father's voice as a sign that he is irritated by her. Or parents and teachers can encourage children to notice connexions already existing in nature (lightning as a sign of thunder, tears as a sign of sorrow) – or engineer events so as to reinforce them (bowling repeated leg breaks, adding spin to a backhand return).

In similar ways *actions and reactions* can become associated, in a more or less automatic fashion, with signs. This can occur without teaching, as when a young child backs away from strangers, seen as indicating some vague danger. Or with teaching, as when children are encouraged to show sympathy for others in distress, or tennis players are trained in a certain sort of backhand return. Mistakes can occur. Learners may fail to notice the connexions they should, or to produce the appropriate responses. Their teachers try to correct them until the seeings-as and responses to them become habitual.

Concepts and definitions

Now to concepts in the more familiar sense, the concepts expressed in language whose learning constitutes so large a part of a child's education. How are these learned?

Sometimes through verbal definition. Children learn that heifers are young female cows, that photosynthesis is the process where a plant changes sunlight energy into chemical energy. Sometimes this happens formally, sometimes informally. A week is a period of seven consecutive days, but children do not learn this concept and its logical connexions, as they might with the concept photosynthesis, in a set lesson. They pick it up through everyday intercourse.

Needless to say, definition-learning cannot be rote-learning of terms not understood. If pupils learn that A is to be defined by reference to B, C, D, they must understand what these terms mean and how A is connected to them.

Learning definitions, with or without understanding, may be out of place – as in Charles Dickens' famous object lesson in concept learning in *Hard Times*. Sissy Jupe, pupil in Mr Gradgrind's class and daughter of a horse-breaker in a circus, is unable to define a horse. Model pupil Bitzer is asked to do so, and describes a horse in terms of its teeth and hooves.

Of course, Sissy already has this concept. She knows what a horse is from her daily experience of horse-breaking. She can both recognise horses and, if pressed, could no doubt give some sort of account of what a horse is. But this would be nothing like the pseudo-scientific definition that Bitzer gives.

Children do not learn definitions of most of the terms they use. They learn what 'table' or 'milk' mean via the roles that tables and milk have in their lives. Tables are things to sit at, to eat from, to draw pictures at. Milk is to drink or to put on Frosties. Connexions with other concepts – sit, eat, draw, drink – certainly come into this picture. But the links are looser than in a definition as such.

Even so, the links exist. Young children build up their understanding of new concepts via concepts with which they are familiar.

Starting from experience?

But this raises a problem. What about the *very first* concepts that children learn? Once the process of concept-learning is well on the way, children have scaffolding they can use to build higher. But how can the upward process ever get started?

It seems there must be ground-level concepts which children learn without the aid of other concepts. A simple colour concept – red, say – is a possible example. Try explaining, using other terms, the difference between red and another colour like green or blue. It cannot be done – not, at least, if we are keeping out of the picture a scientific account of differences in colour in terms of wavelengths of light. And very young children do not learn what 'red' means in *that* way.

How, then, *do* they learn it? If they do not learn it via other terms, must they not do so directly from their experience of red things?

Perhaps it works like this. A very young child sees all sorts of coloured things around her. These include a lot of red things – a plastic spade, a ball, Smarties, a sofa, flowers. What she must do is somehow pick out the red things from the others. Somehow her attention gets drawn to the common property that the red things possess. In this way, by abstracting a general feature from her experience, she comes to acquire the concept red. (We met this account earlier in this chapter.)

In this story the child learns on her own, simply through her unguided experience. In a variant of the story her mother or father also has a role to play. It is they who draw her attention to the feature that the spade and flowers and sweets have in common. 'This is red', they tell her, pointing to a rose. 'And that is not red', pointing to an iris. The child still abstracts the common property from what she sees around her, but this time with help.

This 'abstractionist' account of basic concept learning – especially in its first version – has been prominent in 'child-centred' accounts of education. It is at the root of 'learning by discovery' as this has sometimes been understood. It has provided a theoretical justification for leaving very young children largely on their own in a carefully structured, perceptually stimulating play environment. The idea is that as they gain more experience of different things they will gradually abstract what features go together. Being surrounded, for example, by single objects, pairs of objects or collections of three objects will help them to abstract their first concepts of number. If teachers or parents have any hand in all this, through saying things like 'Here are two things', it is the minimal role of furthering a process on which the child is already spontaneously engaged.

The abstractionist account seems plausible enough until we begin to probe it. How does the singling-out of a common property take place?

Suppose the red things that the child sees around her all have other common features beside their redness. How does she abstract the common feature of redness rather than these others?

Someone may reply that, provided she has plenty of experience of coloured things to draw on, it is highly unlikely that *all* the red things she sees also turn out to be square, or made of wood, or over three inches long. This is true enough, but what about the feature of being spread out in space? The red spade has this property, so have the red rose and dress. So have all red things. How, then, does the child focus on the redness and not on spatial extendedness?

Does this not suggest that she has beamed on to the *colour* rather than the spatiality of the red objects? If so, does this not mean that she must *already* have the concept <u>colour</u>?

But how can this be? We have been investigating how children can learn their very first concepts, the 'ground floor' ones. But <u>colour</u> is a more general notion than <u>red</u>. It belongs on at least the first floor.

To put this another way: we have been assuming that concept-learning begins with the lowest-level concepts and, once they are in place, superordinate concepts are built up from them. But the problem we now face is that the concept <u>colour</u> seems not to be learned *after* <u>red</u>. It must already be in the mind for the learning of <u>red</u> to be possible.

Things are no better if we go by the variant story that the child relies to some extent on someone else pointing to red and non-red things and saying 'Red', 'Not red', etc.

For the teacher in the variant story, the word 'red' is something that belongs to *language*. But for the pupil it cannot be like this. If it were, she would already have to possess the concept <u>language</u>. Once again, as with <u>colour</u>, this is hardly a 'ground-floor' concept.

What is the child to understand when she hears her father producing the sounds 'red' and 'not red' in front of red and non-red objects? What he says is intended to direct her attention to the redness of red things. But how can it do this? Redness is not a property that can be unambiguously pointed to, for whenever someone points at redness they also inevitably point at extendedness in space. The child has to know that it is the *colour* that is at issue. So she must already have the concept <u>colour</u>. By the same token, if she knows what colour is, she must surely also have the concept of <u>property</u>, for colour is a property of things.

We come back to where we were with the first version of the story.

If we pull all these points about abstractionism in its different versions together, it seems that <u>red</u> cannot be a basic concept. To possess the concept <u>red</u> the learner must, it appears, already possess concepts like <u>colour</u> and <u>property</u> – perhaps even the concept <u>language</u> itself.

But how did she come by *these* concepts?

Or before experience? Can concepts be innate?

A tempting answer is that she has never *not* had them. They are, in fact, innate ideas. This is a view popular with philosophers in different ages: Plato, Descartes, and in our own time Chomsky. On this view concept learning cannot be a passive matter of sensory impressions entering the learner's mind and somehow bringing about the formation of ideas. The learner's experience has to fit into a conceptual structure which she has already. This structure is implanted in us innately.

How extensive is this structure meant to be? The more inclusive we make it, the more implausible it becomes. How could we be born with the concepts <u>kebab</u>, <u>floppy disk</u>, <u>jet-ski</u>? These concepts are obviously cultural products in the sense that they are found in some human cultures but not in others. It is hard to see how they could be innate in human beings.

But the concepts which caused problems just now were not <u>kebab</u> or <u>jet-ski</u>, but <u>colour</u> and <u>property</u>. Are we born with *these*?

Although they do not belong to specific cultures, these concepts are still cultural products in that they belong to human language. They aren't part of the non-human reality to which boulders and parsnips belong. So there is still the problem of how something which depends on human culture can be implanted in us biologically.

The innatist view of how we come to have concepts is at first sight no less problematic than the abstractionist. Is there a way out? Or have we reached an impasse?

I think not. We seemed to be driven to the conclusion that there must be innate ideas by the thought that children could not acquire <u>red</u> as a basic, ground-floor, concept. To be able to grasp it, they would *already* have to have the concept <u>colour</u>, and to grasp <u>colour</u> they would *already* have to have the concept <u>property</u>.

What drives us towards innatism is this 'already'. It points to something which must be in place before the alleged first concept. Where else could that be located except pre-birth?

But need we bring in the 'already'? It is true that if a child has grasped the concept <u>red</u>, she must have some understanding that red is a colour and so must have grasped something of the concept <u>colour</u>. But there is no hint of an 'already' in this last sentence. All it has said is that you cannot understand <u>red</u> without understanding <u>colour</u>.

That does not imply that the latter came first. For in principle the two concepts could be acquired together, *at the same time*.

Concept-learning and joined-up thinking

This is indeed what happens in a child's learning. Understanding a concept is, as we saw earlier, not all-or-nothing. It comes in degrees.

Take the child of a year or so, mentioned earlier, who is able to match coloured balls to the relevant hollow in a plastic colour tray. She cannot yet use the words 'red' or 'green', but she understands what to do when asked to put the red ball in the red hollow. She has some understanding of <u>red</u>, therefore. But in getting inside this concept, she is also getting inside the more general concept <u>colour</u>. She is getting the idea that red is a colour, and so are green, blue and yellow.

Around this time she is also beginning to learn what other colour words – 'brown' and pink' – mean as her parents use them with her. Later she will get into more subtle concepts like 'mauve' and 'fawn'. Her primitive notion of <u>colour</u> which revolved around a few dramatically different types like red and green, is becoming subtler, fuller – more attentive to the nuances, the shadings of one colour into another. She is coming to see that the primary colours form a circle, that black and white can also sometimes be counted as colours. Little of this understanding is explicit.

There are all sorts of logical connexions between concepts. <u>Red</u> is a <u>colour</u>. <u>Colour</u> is a <u>property</u>. <u>Spaniels</u> are <u>dogs</u>. <u>Dogs</u> are <u>animals</u>, <u>animals</u> are <u>living things</u>. As a child gets into everyday concepts like <u>red</u> and <u>dog</u>, she is also beginning to get into these larger networks. She knows enough about the difference between a dog and a chair to know that a dog is a living thing. Her idea of what is living and what is not is as yet pretty basic. Only later will she come to see plants as well as animals under the same heading.

There is no need to proliferate examples. These are enough to show that the abstractionist and the innatist are in fact making the same mistake. They are each assuming that when you learn a concept you learn something discrete, on its own.

But <u>red</u> is not a basic concept, an atom from which our larger conceptual system is built up. It brings with it more general concepts. Likewise, we are not born with a framework of more general concepts like property into which we come to fit experientially-based concepts like red. The webs of conceptual relationships cannot be torn apart. They come to be understood and learned holistically.

Acknowledging this can help parents and teachers to avoid some common mistakes. Some people might want to say that a concept like democracy is way beyond the reach of a normal child of five or six. It is something she may well be introduced to at secondary school, but that lies several years ahead.

Once we remember that concepts can be understood in part and to different degrees, it makes perfectly good sense to begin to introduce a notion like democracy to children as young as five. They are able to understand *something* of the idea of making choices. They have *some* grasp of what can happen in different groups when making decisions affecting the whole group – that sometimes it is one person who decides, like the teacher or a parent, while at other times people decide things together, like parents acting together, or children playing. It is on the basis of these and other ideas that *something* of the notion of democratic decision-making can become accessible to the child.

Take a five-year-old I know called Rachel. She came home recently after her first day in big school to announce 'I am the School Council'. It turned out that she had been chosen to be the girls' representative for her class. 'What do you do on the Council?' her father asked. 'I make the rules', she said emphatically. Despite the faintest hint here of a juvenile version of '*l'état, c'est moi*', Rachel is already on the first rung.

Concept-learning as a social enterprise

Children cannot learn concepts on their own. Like some other animals, they are born with a capacity for sign-cognition. Some of the connexions they make here may be as unaided as they are in other animals. But from birth parents also are helping to shape their world, helping them to see what goes with what. They are continually building up and reinforcing expectations. Without such socialisation children would be deprived of so much understanding of their world and of so many opportunities for pleasurable activity that upbringing would be impossible.

Parents and others spend an enormous amount of time in the early years revealing to children what goes with what – in nature, in interpretation of gesture and body language, in the temporal arrangements of day-to-day life. They bring them to hear a ring at the doorbell as a sign of a visitor, to see traffic and roads and electric power points as dangerous, smiles as a sign of comfort, thunder clouds as presaging rain, frowns as meaning disapproval.

If they did not do such things at all, their children's lives would be not so much impoverished as not really human lives at all. The chances of children spontaneously making connexions like these are minimal. Their attention has to be carefully directed onto them and any mistakes they make have to be corrected.

As we also saw earlier, many practical, physical activities that loom large in a human life also depend on sign-cognition: games, cookery, gardening, carpentry, word-processing . . . . These, too, need deliberate induction and correction for left to their own devices learners would never pick up sophisticated associations in these fields.

This building-up of a world of causal relationships provides a background for the child's induction into language and into the new kind of conceptual learning that language makes possible. Not, again, that there is any easy separation here. The early sign-learning is accompanied throughout by language – produced at first by the parents alone but gradually coming to be understood, to some degree, by the infants themselves.

As children begin to understand and then actively use the concepts they acquire in learning their mother tongue, they become inducted into complex webs of interrelationships. They gradually assimilate a new world of logical connexions.

Could they do this on their own? Or do they need parents or other people around them as teachers? As it happens, other people *are* around. But what is their role? Do they just make it easier for the young children to do what they would do in any case? Or is their input indispensable?

Some of the earlier views discussed in this chapter implicitly assumed that children can learn to use concepts on their own – as in the example of the child abstracting the concept red directly from her experience, or the innatist view that children apply their innate concepts to their experience. The general idea that children are the agents of their own concept-learning has long been appealing to educators and educational theorists of a child-centred sort who have opposed the imposition of adult ideas and values on children, sometimes as an affront to their freedom.

But the view that children can learn concepts on their own is unfounded. This is not simply dubious as a matter of psychological fact in the sense that there is no evidence for it. It is something, it seems, impossible even to conceive.

This is a strong claim and needs substantiation. As we have seen, not every term can be exhaustively defined. 'Red' is the name of a colour, certainly, but what differentiates it from other colours cannot be put in words. This is where our experience comes into the picture. Sissy Jupe had the concept <u>horse</u> all right and could no doubt say that a horse is a kind of animal. But neither she nor any of us, Bitzers included, could go on to complete the definition. Sissy, like us, has learned from experience what horses are and how to recognise them.

But what are these experiential criteria that enable us to recognise red things or horses? They are passed on from fully-fledged language users to those being initiated. Parents point out to their children horses grazing in fields, horses in picture books and on television. They talk about what they are like and what they are doing or used for. The children see them swishing their tails, hear them whinnying. In these ways children come to share the concept with their parents and so with wider groups. They pick up insensibly the criteria by which we say something is a horse or not a horse. When they make mistakes – in calling a donkey a horse, for instance – their parents correct them. The children learn to pick out horses correctly time after time. There is an agreed, public understanding of what counts as a horse and children have to be brought to share in this.

This is what actually happens. The question is: could it happen otherwise? Could children acquire such understanding *without* the help of other people? It is hard to see how. After all, they have to learn to be *correct* in their attributions. It cannot be *up to them* what counts as a horse. There is a public understanding about this. It is only because of this publicity that anyone can be right or wrong.

All this brings home Wittgenstein's claim in *Philosophical Investigations* (see Further reading below) that concepts are public phenomena, with publicly agreed standards written into them. They are not private accomplishments which children can accumulate on their own.

Educators and educationists do children a terrible disservice if they deny this, assuming perhaps that anything worth learning must be the product of the child's experience and activity alone. Children need to be inducted into the public heritage constituted by concepts and conceptual systems. If they are not corrected when they go wrong – on the grounds that correction is illicit imposition, how will they ever come to be full members of the community of concept-users?

These truths apply not only to simpler concepts like <u>red</u> and <u>horse</u>, but also to more complex ones, those more the province of the teacher than the parent. Concepts, however simple, however complex, are social institutions. They all have their own standards of correctness into which children have to be inducted.

Many concepts are indispensable elements in people's flourishing as members of a civilised society. What these might be is a big question. But suppose for the sake of argument we agree that – at least in our context – these indispensable concepts include ones like molecule, square root, democracy. If so, educators have an obligation to make sure that pupils grasp the rules which enable them to operate with these concepts correctly, that they do not confuse square roots with squares of numbers or molecules with atoms.

All this implies intervention on the part of the teacher in the shape of explaining, giving examples, monitoring whether pupils have reached the mark and correcting them when they have not. We cannot leave children on their own and imagine that they will pick up such concepts independently. Understanding will not develop naturally within them. If children are brought up under the aegis of such a child-centred ideology, they will find it difficult, if not impossible, to get inside these more complex worlds of academic learning.

This chapter has looked at concepts and the learning of concepts *in general*. This has been important because of the role that concepts play in so much of our mental life, as we saw in Chapter 1. But there is more to say about differences between types of concept – and also about the way concepts enter into our beliefs about and our knowledge of various subject-matters. These things will be found, along with other issues, in the next chapter.

Summary and key points

Chapter 1 showed the central role of concepts in every area of the child's mental life susceptible to education. So what *are* concepts? There are problems with the traditional view that they are ideas in the head, waiting to be linguistically clothed for the purposes of communication. If non-human animals can conceptualise, it is also difficult to equate concept-possession with skills of using language correctly. There is a case for attributing to animals embryonic conceptual abilities in the shape of sign-recognition. These also play a crucial part in human life, not least among pre-linguistic children. With language, children become capable not only of recognising recurring features, but also of understanding logical relationships between ideas.

Turning to the child's acquisition of concepts, there are difficulties both with empiricist accounts – which go back to Locke – in terms of abstracting common features from experience; and with the rationalist view, found in Plato, Descartes and in our own time Chomsky, that concepts are innate. An alternative account, indebted to Wittgenstein, rules out such individualistic perspectives in favour of the view that, as socially-owned phenomena, concepts can only be acquired by deliberate induction into public norms governing their correct application.

The chapter also contains a digression on the teaching of philosophy to young children.

Further reading

Brief philosophical discussions of the nature of concepts are found in Kenny, A., (1989) *The Metaphysics of Mind* Oxford: Oxford University Press, ch. 9; and in Rey, G., (1994) 'Concepts', in Guttenplan, S. (ed.) *A Companion to the Philosophy of Mind* Oxford: Blackwell. John Locke's view that all our concepts come from experience is found in Locke, J., (1690) *An Essay concerning human understanding* Book II, chs 1,2. For a more technical collection of recent essays, see Margolis, E. and Laurence, S., (1999) *Concepts: Core Readings* Cambridge, Mass.: MIT Press.

Perhaps the most stimulating, although demanding, account of the *acquisition* of concepts is Hamlyn, D.W., (1982) *Experience and the Growth of Understanding* London: Routledge and Kegan Paul. This is a comprehensive account of various positions and covers both empiricist and innatist theories. Unlike Geach, P.T., (1957) *Mental Acts* London: Routledge and Kegan Paul, sections 5–11, another work in the Wittgensteinian tradition, it denies that concept-possession depends on the use of language. In this it is closer to MacIntyre, A., (1999) *Dependent Rational Animals* London: Duckworth, ch. 2. On Wittgenstein's contribution, see his *Philosophical Investigations* (1953) Oxford: Blackwell, Part I, sections 27–35 and 242–316. Price, H.H., (1953) *Thinking and Experience* London: Hutchinson, chs 4–6, is interesting on sign-cognition. Winch, C., (1998) *The Philosophy of Human Learning* London: Routledge, ch. 9, presents a more detailed investigation of the issues in this chapter.

There is a critical discussion of the teaching of philosophy to very young children in White, J., 'The roots of philosophy' in Griffiths, A.P., (ed.) (1992) *The Impulse to Philosophise* Cambridge: Cambridge University Press. For a more sympathetic account, see Matthews, G., (1980) *Philosophy and the Young Child* Cambridge, Mass.: Harvard University Press.

Chapter 3

Beliefs: maps by which we steer

Believe it – or not?

A few years ago the young daughter of a friend of ours – she was about four at the time – was worried sick about the Bomb. Older children had told her about it and she was terrified that she and her whole family would be killed. Her mother tried to calm her fears, but unsuccessfully. As a last strategy, she told Jessica that every bedtime she would sprinkle magic dust on all their feet and this would keep them all out of danger. A few shakes of talcum powder later and Jessica's fears had completely evaporated.

As in this case, a large part of upbringing and education has to do with belief. I mean nothing grandiose by this. I'm not talking only about belief in God, in reincarnation or in the inevitable triumph of communism. Jessica's conviction that her whole family would be blown up, though deeply distressing, was less cosmic. So was the belief which replaced it, that they would all be safe.

We each carry around inside us a vast web of beliefs. Some of them are transient, like my belief that it is now raining; others are longer-lasting, like my belief that Tony Blair is the British prime minister. Others again will last a lifetime: that New York is a big city, that molecules are formed of atoms, that $2 + 2 = 4$.

Children have to be inducted into an immense array of beliefs. This is an obvious fact about their education. But what *are* beliefs and how are they connected with what we have already learnt about the mind?

Beliefs are continuants, not occurrences. They do not consist in a present conscious state, like having a pain in the toe, feeling light-hearted, thinking about Friday night. My belief that New York is a big city remains permanently within my network of beliefs. I need not be thinking about New York in order to possess it.

Educationally, this means that belief belongs to the mental *equipment* which we both draw on as teachers and want children to acquire. It does not belong with activities and experiences we encourage them to engage in so as to improve this equipment. Beliefs fit with skills and character traits and not with reasoning something out, listening to a tape, running for a ball.

It has two components. Take a child who believes that Santa Claus brings us presents at Christmas. A somewhat older child believes this is not true. In each case, we can distinguish between the child's *state of mind*, or *attitude*, on the one hand – the believing – and what the *content* of that believing is. In one case this is that Santa brings us presents; in the other, that he does not.

Believing is only one kind of *attitude* to such content. Another is supposing. A child who has long since stopped believing in Father Christmas may play a game of pretending he is real. She lets her imagination wander. She can be described as supposing (or hypothesising or entertaining the idea) that Santa brings us presents. She does not believe it, but for the moment is suspending her usual disbelief. So her attitude is a different one. But the content – that Santa brings us presents – is the same as for the child who believes this.

I will come back to supposing or hypothesising later, in Chapter 7. Sticking to believing meanwhile, we have seen how this consists in a certain attitude to a content. The content is a *proposition*, expressed in words as 'Santa Claus brings us presents' or 'it is likely to rain tomorrow', or '2 + 2 = 4'. It is what follows the 'that' when we are talking of a child believing *that* . . . such and such is the case.

What kind of attitude? If a child believes that *p* (where '*p*' stands for any proposition), she must take *p* to be *true*.

As we know, people can be mistaken about their beliefs. What a child takes to be true – that Santa will come at Christmas – may be false. This helps to bring out something educationally important. Believing is an *intentional* phenomenon (see Chapter 1). Just as being afraid, or listening, or wanting are directed towards objects, so is believing. If a child believes that *girls are stupider than boys*, this proposition is the intentional object of his belief. It is what his believing is directed towards.

As we also saw in Chapter 1, intentional objects are such that they may or may not exist. I may be afraid of the Devil, thinking about people living on Mars, remembering an event that never happened. In each of these cases the intentional object does not exist. The parallel in the case of belief is a proposition that is false – that girls are stupider than boys, for instance.

A large part of education, especially early education, has to do with directing children's minds towards intentional objects that exist rather than do not exist. (There is an important qualification to be made here about developing their imagination. See Chapter 7.) As regards belief, the task is to help them to come to have true beliefs rather than false ones. I will say more about this in a moment.

Meanwhile, a further point from Chapter 1. This stated that if a person's consciousness, or mental state, is directed towards an (intentional) object, the person must conceptualise that object in some way. When I think about something, I must be thinking about *my mother, the spread of foot and mouth disease*, or whatever. If I lacked these concepts, I could not have these thoughts. It is the same with belief. A baby of three months could not believe *that Santa will bring her presents*, for she lacks the concepts <u>bring</u>, <u>present</u>, and <u>self</u>. Our beliefs, true or false, are bounded by the sophistication of the conceptual networks we have so far acquired.

The last example may set one wondering whether a very young baby can be said to believe anything at all. A similar issue arises over non-human animals. Can cats, dogs and pigeons have beliefs?

This is where much of the discussion in Chapter 2, on concepts, comes in again. Whether animals and young babies can believe things depends on whether they can be said to possess concepts. If concepts must be expressible in language, such beliefs can almost certainly be ruled out. But if the kind of conceptualising that comes with sign-cognition is allowed, this leaves room for them in principle.

If so, there *may* be nothing to stop us saying that babies with a certain amount of experience behind them of what goes with what are capable of believing that the breast's appearance leads to food or that a smile goes with comfort and pleasure. As usual, one cannot really put the content of the baby's belief into these – or any – words, if the implication is that the child understands their meanings. She clearly does not. That is why many philosophers are wary about ascribing belief in such cases.

On the other hand, if all sorts of expectations are being built up in children's minds in the first few weeks and months of life, it seems odd to deny them *some kind* of beliefs, even if we cannot put their content easily into words. The uncontroversial kind of believing associated with language does not suddenly appear in human beings out of nowhere. It must be rooted in more basic attitudes that we already possess pre-linguistically – and perhaps share with other animals.

But I will leave this controversy there and restrict what follows to beliefs capable of being expressed in language.

Expanding the web

The education of belief is many-sided. Children need to acquire sets of true beliefs about the natural and social worlds and their place in them. This places two main responsibilities on their parents and teachers. They have to induct the children into a proliferation of new concepts so that more extensive and more complex webs of beliefs can be spun; and they have to steer them away from false beliefs and towards true ones.

About the concepts. These will cover a number of areas. To say what these should be would mean raising ethical, and controversial, matters about the aims of education. But I imagine everyone would agree that children need everyday concepts about the things around them and their properties, about time and space, number, themselves and other people, ethical and moral matters. Assuming they are to acquire beliefs like *If you're going to be my friend, you've got to stop messing me about,* or *It's either a Golf or a Polo,* they will need logical concepts, too, expressed as if–then and either . . . or. As they proceed into the thickets of school subjects, they learn the specialised concepts of those fields. Expanding their conceptual repertoire enables them to possess a wider and wider network of beliefs.

But it is also important that these beliefs be true ones. If children believe that bogeymen lurk in the dark or that foreigners are inferior beings, they have to be disabused.

This is true enough in general, but Jessica's case with which I began suggests a qualification. Whether or not the belief with which she began – that all her family might be blown up by a massive bomb – was true (and it probably was), the belief which came to replace this – that magic dust would make the family safe – was certainly false. So there may be occasions when it makes good educational sense to try to replace a true belief by a false one.

But only for a while. Presumably Jessica's parents did not want her to believe the story of the magic dust *for ever.* At some point true beliefs would have to drive out false.

All this leads towards the thought that we do not want children *just* to believe things. We want them to *know* them.

If I know that Marlene Dietrich was German, I not only believe that she was, the belief is also a true one. I cannot know that Mars is inhabited by living creatures, however much I may believe this, because this belief is false.

Education has a lot to do with acquiring knowledge. Some people would make it all-important, perhaps even definitional of what education is. We need not go along with this: perhaps we want to say, for instance, that education should aim at making good citizens. But whatever aims we write in, they are all likely to accord knowledge an important place. Young people cannot become good citizens without some knowledge or understanding of the society they live in, its political institutions and much else besides.

In the next section I will look at the acquisition of knowledge more fully. Until then, one or two further points about belief.

First, believing can differ in degree of strength. I may half-believe my partner's reasons why she comes home late these days. On the whole I trust her, but there is room for some doubt. Or it is dark. I think I see a cat in the garden, but am not certain. Most of my beliefs, however, are held with greater confidence. With many of these – that human beings die, or that $2 + 2 = 4$ – it is hard to see what might shake them.

Second, beliefs do not exist independently from each other. We have already seen this at the level of conceptual frameworks. If a child believes that her pet Zeus is a cat, she will also believe that he is an animal and a living thing. There are logical links between beliefs. But there are other links as well. The child believes Zeus is old and she believes he is deaf. The two beliefs go together even though one cannot deduce one from the other. More generally, beliefs about Zeus hang together with beliefs about her family, her home, her social and natural worlds. For each of us our total network of beliefs is subjective, in the sense that these are what *we* believe. Our own web of belief is, as has been said, a map by which we steer. This does not mean that, in another sense, our beliefs are not objective. Most of them are true and well-founded. Our personal network overlaps with other people's in that the content of what we believe is and perhaps must be to a certain extent shared.

Knowing

We do not want children to grow up *merely* believers. We also want them to acquire *knowledge*. This goes beyond belief, as we have just seen, because if I believe that p, p may be false, but if I know that p, p has to be true.

But this is not the end of the story. A person may come to have a true belief by accident. A child may have got it into her head that when she gets back from school she will be told that Zeus is poorly. This is exactly what happens: her foreboding is realised. Although she believes that this is what she will be told, can we say she *knows* this?

To ascribe knowledge we require more than true belief that *p*. Most usually, we also need some kind of *good grounds* for *p*. These are what the child worried about Zeus is without, however strong her intuition or feeling of impending disaster. She simply lacks the evidence to support her belief.

Good reasons and the provision of them play a key role in a child's upbringing. They differ according to the type of belief. Empirical beliefs – that Zeus is ill, that George W. Bush is the president of the US – require the evidence of first-hand perception, or perhaps reliable testimony. Mathematical beliefs – such as that $245 + 389 = 634$ – demand logical deduction from other propositions. And what can be said about the backing for ethical beliefs – that it is wrong to steal – or aesthetic ones – she dances gracefully?

Part of a child's education consists in learning to be at home with the different kinds of reasons that support different kinds of knowledge claims. Further questions arise about just how important this kind of learning is in relation to other things that a child might learn. These would lead, once again, into the wider issue of what the aims of education should be, which lies outside this book.

There are also questions about how far we can classify the reasons into discrete types and about the map between any such classification and the way the school curriculum is carved up into different disciplines. These also take the book beyond its brief.

Understanding

Attainment targets in the English National Curriculum set out the 'knowledge, skills and understanding' that pupils are expected to acquire in the different curriculum subjects. We will turn to skills in a moment. But what about understanding? How is it related to knowledge?

We cannot hope for anything like a definition. Partly because we use the term in many different contexts. If I say to someone 'It's a warm day', they will understand *what I mean by these words*. For young children learning their mother tongue this kind of understanding – of the meaning of words – is a major achievement. Later, when they learn

French or German, it will be, too – only this time it will be a matter of grasping what foreign words and utterances mean.

Understanding the meanings of words is often equatable with understanding the concepts which the words express. I discussed acquiring this kind of understanding in Chapter 2. Where a word is a name, though – such as 'Beijing' or 'Margaret Thatcher' – understanding what it means cannot be equated with understanding a concept. This is because we are now dealing with *particular* things, not general kinds of thing like lamps or lumpiness.

Quite different from understanding the meaning of words is the kind of understanding that teachers of science, history or mathematics aim at in their pupils. Here it is a matter of having a fuller and deeper awareness of the field.

In science and mathematics this partly means being acquainted with underlying *principles* (laws, theories) which help to explain or justify other phenomena.

History is different. To understand a particular event – the evacuation from Dunkirk in 1940 – we have to be able to place this within a narrative which makes it intelligible. Historical understanding is not about grasping principles from which lower-order conclusions can be derived, but about seeing how events, including human decisions, are linked together in explanatory stories.

Seeing how parts fit together in a whole is also involved in understanding people. Here, too, we can only explain the things they say and do in terms of a larger picture, a picture which must include a narrative account of relevant parts of their life. Understanding a work of art, too, has partly to do with perceiving interconnexions between parts, and between parts and whole – although a narrative framework comes in only with fiction and drama and sometimes poetry, not usually with music, sculpture or abstract painting.

In all these cases, too, we can in some contexts talk interchangeably of 'understanding' or 'knowledge'. Having a good knowledge of physics or geography is having a good understanding of it. To know a person like the back of your hand is to really understand them through and through. Knowing Beethoven's *Eroica* symphony – where this goes deeper than superficial acquaintance – is partly grasping how the whole is built up of the parts.

The kind of knowledge in question here is knowledge *of* something: an academic subject, a person, a work of art. This should be distinguished from the sort of knowledge discussed in the last section, e.g. knowing that Marlene Dietrich was German or that $2 + 2 = 4$.

Knowing *that p* is not the same as knowing *something or somebody*. For one thing, these latter things require acquaintance with the object of knowledge. I cannot know Tony Blair without having met him or seen him, for instance, on television. This is true however many facts I know about him – that he lives in London, is such and such an age, has four children . . . – without being acquainted with him.

Skills

Skills, too, are a kind of knowledge – again, a different sort from knowing *that something is the case*. Having a skill is knowing *how to do something* – do joined-up writing, read, swim, send an e-mail, solve a mathematical problem. However many facts a child knows about swimming, he does not know how to swim unless he can actually swim.

Back to belief

In this quick sketch of knowing that *p*, understanding, knowing persons and subjects, and skills, I seem to have come a long way from belief. But belief is still at the heart of all these other things. This is because believing that *p* is a component of knowing that *p*, and knowing that *p* is a component of the other things.

If a student knows geography, she plainly must know all sorts of geographical facts. But even if she knows a non-factual subject like music, she must know that musical works have structure, that symphonies are different from string quartets or pieces of jazz. If I am well acquainted with Tony Blair I must know a lot about him – that he is a father, likes eating shellfish (or whatever).

Likewise, a child cannot know how to climb a rope without some knowledge of relevant facts – that this is a rope, that you have to start by gripping it. . . .

So *knowledge that* is an essential ingredient in these other forms of desirable educational equipment – knowing a subject, knowing how to do something. Given, as we saw, that believing that *p* is one component of knowing that *p*, belief is equally embedded in these other things.

I come back to our webs of belief and their significance in children's lives. They are key to what they know about the world, and also to their physical and mental abilities. As will be seen later, they have a central place, too, in their emotional life and in their imaginativeness. Children draw on them in their thinking as well as in their outward behaviour. More of this later.

We often take it in our kind of society that children need to learn not to accept blindly all the beliefs they have been taught, but, where appropriate, to test their credentials. This does not come naturally to human beings. Biologically, we have evolved needing maps in our heads to guide us – just as some other animals need whatever proto-beliefs are in theirs. Believing is, as it were, our default state of mind, not least as children. Yet beliefs can mislead. Children need to be taught how to assess them and to reject them if untrue or ungrounded. Knowledge-maps are more reliable than mere belief-maps.

All this assumes a certain picture of a human life and a human society. It pictures children growing up to think for themselves and not take everything on trust. It fits into a wider, liberal, ideal of life – of people making their own way in the world in a society of equally autonomous individuals.

But not all education systems have been so attached to these values. It is not only hyper-traditional societies that have sought to induct their new generations into accepted ways of thinking where critical appraisal does not come into the picture. Lenin's early education at his Simbirsk grammar school was designed – but arguably failed in his case – to inculcate respect for the Tsarist regime. English elementary schools in the first part of the twentieth century reinforced in pupils the idea that they were destined to remain in the world of manual work. The tyrannies of Hitler, Stalin and Mao cultivated believers, not dissidents.

Are there more benign ways in which education can celebrate belief at the expense of knowledge and critique? For some religious parents and perhaps for some teachers of religion, *faith* is a central virtue. Belief *in* God – or Allah – brings with it various kinds of belief *that* such-and-such is the case – that God is good, will hear your prayers, is merciful. But it goes further than belief *that*. Believing in God is also putting your *trust* in him as director of your life.

I have mentioned belief in God or Allah, linking this with trust in Him as your guide through life. Belief *in* is not always an explicitly religious notion. Jessica believed in her mother when she told her that the magic dust would protect them all. When I was in my last years at secondary school, I believed in my teachers. I trusted that they knew best about what it would be good for me to do at university. They could not have been more wrong. At which points or on which occasions should belief in other people cede to scepticism or even mistrust?

To come back to religion. Are attempts to make children's faith rock-firm a last – and jettisonable – relic from a hyper-traditional era?

Indoctrination is trying to fix or reinforce beliefs in learners' minds in such a way that they do not reflect on them. Is this kind of religious upbringing indoctrination? Is indoctrination justifiable if it impedes the development of free thinking? Or is inculcating faith to be welcomed as a way of countering the disintegrative tendencies of the age?

More questions. Questions springing from a central concern with the nature of the child's mind but leading in other directions. I turn instead to memory.

The Memory Man

Some years ago there was an entertainer called Leslie Welch, known as The Memory Man. Assuming they were not planted for the purpose, people in the audience would ask him who came second in the 2.30 at Catterick on 18 June 1922 or who played outside right for Blackburn Rovers in 1897 – and he invariably got it right.

Was this a natural gift, or did his teachers have some hand in developing his ability? I do not know. Certainly, the idea that one of the purposes of education is to strengthen the memory was popular in some quarters in the late nineteenth century and into the twentieth. In British elementary schools plenty of practice at learning lines of verse or historical, geographical and other facts was seen as essential for building up this mental muscle.

Should we think of the memory in this way – as a faculty to be specially trained? What is it, after all, to remember something?

Suppose Leslie Welch remembers that Captain Dreadnought won the 2.30 at Catterick on such-and-such a day. He remembers a fact. Assume, that is, that he gets the answer right and is not misremembering. Remembering – *really* remembering – that *p* requires that *p* be true.

If this formulation looks familiar in the light of earlier points made in this chapter, it should. To remember that Captain Dreadnought won the race, or that Quito is the capital of Ecuador, is to *know* these things. It is to know them because one knew them in the past.

Just as there is knowledge *how* as well as knowledge *that*, so there is also *remembering how*. I can remember how to use an electric tooth-brush (where would I now be without it?) because I came to know how to do so a couple of years ago and have not forgotten it.

We also remember other things – Marlene Dietrich's voice, the sunshine on the Costa del Sol. We know them because we were acquainted with them in the past. The type of knowledge involved here is what I called above knowledge *of* something.

We remember these different kinds of things – facts, how to do things, experiences – even when they are not in our mind. This is not surprising, since remembering is a kind of knowing and knowing involves believing. I remember even when I am asleep that my aunt used to live in Raynes Park and kept a pet tortoise. When asleep I also know and believe these things.

We have been talking about remembering as a continuant. But it also comes in occurrent form in the shape of recall or recollection. I can call up – now – the memory of ice packed under warm lava on Etna. I can suddenly remember the name of someone which has been on the tip of my tongue all morning.

What part does and should memory play in children's education? We do not want what we teach them to go in one ear and out of the other. We want it to stick. So memory must come into the picture, whether it is of facts or of skills. The only question is whether we need to make remembering things a *separate* objective over and above the acquisition of knowledge.

An art teacher teaches a pupil how to throw a pot. After a few lessons she is able to do this with a certain amount of skill. No one would be happy if the child immediately forgot how to do it once the last lesson was over. The teacher wants the child to retain the knowledge at least for some time in the future – which is to say that he wants her to remember how to do it.

The same is true in other areas. When children learn that ions are charged atoms or that Britain's population massively increased in the nineteenth century, they are expected to retain this knowledge for some time at least. In the shorter term, they are expected to remember what they have learnt in one lesson until it can be reinforced or built upon in the next.

All this suggests that once we have knowledge objectives, memory objectives are otiose. Alternatively, of course, one might say that precisely because the knowledge is intended to be retained, the key aim is that children remember what they have learnt.

Whichever way, we no longer think in terms of special lessons on training the memory as if it were some mental organ which grows stronger on a diet of rote-learnt names and facts. Having said this, I remember from the early 1980s a primary teacher getting his ten-year-olds to take home once a week an 'information worksheet' to mug up. It consisted of a page of text on anything from the story of Bonnie and

Clyde to details of eruption of a volcano in Iceland. Back in class, Mr P. would read out a sentence from the text with a missing word in it which the children had to fill in. This *did* seem to be a pure exercise in short-term retention and recall: the content of the knowledge was not important. What the educational point of all this was never became clear.

I said just now that teachers want pupils to retain the knowledge they have acquired *at least for some time in the future*. For how long? For a lifetime? Until they have sat their end-of-school exams?

This takes us back – once again – to the aims of education and of schooling in particular. Some things learnt are meant to stay for life. Knowing how to read and write, most obviously, but also being kind, considerate, tolerant and no doubt much else besides in the realms of history, the arts and sciences.

Other things are jettisonable. Children who learn piano are not all expected to keep this up into their nineties. It is up to them after a certain point whether they choose to keep up the activity or drop it. Retention objectives are subordinated here to autonomy objectives.

At other times they are geared, more narrowly, to passing tests and exams. Whether their pupils are going to use mathematics throughout their lives – or whether they are to decide for themselves whether or not they want to follow it up – may not exercise some teachers nearly as much as whether they can remember how to solve quadratic equations sufficiently well to pass the upcoming exam. Strictly speaking, the aim is not simply that they continue to know how to do this at least for the next five months. They must also *recall* the knowledge at a specified time. Mental occurrences as well as continuants form part of the objective.

There are ethical questions about the point and value of all this. These are not the focus of this book, so I will leave them here – except to say that these questions *do* need answering. Parents, teachers, pupils and policy-makers have come to take it for granted that tests and exams are enormously important features of the educational landscape. This brief look at the place of memory in education may help them to see more clearly what this belief commits them to. How long is remembering supposed to be for?

Summary and key points

Central to children's learning is their acquisition of interconnected webs of belief about themselves and their world. These depend on an expanding and deepening conceptual understanding. As an intentional phenomenon, believing may take as objects false propositions as well as true ones.

Children's early education has partly to do with helping them to make distinctions between truth and falsity, and thus be able to acquire not merely belief but knowledge. Their acquisition of knowledge and understanding in different fields depends among other things on their grasp of the different patterns of argument used to support knowledge claims. Belief is an essential element in propositional learning of this sort, and also – thereby – in skill-learning.

Memory is a form of knowledge, covering skill-knowledge as well as memories of facts and of events. Memory training has been held in the past to be an important educational objective, but it is doubtful whether, given the link between knowledge and memory, the cultivation of memory needs to be a *separate* educational task. This has relevance for attitudes towards the use of tests and examinations in schools. See also Chapter 10 below for further discussion of the role of memory in children's self-understanding.

Further reading

For brief discussions of the concepts of belief, knowledge and memory see the alphabetically-arranged items on these three topics in Dancy, J. and Sosa, E., (eds) (1992) *A Companion to Epistemology* Oxford: Blackwell. See also the two entries on belief and one on memory in Guttenplan, S., (ed.) (1994) *A Companion to the Philosophy of Mind* Oxford: Blackwell. On beliefs in animals and pre-linguistic infants see MacIntyre, A., (1999) *Dependent Rational Animals* London: Duckworth, ch. 4. For a slightly fuller essay on the concept of knowledge, see Scruton, R., (1994) *Modern Philosophy* London: Sinclair-Stevenson, ch. 22; and for a book-length treatment of these topics, Audi, R., (1998) *Epistemology* London: Routledge. On memory in particular, see also Warnock, M., (1987) *Memory* London: Faber and Faber, as well as Winch, C., (1998) *The Philosophy of Human Learning* London: Routledge, ch. 10.

On the educational side more generally, a classic account of education as progression from belief to more and more adequate states of knowledge is in Plato's *Republic* Books 6, 7. Plato's *Meno* contains his view of learning as the remembering of innate ideas. There are problems in applying Plato's ideas on these topics directly to upbringing and schooling today since they are heavily dependent on a metaphysical position which is both complex and controversial. More recent philosophical writings on education have focussed mainly on knowledge, rather than belief or memory. Hirst, P.H., (1974) *Knowledge and the Curriculum* London: Routledge and Kegan Paul is a well-known text in philosophy of education, examining the curricular significance of different kinds of truth claim in different areas of knowledge. The place of knowledge-aims in education against the wider background of aims in general is discussed in White, J., (1990) *Education and the Good Life* London: Kogan Page, ch. 7. For a recent work in philosophy of education on epistemological topics, see Carr, D., (ed.) (1998) *Education, Knowledge and Truth* London: Routledge.

Chapter 4

Do minds develop?

From little acorns

The topic of the child's mind lends itself to metaphor. On one traditional view, the mind is a kind of eternally enduring entity, a private, unobservable, ethereal something, whose content is known only to its possessor. Our less religious age has often favoured something more scientific. On one view, minds are not spiritual substances but biological ones. They are seeds.

Like acorns, embryo minds grow – or develop – into more complex mature forms. A whole branch of educational theory called 'Child Development' came into being in order to study the laws and processes by which children's minds grow. Well-known educationists have embraced the developmentalist perspective: Rousseau in the eighteenth century, Pestalozzi and Froebel in the nineteenth, Jean Piaget in the twentieth, and in our own age Howard Gardner.

It is only in recent years that we have begun to speak of schools' 'mission statements'. But the basic idea was there before the word. For much of the twentieth century a key aim for many teachers was *the development of pupils' potentialities to their fullest extent.*

Development is a familiar biological notion. A human body develops in stages from an embryo into a mature physical specimen. Mature night-scented stocks develop in stages from the seeds in a seed packet. In the same way, according to developmentalism, a child's mind passes through stages of growth.

A conclusion that many have drawn from this view is that children's education can to a large extent be left to natural processes. For them the idea of the teacher imposing external objectives on the learner is anathema. Direction is given from within. The teacher is like a gardener tending seeds and seeing them grow into healthy plants.

Children need teachers, certainly, but only as plants need gardeners. The teacher's role is to provide the right conditions – the school's equivalent of soil, water and sunlight – in which learning can occur. Hence the notion of the 'kindergarten', or children's garden.

The assumption here is that children develop mentally as they develop physically. But do they?

What *is* development? In English the word has a transitive and an intransitive use. A teacher can try to develop in her charges a love of learning or non-racialist attitudes. That is the transitive sense. The developmentalist notion is intransitive. Children develop, full stop – just as eggs develop into chickens, full stop and bulbs into daffodils.

Development in the transitive sense raises few pedagogical eyebrows – except among those for whom any suggestion that teachers instil content from the outside is anathema. But development in the intransitive sense is a different story.

It is a biological notion, to do with the *unfolding* of an organism. This brings with it two further notions: *the seed*, or *initial state*, from which the unfolding takes place; and *the mature state*, towards which the unfolding proceeds.

There is no problem about locating these three elements in the growth of plants and of animal bodies. We have acorns and we have full-sized oaks, the former unfolding by stages towards the latter. We have the combination of sperm and ovum and we have the fully-grown horse or human being, the former unfolding, again, into the latter.

The big question is whether these features are also discoverable in the mental world. Of course, if minds are purely physical things and have no other than physical characteristics, things should be straightforward. Brains develop as the body develops; so if minds are brains, minds can develop. (See the Appendix for more on physicalist accounts of mind.)

But suppose mental phenomena are not equatable with physical. (See the Appendix on this, too.) What sense could we then make of mental development? Could we locate the crucial three elements? Is there an initial state, counterpart to the seed? Is there a mature state? Is there unfolding from the first to the second?

Mental seeds

The initial state, first. What might count as mental seeds? Could innate ideas (see Chapter 2) fill the role? The signs are not hopeful, partly because, as we saw earlier, there are serious doubts about whether innate ideas exist, or indeed could exist. But even if they could, would they be the *sort* of thing that fitted the bill? Would they be sufficiently seed-like?

The problem has to do with *unfolding*. Are concepts the kinds of thing that can unfold into more complex forms? It is hard to make sense of this. The nearest we can get to it is in the idea that concepts can *change*. A sixteen-year-old can have a very different concept of a bird from a two-year-old. She has a more definite idea of the place of birds in the animal kingdom, perhaps her views have been shaped by evolutionary ideas. Her concept of a bird has certainly become more complex. But this is not enough to say that it has *unfolded*. Dead bodies change, but do not unfold, when they decompose. A house begins as excavated earth and months later is a complicated structure of brick, wood and metal, but there has been no unfolding into the latter.

Mentalité sans frontières?

There are problems, therefore, about identifying the initial state. What about the end of the process – the mature state? We grasp this notion easily enough in physical contexts like fully-grown hollyhocks or human bodies. Can we understand it in the mental sphere? Would it commit us to minds as some kind of entity?

There are other problems. A fully-grown human body is one which can grow no further: it has reached the limits of its development. The same is true of delphiniums and oak trees. Like these, the human body can certainly go on *changing*, but the changes are to do with the maintenance, and later deterioration, of the system, not with its further growth. If we apply these ideas to the mind, do we want to say that all human beings have mental ceilings beyond which they cannot progress?

Taken literally, this does seem to be implied in the well-worn view that education is about the *fullest possible* development of pupils' potentialities. But the idea of mental ceilings goes against the grain for many teachers and indeed for many laymen. They like to think of mental life as expandable and deepenable in all sorts of directions. True, psychologists of intelligence and the IQ have often built the notion of mental ceilings into their notion of intelligence, but their views have been trenchantly criticised. I will come back to this in Chapter 5.

Can we hang on to the notion of mental development without commitment to the idea of an end-state? It has been suggested to me that we can – that what makes mental development different from physical is precisely that it has *no* ceiling, at least in non-brain-damaged individuals – that its trajectory is potentially endless. Mentalité sans frontières.

What grounds could there be for this? All other examples of biological development that we know have limits. If the evidence comes, as is likely, from our own and others' experience of expansion and deepening, why leap to a developmental interpretation? For other explanations are possible: cultural, rather than biological, for instance. The drive to conquer new heights and new fields is part of our non-stick-in-the-mud-culture. The open-endedness of our mental horizons is dubious evidence for this version of developmentalism.

In any case, it still has some notion of maturity built into it. Limitless mental unfolding from within is still *in a certain direction* – away from the less developed and towards the more developed.

Whichever way we take developmentalism, we are still left with the question: what *counts as* maturity in the mental case? With oak trees and human bodies, we know when maturity has been reached through the use of our senses. We can see that a person is fully grown, physically speaking, or that an oak tree has reached its full dimensions. What equivalent is there in the mental realm? How do we know either that people have reached their mental ceiling or, on the ceiling-less view, that they are more mentally mature than they were?

We do not just use our senses. We cannot *see* a person's intellectual maturity as we can see that he or she is physically fully grown. So how *do* we tell?

In ordinary life we make all sorts of judgements about people's intellectual maturity or about how far they have got in, say, their understanding of morality. What is significant about these judgements is that they tend to be controversial. Some people would see intellectual maturity in *Mastermind* terms, as being able to marshal and remember heaps of facts. Others would emphasise depth of understanding. Yet others a synoptic grasp of connexions between many different fields. And so on.

What counts as greater maturity in a more specific area like moral understanding is similarly contentious. For certain ex-ministers of education in the UK, this is a matter of having seen the need to conform to certain absolute rules – that you should never lie, steal, break your promises, etc. Other people might put more weight on sensitivity to others' needs, others again on an awareness of the great plurality of moral values and the need to strike balances among them.

Ordinary judgements of mental maturity lack the universality of agreement that we find over fully-grown pine trees or badgers. This is because we are in the realm of value judgements rather than of observable facts. Judgers apply their intellectual and moral values to their decidings. They differ among themselves because of the different weights they each apply to the multiple criteria operating in these areas.

Unwanted growth

Whether we look towards the beginning or towards the end of the development process, towards the seed or towards the full flowering, we find apparently insuperable problems in identifying a mental counterpart to physical growth. There are further problems, too, concerning determinism and predeterminism. Plants and animal bodies cannot help, given an appropriate environment, developing towards certain, usually rigidly prescribed, pre-set ends. How far can something like this be paralleled on the mental side? It conflicts with intuitions about free-will, in particular with the belief that individuals can have some autonomous input into the intellectual directions that they follow.

I shall leave such larger questions on one side. Without them there are doubts enough about the developmentalist project.

None of this means we should stop talking about the growth of children's minds, as long as this is not interpreted in a biological way. The mental capabilities and achievements of a well-educated sixteen-year-old are very different from those of a six-year-old. The older child has more complex conceptual schemes, a deeper understanding of many matters, vastly more factual knowledge about the human and physical worlds, greater emotional refinement. If we like to put things that way, we can say that he or she has a more developed mind, or that his or her mental powers have grown appreciably. But this way of speaking does not point unequivocally to developmentalism. It is compatible with belief in careful shaping by parents and teachers.

Very young children are sometimes portrayed as beings whom we find it difficult to fathom, creatures whose minds work in very different ways from ours. Getting inside the bizarre judgements they make is sometimes made to seem like an anthropological investigation of the thought-patterns of some primitive tribe. This perspective on the child's mind comes down to us from developmentalism.

It coloured a television programme I recently watched about the child's world. Children aged between three and five were asked to arrange objects on a table into two categories according to whether or not they were living things. The younger ones put the robot dog and the doll along with the live, caged rat and the wriggling maggots in the set of living things. A five-year-old put the potted plant at the non-living side of the table. Not until children grow older, we were told, does their concept of life exclude representations of living things and include plants as well as animals.

The child's world is not as alien as programmes like this suggest. Children's concepts of life or time do not slowly unfold from the utterly unfamiliar into the concepts we have as adults. It is not really surprising that Euan and the other boys and girls made the decisions they did. Would it not have been *much more amazing* if they had all confidently classified animals and plants together and excluded toy animals and dolls? We know already that pre-school children have not been introduced to the scientific concept of life we have got from biology. Their judgements are perfectly intelligible to us once we remember what they are likely to have been told about how the world is.

The programme claimed that the youngest children were at a stage where they could not differentiate between living things and representations of living things. This would make their thinking seem extremely primitive. But was it? Since their instructions were simply to put living things together, it is *quite understandable* that they should include dolls and toy dogs. For all we know, they might have acted very differently if the instructions had been fuller: 'Put just the *really* living things – not toy living things – on this end of the table'. If they could have understood this, the very fact that they did would show that they had *some* idea of the distinction which the programme claimed they did not have.

The central features of young children's minds are not biological phenomena best studied by the experimental or observational methods of science. We have a good idea of the beliefs, judgements, decisions, emotions of which they are capable once we know the concepts they have learnt and those they have not – always bearing in mind that concept-understanding can be a matter of degree. For the most part the methodology we should follow involves finding out the extent to which they have already been inducted by their parents and others into our shared conceptual world. Here we can take certain things as read – that children of four or five will not yet have a scientifically informed conception of living things, for instance.

One last point. Although developmentalism may have been under-mined, and therewith the thesis that minds grow as plants and animal bodies grow, this does not mean that minds are not in *any* way biological. Mental life is a feature of some animals, including human beings. It requires a brain, sense-organs and organs of locomotion. It has the biological function of helping the organism to survive. How it came to exist, on an evolutionary time-scale, in a previously non-mental world is a question to which neither I nor anyone else has the answer. Minds are biological in origin, even though not in the full-blooded way that developmentalism claims.

In human beings mental life has biological roots but is shaped according to social expectations. Earlier chapters have established this point firmly enough. A weakness in developmentalism is its individualism. It sees children as atomic organisms. It misconceives education as unfolding from within – instead of induction from without.

Despite political and press statements to the contrary, child-centred, or progressive, education in its developmentalist form has never been a major player in the classroom – as distinct from now defunct teacher-training colleges. This is all to the good, since it is more likely to be a hindrance to children's learning than a help. The more it demotes the careful, painstaking initiation of children into correct or appropriate ways of conceptualising, believing, feeling, and behaving, the more it sets them back.

Summary and key points

The idea, deriving from Rousseau, Pestalozzi and Froebel, that children's minds follow biological laws of development, has influenced child-centred views of psychology and of education down to our own time: Jean Piaget and Howard Gardner (see Chapter 5) are developmentalist theorists. The central idea is built on the assumption that what is true of the physical growth of plants and animal, including human, bodies also applies to human minds.

The claim is tested here by looking at what is presupposed in the notion of biological development – that an initial phenomenon, e.g. a seed, unfolds by stages into a mature entity. On the mental side there are problems about locating appropriate initial states. Innate ideas (see Chapter 2) do not seem to fit the bill. There are also difficulties about identifying mental maturity – and, in the specific case of moral development, moral maturity. These have to do mainly with the objectivity of claims about maturity, the alleged maturity of the mind being in this respect unlike the maturity of a fully-grown oak tree.

The theory is also often taken to imply that there are individual ceilings on children's mental growth – just as, from a physical point of view, they cannot grow beyond a certain height. The individualistic way of conceiving of the growth of children's understanding implied in developmentalism is at odds with the view, discussed in Chapter 2, that learning must be a matter of social induction.

Further reading

The seminal work in philosophy of education on developmentalism began more than thirty years ago, criticising the tradition originating in Rousseau's *Emile* (1762) and continued by Pestalozzi and Froebel in the nineteenth century. See Dearden, R.F., (1968) *The Philosophy of Primary Education* London: Routledge and Kegan Paul, ch. 3. The notion of development is discussed in Hirst, P.H. and Peters, R.S., (1970) *The Logic of Education* London: Routledge and Kegan Paul, ch. 3; as well as in an essay on 'The concept of development' by Hamlyn, D.W., and a reply by Elliott, R.K., in *The Proceedings of the Philosophy of Education Society,* Vol. 9, 1975. Both these latter essays are included in Hirst, P.H., and White, P., (eds) (1998) *Philosophy of Education: Major Themes in the Analytic Tradition* (four vols) London: Routledge, Vol. 2. Winch, C., (1998) *The Philosophy of Human Learning* London: Routledge, ch. 7, looks at development in relation to learning and includes a discussion of Piaget's theory. For a fuller critique of the latter see Hamlyn, D.W., (1982) *Experience and the Growth of Understanding* London: Routledge and Kegan Paul, ch. 4. A defence of child-centred views in general, which includes a discussion of the 'growth' metaphor, is in Darling, J., *Child-Centred Education and its Critics* (1994) London: Paul Chapman, especially pp. 75–82. See also White, J., (1998) *Do Howard Gardner's Multiple Intelligences Add up?* London: Institute of Education, pp. 6–12.

Chapter 5

Who needs intelligence?

[Lenin's sister] Maria Illinichna was to try to warn him that his opponent [Josif Stalin] was more intelligent and therefore more dangerous than he imagined. But Lenin would have none of it: 'He is absolutely not intelligent!' Thus spake the brilliant gymnazia student, the polyglot emigré and chief party ideologist. He was about to learn, in the last lesson of his political life, that intelligence was not monopolised by those who had formal cultural proficiency.

Robert Service (2000) *Lenin*, p. 454

Introduction

Intelligence is a topic more written about by psychologists than philosophers. In philosophical works we can find discussions of consciousness, perception and sensation, thought, action, memory, emotion, and imagination, but rarely anything on intelligence (unless it is on the technical topic of 'artificial intelligence'). Psychologists, though – many of them at least – cannot keep off the topic. It is a staple in every two-kilo textbook of psychology found in public and university libraries across the world.

Since all the running has been made in psychology, it makes sense to begin there. Everyone will know about the controversies over the IQ that have preoccupied psychologists for most of the twentieth century. They have been prominent in educational thinking and policy-making, largely as part of a theoretical justification for selecting children for schooling pitched at different intellectual levels. According to many psychologists, intelligence is what is measured by the Intelligence Quotient, as revealed by intelligence tests.

In one version, intelligence is something wholly innate. Cyril Burt (in Wiseman 1967, p. 265) defined it as 'innate general cognitive ability'. He saw it as an intellectual capacity, one closely connected with our powers of theoretical reasoning – which is why logical and linguistic problems form the staple of intelligence tests. Other psychologists have championed the role of environment over heredity in determining IQ.

More recently, yet others have claimed that intelligence is too narrowly defined in terms of abilities connected with IQ: there are 'multiple intelligences'. Howard Gardner identified seven of them by 1983 and discovered at least one and a half more – according to his own reckoning – by the mid-1990s. On the back of growing public interest in this proliferation of hitherto undiscovered abilities, a book entitled *Emotional Intelligence: Why it Can Matter More Than IQ* (Goleman 1996) became a number one best seller in the late 1990s. Meanwhile, advocates of innate intelligence as measured by IQ had come back to prominence via the also fast-selling *The Bell Curve: Intelligence and Class Structure in American Life* (Herrnstein and Murray, 1994).

For all their differences, these century-long disputes have at least given people to believe that intelligence is a key mental category. But this truth, if it is a truth, does not seem to have got through to the philosophers, even those who specialise in the philosophy of mind. With few exceptions, they scarcely mention the term.

How can one try to sort out whether intelligence is or is not a central feature of children's minds? A starting-point could be how we use the word 'intelligent' in ordinary language. A problem here is that over the last hundred years popular usage has been influenced by the psychological debates themselves. Because of the association of high IQ with selective education and vocational 'success', intelligence has become a socially prized attribute. Calling someone an intelligent person rather than a stupid one is not simply to say something descriptively about their mental life. It is to surround them with an aura of social approval.

Philosophers

Can we detach ourselves from such judgements? Those philosophers who *have* had things to say about the concept of intelligence have more often than not associated it with the flexible adaptation of means in the pursuit of one's goals On this view, there are as many types of human intelligence as there are types of human goal. Intelligence is displayed in countless different ways. A bowler wants to get the batsman out, so he varies his delivery. A motorist on the motorway wants to get home safely and adjusts her speed, lane and signals appropriately to road conditions.

Intelligence on this view has nothing particularly to do with the logical thinking allegedly measured by IQ tests. We all draw on it every day in the practical tasks and projects that make up most of our lives. We want to sort out a family holiday and think through different possibilities. We want to split up with our partner and wonder how most painlessly we can do it. As citizens, we want a housebuilding policy but are worried about the environment – so what is the best way through?

Perhaps through the impact of the IQ on twentieth century culture, intelligence has become popularly connected with skill in reasoning; but it is only in some cases that reasoning occupies a central place. When planning a holiday, people have to think things through. 'Switzerland would be idyllic for walking . . . but it's expensive . . . and July could be wet . . . who was it talking about North Portugal?' No doubt some trains of thought on this pattern can go on when driving on the motorway ('Why are they all slowing down? Roadworks ahead? Or accident? In any case, I'd better follow suit.'). More typically, however, the varying actions the driver takes in proceeding towards her destination are more immediate than that: she sees a red tail light ahead, a car coming into her lane, a derestriction sign and automatically, as it were, slows down, pulls out, accelerates.

Not that what she does is automatic in the sense that a washing machine works automatically once switched on. She has a mind and a washing machine has not. She has to *see* something happening in order to produce the reaction she does. Her consciousness is at work. In this case this does not take the form of thinking something through, but of seeing something and acting accordingly. Her long experience of driving has provided her with a number of repertoires, habitual responses to situations which obviate the need for reasoning.

If asked after the event, 'Why did you slow down just now?' she will reply 'Because I saw the cars ahead slow down'. She will, in other words, be able to articulate her reason for action. If she were unable to give some such answer we might indeed begin to doubt that she had acted intelligently. But although she *had a reason* for behaving as she did, no *reasoning-through* was necessary at the time. Reliance on her learnt repertoires was enough.

Observing intelligence

If we look at intelligence in this way, could it be something an observer could see exhibited in a person's behaviour? If we wanted to assess children's intelligence in a certain field, could we do this wholly from the outside?

A philosopher of behaviourist inclination like Gilbert Ryle would go along with this. Take his example of the soldier exercising his intelligence in scoring a bull's eye: 'Was it luck or was it skill? If he has the skill, then he can get on or near the bull's eye again, even if the wind strengthens, the range alters and the target moves' (Ryle 1949, p. 45). Intelligence, for Ryle, is a capability, or skill, underlying particular manifestations. You cannot tell from a single action whether or not it is intelligent. You have to look to a number of actions performed in different circumstances. Intelligence is a continuant. In Ryle's view, observable behaviour is all you need to, and can, go by – not one instance of it, but many instances in varied situations.

Ryle's general target is Cartesianism. He rejects the view that human beings have privileged access to their own minds. We are not necessarily the best judges of whether or not we possess a mental attribute like intelligence. Those who witness our behaviour are in a better position to say.

Yet it is doubtful whether intelligence in Ryle's sense *is* something that can be observed wholly from the outside. It is not on a par with observations a scientist makes about geological structures or the make-up of the Moon.

Suppose a chess-player puts her queen in the way of a pawn and then makes other disastrous moves. An observer is not likely to call this intelligent play. But add to this that she is playing with a sick child whom she wants to win and this judgment is reversed. This shows that the verdict has to take into account what agents *have in mind* – the goals they are trying to attain and the way they see what they are doing as means to these ends. Intelligence can only be understood by adopting the perspective of the subject. Observed behaviour is not enough (MacIntyre 1960).

Intelligence and flexible behaviour

One advantage of looking at intelligence as the ability flexibly to adapt means to ends is that it helps to make sense of attributing it to certain animals. We may not be secure on whether scallops or red ants are intelligent creatures but we tend to have less hesitation over cats and monkeys. Agreed, they lack the knowledge human language-users have of how what they are doing is connected to their goals. They do not have *reasons* for behaving as they do. They cannot, either before the event or retrospectively, think or say 'I am doing/have done X in order to bring about Y' (see Chapter 8). Even so, the roots of human practical rationality lie in our non-human ancestry. We share with certain other animals the ability to vary our behaviour in relation to goals. The place of sign-cognition in this was brought out in Chapter 2 in comments about its role in non-human behaviour and indeed in some sophisticated human performances. (It plays a part in the example just above about the driver slowing down on the motorway.)

Philosophical accounts of intelligence, sparse as they have been, have tended to assimilate it to a kind of practical rationality to do with means and ends. This may cast light on the question with which I began this chapter – *why* philosophers have not shown much interest in intelligence. Could this be because it boils down to something they have traditionally dealt with using other language – the language of 'thinking', 'means and ends', 'reasons for action', 'seeing X as a sign of Y'?

This question aside, will the account of intelligence in terms of flexible behaviour in relation to our goals really do? Suppose a latch-key child comes home from school and tries to unlock the front door. At first he finds himself using the garage key by mistake, so he switches to the house key. Then he cannot get this key into the keyhole because it is upside down, so he turns it round the right way. In all this he is behaving flexibly, varying what he does to the situation. But who on earth, seeing all this, would say 'Gracious, how intelligent!'? This is because we usually only call behaviour 'intelligent' if it in some way *transcends normal expectations* – if, for instance, a child applies her understanding in judgements which are abnormally quick or abnormally sophisticated.

This objection focuses on the kinds of occasions when we use the word 'intelligent'. But it is not clear how much light observations of this sort throw on what a concept involves.

To take another example. We talk about people's motives when there is, or may be, something untoward about what they are doing. We ask for the motives of a criminal, but not of a child going into a canteen. But the fact that we would never *talk* about people's motives for the quite ordinary and readily intelligible things they do does not imply that they do not *have* motives for these things (see also Chapter 8). The child's motive in going into the canteen is his desire to satisfy his hunger. The very obviousness of the motive explains why we have no need to mention it. We must beware of the same fallacy in writing into the meaning of 'intelligence' something to do with transcending normal expectations. Putting a key in a door is never *called* 'intelligent', but this does not imply that it *is not* intelligent. It is the very obviousness of its being an intelligent thing to do which makes it not worth saying that it is. Intelligent performances, like actions from motives, are such omnipresent features of our lives that it is scarcely surprising that we do not often trouble to call them what they are.

This discussion has been built around the view that intelligence is a matter of *practical* rationality to do with means–end links. But is this necessarily so?

Wider horizons

A man who has recently made an amateur film about Edward Jenner, the discoverer of vaccination, is reading the nursery rhyme 'Where are you going to, my pretty maid?' to his little grand-daughter, and comes across the line,' "My face is my fortune, Sir", she said'. He connects this with the fact that in the old days milkmaids were known to be immune to smallpox. This is an intelligent thing to do; but although the connexion he makes is itself no doubt connected with his wider interests, the intelligence this reveals has nothing to do with adapting means to ends. He has made a connexion of a theoretical rather than practical sort.

Is intelligence, then, something more general than either practical or theoretical rationality? Is it to be defined as the skill that manifests itself in acts of thought? (see Chapter 6). But this is problematic, too. Thinking is an activity; and many manifestations of children's intelligence – riding bicycles, playing tennis, turning keys in locks – are not accompanied by thought acts.

It looks as if intelligence must be something still more general. We must be careful here. It would be silly to fall into the trap of thinking that there must be some *essence* of it which we may find if we look hard enough. We call children or their performances 'intelligent' when they use their conceptual equipment appropriately in making theoretical or practical means–end judgements, especially where these are non-routine. We do also use the word – compatibly with the above – in a less determinate sense when we refer to human beings and some animals as intelligent creatures – where we mean by this that they have a mental life. Being intelligent on this view is simply having a mind.

But suppose there were an animal capable of feeling pain but having no other kind of mentality. Would *it* be an intelligent creature? There is some inclination to think not. There is nothing intelligent about being able to feel an ache in your leg. It is a more active notion than that.

In what way? In Chapter 1 I drew a sharp division between two sorts of mental phenomena: sensations, and those involving concepts. We seem to be homing in on the idea that intelligence has to do with the ability to operate conceptually.

I suspect we are at the end of the road. The term 'intelligence', as used in non-technical contexts, is very elastic. At its furthest stretch, it is equivalent to mentality in general or to that part of mental life which goes beyond sensations and into conceptualising. More restricted uses have to do with concept-using activities of a theoretical and particularly of a practical sort, in the latter case about means and ends. More restricted still is the term's employment to pick out only performances which are supranormal in some way – in speed, depth, breadth, etc. of connexions made.

All this throws a lot of light on philosophers' apparent lack of interest in intelligence. There is no Newfoundland of the mind which they have wilfully declined to explore. If intelligence is mind, they have been interested in this since the Greeks. If conceptual ability, ditto. If means–end rationality, ditto again.

Three levels of intelligence

A trichotomy whose origins go back to Aristotle is useful at this point.

Paperclips

(i) Some things are not intelligent at all: paperclips, boulders, loaves of bread. We could have added daisies and sequoias and perhaps hornets and clams as well, but instead of climbing further up the phylogenetic tree to animals like rabbits and antelopes where some kind of intelligence in the form of flexible behaviour seems undeniable, let us stay well clear of the biological world and concentrate on our plainly intelligence-less paperclips and rocks.

When we say a paperclip lacks intelligence, we are surely not saying that it is thick or stupid or unintelligent. We are dealing with a different sort of contrast.

Paperclips and rocks are not unintelligent; they are non-intelligent. They do not have the wherewithal ever to be able to conceptualise or display flexible goal-directed behaviour. They are constitutionally incapable of this, not being made of the right kind of stuff.

Human beings and some other animals are – nearly always – born with the ability to acquire concepts/flexible forms of behaviour as they grow up. They are intelligent creatures in a way that filing cabinets and sausages are not. To say that human beings are intelligent is to say that they are *constitutionally* – genetically – equipped with the ability, or capacity, to acquire such skills as speaking, playing hockey, driving cars, planning holidays, doing algebra, and an unlimited host of other things.

Non-drivers

(ii) A young person who has learned to drive has acquired a form of intelligence that a non-driver lacks. She can appropriately adapt her behaviour to road conditions. Both driver and non-driver are intelligent creatures as in (i), in that they are both born with the capacity to acquire a skill like driving. Only the driver manifests driving intelligence. How shall we characterise the non-driver?

In a way he is lacking in intelligence. In what way? Not, as we have seen, in the paperclip's way. He is not a non-intelligent creature. Is his lack of intelligence equatable with unintelligence? Surely not. We are not saying that just because he has not learnt how to drive he is stupid or a dimwit. His lack of intelligence is simply his not possessing the skill in question. We all lack intelligence in this sense in a million and one ways. Children from deprived backgrounds often lack intelligence in many areas where their more fortunate coevals are already adept. This is not at all to say they are 'thick'.

Plumbing disasters

(iii) The final contrast is between intelligence and unintelligence or stupidity. It is embarrassing and demeaning to have to admit it, but a year or so ago when I was trying to fix a leaking tap, I managed to project an unstoppable jet of scalding water across the kitchen and tried vainly to get near enough to smother it in a wodge of teatowels and handtowels. If I had thought for a moment and not panicked, I would have remembered to turn on the upstairs taps to reduce the pressure. It was really stupid not to do so.

We are all stupid from time to time (I tell myself). Stupidity consists in a lapse, a failure. We have the relevant conceptual abilities – knowing how to control the water system in my own case – but fail to apply them on a particular occasion. Just as lacking intelligence in sense (ii) presupposes possessing intelligence in sense (i), so lacking intelligence in sense (iii) presupposes being intelligent in sense (ii).

All this bolsters the claim that stupidity does not run through us like letters through a stick of Blackpool rock. Children may sometimes think of themselves as thickos, but they are logically awry in doing so. Stupidity is not a personal quality, on a par with such vices as meanness or intolerance. It is not an enduring feature of our personality, but a one-off or occasional failure – through tiredness, anxiety, panic or whatever – to activate the know-how we possess.

In a formulation whose general schema, if not this specific version, has been familiar to the philosophical world since Aristotle, we may conclude that we operate with three, related, concepts of intelligence. Beginning with the clearly biological one, we have:

(i)   Intelligence as the innate capacity to acquire specific intelligent abilities or capacities. Its opposite is non-intelligence.

(ii) Intelligence in an area as a specific, learned capacity (to speak, forage for food, swim, drive, etc.). Its opposite is the non-possession of this capacity.

(iii) Intelligence as the realisation, the successful application, of a specific capacity in a particular instance. Its opposite, stupidity or unintelligence, is a failure to apply this acquired capacity.

One last point before leaving the philosophers. The quotation about Lenin at the head of this chapter is a reminder that intelligence can be used for evil as well as good ends. Stalin was a flexible thinker all right when it came to working out the most effective ways of attaining or keeping power. The men behind the Great Train Robbery or the Brinks-Matt bullion theft were no woodenheads.

This should make educationalists think twice before placing intelligence on the pedestal it has so often occupied these last hundred years. It is an ethically neutral capacity. Aristotle himself did not consider mere cleverness a virtue. It is part of something else. The virtue of which it forms a part, for him, is practical wisdom. The practically wise person is one who uses reason practically in the conduct of his life – for the sake of his own flourishing as well as the flourishing of others within his community. This *includes* the flexible adaptation of means to ends (intelligence), but goes beyond this. For the practically wise person also thinks about the desirability of the ends themselves. The starting point is the good life. Intelligence comes in further down the road. Once the ethically good ends are in place, attention turns to – equally ethically acceptable – ways of realising them.

In our own age intelligence itself has sometimes been treated as an unequivocally desirable quality to possess. It has been *severed* from the wider notion of practical wisdom within which it has traditionally been embedded – but it has retained the aura of desirability it used to have as a part of something larger.

Psychologists

Intelligence and the IQ

I turn to the concept, or concepts, of intelligence used by *psychologists* over the last hundred years. Theories of all kinds have mushroomed, but have tended to veer towards one or other of two poles. On the one hand, towards the view best exemplified in Cyril Burt, that intelligence is 'innate, general, cognitive ability', where this is associated with the kind of logical reasoning allegedly tested by intelligence tests. On the other, towards the far more catholic position that intelligence can take many different forms – as in Howard Gardner's theory of 'multiple intelligences'.

In this way psychological treatments reflect the elasticity of the concept, mentioned above. Burt's view has strong affinities with Cartesianism. His version of intelligence is close to the innate power of ratiocination that Cartesians attribute to the mind – which for them is, indeed, the mind's *sole* attribute. For them, too, it is what makes us distinctively human. Something of this has attached itself to psychological work on the IQ. Intelligence tests have been seen as tapping into a power at the core of our humanity. In their early days they were associated, in Burt not least, with eugenic visions of an improved human race. Even after the demise of the eugenic project in post-Nazi times, the notion that children with very low IQs are somewhat less than fully human has stuck like a burr to the popular mind.

The rejection of Burtian intelligence towards the end of the twentieth century in favour of 'multiple intelligences' can be interpreted as a rejection of one account of what it is to be human in favour of another. Like Ryle's rejection of Descartes, this later view sees human beings as practical creatures, whose interests in getting things done may take many different forms. We have here a typically late twentieth century notion of human nature – a pluralistic, go-getting conception in which sportsmen, business people, artists, teachers can all be living a full human life. The human animal is no longer archetypically a theoretical thinker, a *penseur* as Ryle put it. This is now only one kind of social practice in which he or she might be engaged.

Similar remarks may be made about creativity. This began to fascinate some psychologists of the late twentieth century disillusioned with the IQ approach. Like other colleagues in their discipline in that century, their researches have not so much uncovered previously unknown facts about our mental life as thrust forward a challenger for the title Essence of Humanity. (See Chapter 7 for more on creativity.)

The endless spats earlier in the twentieth century among those within the IQ tradition over whether intelligence is innate or acquired took for granted the metaphysical importance of their concept in defining what we are. The centrality of abstract reasoning to specifically human nature was not in question, only the extent to which the power to do this is inborn or needs to be learned.

On the basis of the three-fold, 'Aristotelian', account of intelligence at the end of the last section, it looks as if there may be a pretty simple way of resolving these difficulties over nature versus nurture.

Is children's intelligence an innate capacity? Well, does it not depend on which sense of the term we take? Intelligence as the capacity to acquire capacities is clearly innate; intelligence in the other two senses is acquired.

It would be gratifying to think one could dispatch the 'nature–nurture' issue as quickly as this. But it would be odd if we could. For it would be surprising in the extreme if this long-standing controversy has turned on no more than a simple ambiguity in the word 'intelligence'.

Mental ceilings and the existence of God

In fact it goes deeper. Take the claim, born with Francis Galton in the nineteenth century, picked up in Cyril Burt's writings in the early twentieth, and at the basis of *The Bell Curve* arguments today (Herrnstein and Murray 1994), that intelligence is an innate capacity of some sort. In Burt's formulation it is 'innate, general, cognitive ability'.

Despite appearances, intelligence as so defined is *not* intelligence in the first of the three Aristotelian senses, i.e. is not intelligence as the (innate) capacity to acquire capacities. For intrinsic to the Galtonian concept is that individuals may *differ* in intelligence. One person may be more intelligent than another. The notion of possible degrees of intelligence is *not* written into the concept of intelligence as the (innate) capacity to acquire capacities. Animals, including human beings, either have this capacity or they do not. Human beings (in almost all cases) have it.

I have claimed, against Galton or Burt, that normally human beings do not differ in innate capacity. But 'capacity' is an ambiguous word. In one sense, it simply means 'power'. Human beings are born with the power of acquiring learned abilities, a power not found in plants and rocks. In another sense, it means more than this. In saying, for instance, that a milk bottle has a 'capacity' of one pint, I imply not merely that it has the power of holding one pint, but also that it *lacks* the power to hold more than this. There are upper limits on the amount it can hold.

The Galtonian concept of intelligence sees it as an innate capacity in this second sense. We are born not simply with conceptual powers, but with individually varying upper limits beyond which we cannot develop.

We can each hold only just so much intellectual substance. Some of us may be quart-size, others pint-size, others quarter-pint-size. Cyril Burt defined intelligence as 'innate, general, cognitive ability'. He wrote: 'The degree of intelligence with which any particular child is endowed is one of the most important factors determining his general efficiency all throughout life. In particular it sets an upper limit to what he can successfully perform, especially in the educational, vocational and intellectual fields' (Wiseman 1967, p. 280).

I cannot stress too strongly the difference between this Galtonian concept of intelligence and the first of the 'Aristotelian' senses. To say, in the Aristotelian way, that we have an innate capacity to acquire learned abilities does not imply that there is any upper limit, peculiar to the individual, on the abilities attainable. It does not imply an innate capacity in the milk-bottle sense of 'capacity'.

Does intelligence in the Galtonian sense exist? We cannot take it that it does without evidence. What kind of evidence would be necessary to confirm or refute this claim? What criteria would have to be satisfied to show that a person has an upper intellectual limit?

Poor achievement on its own would not be a criterion. If a child fails to understand a certain theorem in geometry – Pythagoras's perhaps – we cannot assume such understanding to be forever beyond him. He may well come to grasp it tomorrow – perhaps because his teacher has tried to explain it to him in a different way, or for some other reason.

But suppose all sorts of teaching methods are tried and none of them work. Would this be enough to show he had reached a ceiling? Is there not still always the possibility that some method may work of which we are now not aware? I suppose there always is. But it seems to me that, beyond a certain point (and I am not clear where that point is) doubts like this may become otiose. Some children with severe learning difficulties do seem to have intellectual ceilings, in that they are unable to acquire even a rudimentary grasp of language. Here the evidence is the failure of all sorts of different methods of helping them over this hurdle. Perhaps this evidence is insufficient. If so, we might conclude that the claim that at least some people have upper intellectual limits is unverifiable. I do not think I want to say this.

But the Galtonian claim is in any case stronger than this: not some, but *all* of us are so limited. Is *this* a verifiable proposition? A difficulty is that this now applies to normal people as well as those with severe learning difficulties. With the former it is so much more difficult to tell when the criterion has been satisfied. This is because they possess conceptual equipment which teachers can make use of in trying to devise different methods of getting them over intellectual hurdles. It is not clear to me just when, if at all, one would be justified in concluding that a normal person had reached his or her ceiling and that no further teaching efforts would be of any use.

It looks, therefore, as if the claim we are examining is in principle *unverifiable*. But neither does it seem to be in principle *falsifiable*. For what could possibly falsify the proposition that we all have intellectual ceilings? Nothing, as far as I can see. If one took the most brilliant person in the world, whose grasp of new ideas seemed boundless, even this would not be enough to falsify it. Even she might have her Pons Asinorum somewhere – even though no one could ever know what it was.

If this argument is correct, the belief that we all have our own upper limits of ability is both unverifiable and unfalsifiable in principle. So, too, therefore, is the belief that we all have innately determined upper limits, i.e. that there is such a thing as Galtonian intelligence. So too, indeed, is the more specific claim that we all have upper limits which vary along a normal curve. To say that these propositions are unverifiable and unfalsifiable in principle is to underline that they cannot be empirical hypotheses and therefore subject-matter for scientific investigation.

They are, rather, metaphysical speculations in the Kantian sense that they transcend the bounds of any possible experience. In their unverifiability and unfalsifiability, they are similar to the claim that there is always some unconscious motive for what we do. Or to the claim that every historical event is the product of economic forces. Or to the belief that God exists. All of these, as far as I can see, may be true. But no possible evidence could prove them right or prove them wrong.

Claims like this are often found at the centre of ideological systems of belief – psychoanalytic theory, Marxism, Christianity. This is not surprising. To say that a statement like 'God exists' cannot be falsified is to say that no one can produce any good reason for claiming that it is not true, or if you like, it is to say that its truth cannot rationally be denied. But if its truth cannot rationally be denied, its truth is surely undeniable. In which case one might be inclined to conclude it surely must be true.

This line of thought may help to explain why adherents of different ideological systems often cling so tenaciously to their beliefs, even where these depend on unverifiable propositions like the one mentioned. But it is fallacious. What is undeniable in the sense that it cannot be falsified is not necessarily undeniable in the sense that it must be true.

Like the religious and political claims I have mentioned, the proposition that we all have innately determined upper intellectual limits has become the hub of a new ideological system. Around it, too, have accreted all kinds of other propositions, both descriptive – for instance about the constancy of IQ, normal distributions and so on – and prescriptive – for instance about the different kinds of educational provision that ought to be made for children of different 'innate capacities'. As such a system grows in complexity and as its supporters occupy themselves more with discussions about details, the greater the likelihood that the basic beliefs, presupposed to these peripheral ones, get taken for granted. This makes them all the harder to question or relinquish. If two people, for instance, are arguing whether God is one person or three, they are each committed to the belief that God exists. If two others are arguing whether their IQ is a valid indication of their intellectual ceiling, they are each committed to the belief that we have such ceilings.

Multiple intelligences

How many of your intelligences have you used today?

An odd question? Not to the students in an Australian school who pass this message on a board each day on their way out of the building. For their schooling is based, like that of a rapidly growing number of pupils in the US, Britain and elsewhere, on the theory of Multiple Intelligences (MI) produced by the Harvard psychologist Howard Gardner.

Howard Gardner published his book *Frames of Mind* in 1983. In it he argued for the existence of a small number of relatively discrete 'intelligences' in human beings, combinable in different ways to form the intellectual repertoire of different individuals. Two of these, logico-mathematical intelligence and linguistic intelligence, are what IQ tests have focussed on. But intelligence is more multifaceted than this. Other intelligences include the musical, the spatial, the bodily-kinaesthetic, the intrapersonal and the interpersonal. His recent research has added to the original seven both the classificatory intelligence of the naturalist and – he has some doubts on this one – spiritual intelligence. He says, half seriously, that while Socrates viewed human beings as rational animals, he himself sees them as animals possessing eight-and-a-half intelligences.

Gardner's views about multiple intelligences have grown increasingly influential over the years. He is now one of the most well-known experts on intelligence not only in the US, but across the world. In addition, thousands of so-called 'MI schools' have sprung up in recent years in the US, Canada, Australia and elsewhere, all based on his theory. Some of Gardner's disciples, as in the Australian example with which we began, believe that the curriculum should be based on the development of all the 'intelligences'. Gardner himself (1993, p. 71) sees more educational mileage in recognising that pupils 'have quite different minds from each other', and that 'education should be so sculpted that it remains responsive to these differences'.

His ideas have also been influential in Britain. In the late 1990s MI theory became a liberating force in school improvement projects across the country, from Sandwell and Birmingham in the West Midlands to Govan in Scotland. It is not difficult to see why such a notion should appeal to teachers and policy-makers working in deprived areas and faced with underachievement. Many children in these areas are held back by a low self-concept. They see themselves as dim or thick. But this is within the framework of the traditional version of intelligence –

they are poor at the kind of abstract logical thinking that IQ tests target. Broaden the picture and their perceptions are transformed. 'Children are born smart', as a project leader from Birmingham put it. Their abilities may lie in physical activities, in music, in the visual arts, in interactions with other people. Extended learning schemes in West Midlands, Glasgow and other schools have tapped into these and other areas. Once children become aware of how intelligent they are in this field or that, their self-esteem has been said to increase amazingly.

None of the projects mentioned has been slavishly attached to Gardner's theory. They have all used it more as a catalyst for unlocking pupils' – and parents' – minds. This is just as well, because the theory itself is decidedly flaky.

I suspect that many of Gardner's supporters on the ground have had, as busy people, little opportunity to go through his theory with a toothcomb. The idea that intelligence is not restricted to abilities tested by IQ tests but is found in all sorts of areas has wide appeal in the education world. It is a vital support in the work that teachers do in trying to overcome pupils' perceptions that they are unintelligent.

But so far this has nothing specifically to do with Gardner's theory of MI. We should distinguish between the *general* claim that intelligence takes many different forms – not being restricted to the kind tested by IQ tests – and the *particular* version of this claim embodied in MI theory. The former is not new. Ryle (1949, p. 48) had reminded us that 'the boxer, the surgeon, the poet and the salesman' possess their own kinds of intelligent operation, applying 'their special criteria to the performance of their special tasks' (ibid.). There are, as I said earlier, as many types of intelligence as there are human goals.

And more than two thousand years ago, as we have seen, Aristotle had distinguished the merely clever person, who is good at adapting means to ends whether the ends are desirable or not, from the practically wise person, who makes sure the ends are good to start with.

As we also saw earlier, intelligent action has to do with the flexible adaptation of means in the pursuit of our goals and there are as many types of human intelligence as there are types of human goal. Once unbewitched by IQ, we should find this familiar enough. Gardner has always admitted the great number of different ways in which intelligence is manifested. Yet he has sought to *regiment* this variousness, to corral it within a small number of categories, within what he has called his 'charmed circle of intelligences' (Gardner 1983, p. 60). The seven (in later versions, eight or more) intelligences are the relatively autonomous basic building blocks of all the rest, several of them participating in the boxer's skill, another combination of them in the surgeon's, and so on.

What criteria guide Gardner in distinguishing his areas of intelligence? They embrace the following (pp. 62–9):

- The potential isolation of the area by brain damage
- The existence in it of idiots savants and other exceptional individuals
- An identifiable core operation/set of operations
- a distinctive developmental history, along with a definable set of expert 'end-state' performances
- Evolutionary history and plausibility
- Support from experimental psychological tasks
- Support from psychometric findings
- Susceptibility to encoding in a symbol system.

I will not go into a detailed critique of these criteria, partly because I have already done this elsewhere (White 1998). To a lay person it may look as if scientific discoveries in these different fields have all converged on the conclusion that the human mind is structured around the seven (or so) intelligences. But this is far from being so.

This is partly because at least two of the criteria depend not on empirical evidence but on psychological or philosophical *theories* whose credentials rest on shaky foundations. One of these, the developmentalism presupposed in the fourth criterion, was subjected to radical critique in Chapter 4. The other – which lies behind the final criterion – is the philosopher Nelson Goodman's theory of symbol systems in the arts and other areas. His is a highly controversial position which many philosophers, including leading aestheticians, would reject.

There are also problems about how the criteria are to be used to pick out the intelligences. Gardner's writings, as I substantiate elsewhere, fail to make it clear whether they are all intended to be necessary conditions or whether a weaker requirement is at work. Sometimes he suggests they *all* have to be satisfied; while in other places he seems content with a *majority* of them. (Any five?) Elsewhere again he tells us that there is no 'algorithm for the selection of an intelligence, such that any trained researcher could determine whether a candidate intelligence met the appropriate criteria' (1983, p. 63). Rather, he goes on, 'it must be admitted that the selection (or rejection) of a candidate intelligence is reminiscent more of an artistic judgement than of a scientific assessment' (ibid.). I do not know if there is anything more to this admission than the thought that the identification of intelligences is a subjective matter, depending on the particular weightings that the author gives to different criteria in different cases.

But the most fundamental problem with Gardner's scheme is this. How does he *justify* the *particular criteria* he lists to pick out intelligences? I have not been able to find any answer in his writings.

An overall verdict. Gardner was right to challenge the identification of intelligence with what IQ tests test, and to claim that it takes more varied forms than the linguistic and logico-mathematical abilities required by those tests. But he goes adrift in trying to pigeonhole this huge variety within his seven or eight boxes. His success in opening teachers' and project workers' eyes to new possibilities deserves our gratitude. It is aided by the fresh and accessible way in which he presents his ideas. But there are dangers in taking MI theory on board. The seven or eight categories are too close to familiar curricular areas for comfort. We may escape the shackles of IQ intelligence only to find ourselves imprisoned within another dubious theory.

Can we do without it?

So do teachers and parents *need* the concept of intelligence? Is it helpful or confusing to them in thinking about children's minds?

All the running, as has been seen, has been made by psychologists. It is they who have written about it, unstoppably, for over a century. It is they who have seen in enquiry into its nature and its measurement the key to human nature and, in some cases, the improvement of the race. Their enduring internal differences, on the innatist–environmentalist and the monist–pluralist dimensions, have reinforced the lay perception that matters of great importance are at stake and that one day science will resolve all the difficulties.

But reality has been otherwise. It is doubtful whether a century of psychologising about intelligence has advanced our knowledge beyond what was already grasped by Aristotle. It has certainly given us ideologies, unjustified claims and confusions aplenty, but that will be no comfort to parents and teachers looking for clarity and enlightenment.

We cannot dispense with the notion of intelligent behaviour as the flexible adaptation of means to ends. There should be no question about that. The only real issue is whether we need the notion as *the self-standing, truncated thing it has now become,* since the ethical framework in which it was located as part of the wider notion of practical wisdom has fallen away. Detached cleverness in this or that area is what for obvious reasons political and business leaders want to encourage in – at least some – school students. Young people who have been blinkered from ethical reflection on ends can be useful tools.

But whether a civilised society still needs to put so much weight on this denuded notion of intelligence rather than the more all-embracing concept of practical wisdom is another question.

Summary and key points

How useful is the notion of intelligence in understanding the child's mind? Psychologists, not least those interested in measuring IQ, have worked extensively on the topic for a century, while philosophers have rarely referred to it.

Those philosophers who have, have often understood intelligence in terms of flexible adaptation of means to ends, and thus as a broader notion than the collection of intellectual abilities assessed in intelligence tests. On this view, many actions can be intelligent without our ever having reason to refer to them as such. A behaviourist approach to the topic is problematic. So, perhaps, is the whole attempt to pin down *the* meaning of intelligence, since the concept can be used in wider and narrower senses. At its widest, it is equatable with mind itself, at least in its concept-involving aspects.

Adopting an Aristotelian approach, we can distinguish three levels of intelligence. The first is innate in human beings and some other animals, the second to do with abilities acquired through learning, the third, with the application of these learned abilities in judgement.

Turning to psychological accounts, Cyril Burt's account of intelligence as 'innate, general, cognitive ability' assumes that this innate ability sets ceilings on the intellectual level which individual children can attain. (See Chapter 4 for the role of ceilings in developmentalist accounts of the mind.) This assumption appears, perhaps like claims about the existence of God, to be both unverifiable and unfalsifiable. Howard Gardner's recent theory of 'multiple intelligences' rejects the narrow focus on logical and linguistic skills found in Burt and other IQ theorists, but is itself open to philosophical critique.

Aristotle was critical of cleverness as a faculty taken in isolation from practical wisdom. The latter is a moral virtue and is wider than cleverness, requiring reflectiveness about the goodness of ends as well as about effective means to ends. This bears on the extent to which intelligence is indeed a key concept in understanding the child's mind.

Further reading

As stated in the main text, philosophical discussions of intelligence – at least where this term is used explicitly – are rare. There is no item on the topic, for instance, in Guttenplan, S., (ed.) (1994) *A Companion to the Philosophy of Mind* Oxford: Blackwell. But a classic philosophical discussion, from a behaviourist perspective, is Ryle, G., (1949) *The Concept of Mind* London: Hutchinson, ch. 2. See also MacIntyre, A., (1999) *Dependent Rational Animals* London: Duckworth, ch. 4, on 'the intelligence of dolphins'. For a more general account of abilities and dispositions, see Kenny, A., (1989) ch. 5. Aristotle's distinction between cleverness and practical rationality is found in his *Nicomachean Ethics*, Bk 6, section 12 [1144a18]. The three-fold 'Aristotelian' distinction derives from Aristotle's *On the Soul* Bk II, 5 [417a21].

As a more educationally orientated text, White, J., (1998) *Do Howard Gardner's Multiple Intelligences Add Up?* London: Institute of Education, on which this chapter draws, includes a general account of the concept as well as a critique of Gardner, H., (1983) *Frames of Mind* London: Heinemann; and Gardner, H., (1993) *Multiple Intelligences: the Theory in Practice* New York: Basic Books. For a short philosophical critique of psychological work on intelligence and the IQ, see Kleinig, J., (1982) *Philosophical Issues in Education* London: Croom Helm, ch. 11. For a longer critique, see Winch, C., (1990) *Language, Ability and Educational Achievement* London: Routledge, chs 1–6. Barrow, R., (1993) *Language, Intelligence and Thought* Aldershot: Edward Elgar, is a longer discussion of intelligence and its place in education. Barrow's account of intelligence, unlike the one in the present chapter, ties it more to intellectual enquiry.

Chapter 6

What is thinking?

A chastening chapter title. It reminds me of an episode in bringing up my daughter that I would rather forget. It may have been the Milwaukee Maulers or the Chattanooga Cheetahs – I don't recall exactly – but whichever team it was figured in an exercise on syllogisms in a logic text. I had got hold of it to hone my nine-year old-daughter's thinking skills. How I cajoled her – and her mother – into working through examples like these and spotting invalidities I cannot now imagine. Quite likely I presented it as a new kind of family fun(!). At all events, it was hard going and I soon gave up syllogisms for logic puzzle books from our local newsagent. I thought they would be closer to real life, but working out whether Andrew who is vegetarian, likes fishing and volleyball but not soccer or swimming, and is free only on Mondays and Thursdays is taller than Brian, who . . . proved to be, if anything, even less riveting.

A philosopher should know better than to believe that the improvement of thinking in general is likely to come about through exercises in logic. These demand a highly specialised form of thinking. It is not focussed on clashes between competing commitments, on hitches in personal relationships, on how to fix a broken bicycle, on the flooded garden – or any of the other things we commonly think about. It is directed on to *certain abstract relationships between statements*.

While we may not want children to become formal logicians, we *do* want them to tackle practical problems in everyday life, think mathematically or historically, engage in creative writing, think how they should live a fulfilling or a morally good life.

What do such things have in common which makes them all kinds of thinking?

Thinking as an activity

Let us get an obvious distinction out of the way.

- If a child *is thinking*, about some problem in algebra, say, she is engaging in a kind of activity. Something is presently going on in her mind.

- If a teacher asks a student what he *thinks* about a point just raised in class, she is asking about what he believes, not about what activity he is engaging in.

In the language of Chapter 1, the difference is between thinking as an occurrence and thinking as a continuant.

As we saw there, teachers aim at modifying and improving continuant states of mind – beliefs, skills, personal qualities – by involving students in ongoing mental activities – looking at things, thinking about problems, feeling sympathy with others. On one side aims, on the other pedagogical procedures.

The distinction between thinking as an activity and thinking as believing fits this. Through involving children in thinking activities teachers enable them to gain new beliefs and modify old ones. Thinking hard in a civics lesson about how to handle problems of pollution may bring a child to believe there are no easy solutions.

Thinking activity in the classroom is not always targeted on *beliefs*. Teachers may also want to develop *skills* of argumentation. Encouraging children to think more carefully about how they should behave towards other people may be part of fostering certain *personal qualities*.

Kinds of thinking activity

There are many kinds of thinking activity. Some are more relevant to educators than others. Thinking can be undirected. Daydreaming, unlike thinking about a problem, is not consciously focussed on a goal. One thought triggers off another in an often haphazard way. Whether daydreaming has any place in education is moot. It can be a distraction from serious business. On the other hand, if Yeats had been jolted out of his childhood daydreaming and forced towards something more productive, perhaps he would not have become a great poet.

Other thinking is directed, focussed perhaps on a task or goal. Not that there is a clear-cut line between undirected and directed thinking. There may be all sorts of borderline cases.

There is no unique way of classifying types of directed thinking. It depends on your wider purposes. In an educational context, there are good reasons for beginning with the traditional distinction between theoretical and practical thinking.

Theoretical thinking is directed towards the discovery of truth. It features, for instance, in curriculum activities which have that aim, such as mathematics, history, geography and science. It takes different forms from domain to domain.

Practical thinking is about deciding what to do rather than finding out what is the case. If I am stuck in a traffic jam and apply myself to how best to get out of it, I am engaging in practical thinking about the most effective means of achieving my end. Students in a practical science lesson asked to devise an experiment to test a hypothesis are also doing this. So is a civics class discussing how to reduce pollution. All these are forms of practical thinking.

So is thinking about *ends* as well as means. The teenager who wonders whether he should be spending so long studying instead of socialising (or vice-versa) may just have instrumental considerations in mind (he wants to be accepted in his group, or he wants to get into higher education); but he may also be beginning to weigh up what things are important to him for their own sakes, or what priorities there should be among human ends in general.

The links between theoretical and practical thinking are important, too. Practical thinking draws at many points on the *results* of previous theoretical thinking. Deciding what is to be done about pollution, for instance, depends on factual data on its nature and extent. But practical thinking can also *incorporate* theoretical – truth-seeking – thinking within itself. In deciding how to get out of the traffic jam, part of my reasoning may include (although probably not in such an articulated form, given the scrappy nature of my actual thinking processes) such a sequence as 'If I turn off at Redland Road, will I get held up at the T-junction? I'd better not risk it, so it would be better to . . .'.

Are there any other types of directed thinking beyond the theoretical and the practical? A common feature of both is that they are, for the most part, forms of *reasoning* – about what is the case or about what is to be done. Contemplation is different. A religious person at prayer is focussing his mind on God or on nirvana. This is directed thinking, but not thinking harnessed to some further purpose like truth or action. It is thinking undertaken for its own sake, with its own intrinsic rationale. Or take someone looking at a Rubens painting in an art gallery. She contemplates its different features and their relation to the whole work, again not with any extrinsic purpose in mind but as an end in itself.

And what shall we say about physical activities – playing tennis, driving a car, making a pot, painting a picture? Does thinking come into these at all? To be sure, they may all involve some element of practical reasoning. Between games a young tennis player may think out strategies to help her win the match, but is she thinking when she is in the thick of an exciting rally and has no time to reason things out?

If she is playing well, she has her mind on her task: she is thinking what she is doing. And in so far as she is thinking, this must be directed thinking rather than the freewheeling variety we find in daydreams. More on this in a moment.

Have we now covered every sort of thinking? What about a scientist or historian searching for a hypothesis, or a poet coming up with an appropriate metaphor? This is directed thinking, but its products are not wholly generated through a process of reasoning. They come via 'imaginative leaps'. As the example of the scientist shows, imaginative activities are not to be put in a different pigeon–hole from theoretical thinking. Hypothesis-making in science is part of a larger enterprise aimed at discovering truth.

Four theses about thinking

Thinking is intentional

We cannot just think, full stop. Our thinking is always thinking *of* or *about* something, or thinking *that* something is the case. A child can be thinking about her mother, or thinking that the weather has been horrible recently. Thinking, in other words, is an intentional phenomenon (see Chapter 1). In the examples just given, the object of her thinking actually exists (in the case of her mother), or is true (in the case of the weather). But this need not be so. A child can be thinking about werewolves even though they do not exist. In Chapter 1 I discussed this feature of intentionality in general: that its objects may or may not exist.

This is of obvious significance for parents and teachers. A large part of their task has to do with weaning children from what is false or non-existent and directing them towards what is true and real. But this is not the whole story. If thinking were always tied firmly to actuality, there would be no room for children to enjoy *Alice in Wonderland*, putting themselves in others' shoes, or producing speculations about why birds migrate.

Thinking is an activity

Thinking is distinguished from certain other intentional phenomena, like feeling grief, for instance, in that it is an *activity* – something that we do as distinct to something that happens to us, overcomes us. The activity is sometimes undertaken as a means to a further end – the discovery of truth or decision-making; and sometimes as an end in itself – as in religious or aesthetic contemplation.

In the former, means–end, case, the immediate intentional object of our thinking is in a sense incomplete. It forms part of a larger object which includes the further purpose we have in mind. If, for instance, a child is working out a long multiplication sum, say 314 × 569, and at a particular moment is thinking about what nine times four makes, her immediate object of thought is the sum of 9 × 4, but this is part of a larger project.

In the case of contemplation, the immediate object of our thinking may be complete in itself if, for instance, our attention can be focussed on God alone. But contemplation can also embrace incompleteness, although incompleteness of a different sort from that found in theoretical or practical reasoning. The student looking at a Rubens painting of the Last Judgement may be thinking of the beatific expression on the face of a saved woman. However, this is not an atomic activity, but rather one that forms a part of the larger enterprise of appreciating the work as a whole. The reason why aesthetic contemplation is different in its incompleteness from reasoning activities is this: in the former the incomplete object is related in a *part–whole* way to the larger concern, while in the latter the relationship is, more specifically, *means–end*.

Thinking employs concepts

I remember from way back my former colleague Richard Peters's wry remark about a recent book about teaching children to think, called *Thinking with Concepts*. 'As if you could do anything else!' he said.

The idea that thinking must involve the use of concepts seems unproblematic. An intentional object, as we saw in Chapter 1, brings with it the use of concepts. Thinking of x must be thinking of x under some description, that is, *as* such-and-such. So when a girl thinks about her mother, she thinks of her not as others may do — as a pleasant neighbour, an old friend — but as her mother.

Concepts are also required in thinking for a further reason. If thinking is an activity, thinkers know what they are doing when thinking. They have an understanding, not necessarily a very explicit one, of their purpose — whether this is extrinsic as in the case of reasoning, or intrinsic as in contemplation. This purpose is also something that comes conceptualised. The child thinking out the answer to 314 × 569 is aware that she is working out a multiplication sum. Unless she had that latter concept, she could not engage in this type of thinking. Moreover, in this and in other cases of reasoning, the young thinker needs concepts in order to be able to operate with the propositions which come, again not always explicitly, into the chain of reasoning ('nine fours make thirty-six, so put down six and carry three').

Can there be conceptless thinking? Some religious or aesthetic ideals of contemplation may suggest this, but it is inconceivable that they could dispense with conceptualisation altogether. Given the contemplator is attentive to something, there must be some aspect under which he thinks of this. More generally, he must also have some kind of conception of what he is about in contemplating in the first place. Concepts do seem to be indispensable in thinking.

The immediate educational relevance of all this is that if children are to learn to think, they must possess the concepts necessary for the thinking in question. I will come back to this point later.

What are we to make of the view that thinking is displayed in physical activities like playing tennis, even where no reasoning is occurring? If thinking does indeed take place, where are the concepts?

Given the argument in Chapter 2 is sound, there is no problem. We are dealing with sign-cognition. A learner playing tennis properly is thinking what she is doing. When she sees the ball flying back over the net, she sees it as about to go deep, land with spin, or whatever, and gets set to react accordingly. Her thinking is directed onto an object — the flight of the ball — that she sees in a certain way, as a sign for a response of a certain sort.

True, her thinking is not autonomous, in the way that reasoning and contemplating are. It is tied to her perceptions, only coming into play when she is watching the ball or the reactions of her opponent. It is not thinking that she can carry out when and where she likes. It is not directly linked to possessing language and the structures of logically interrelated concepts this brings with it.

Thinking is a skill

Thinking is an activity. It is something that goes on in the mind. It is an occurrent phenomenon. But it is also something at which children can improve. The activity can get better with practice. This is why thinking is sometimes characterised as a skill. It has a continuant as well as an occurrent side to it. Part of the educator's task is to build up children's thinking skills through engaging them in thinking activities.

We could use the word 'intelligence' to label the skill, or skills, of thinking (in the second of the 'Aristotelian' senses of 'intelligence' picked out in Chapter 5). But because of controversies surrounding intelligence sketched in that chapter, it is probably better to stick to the expression 'thinking skill'. Thinking can improve through practice. Children can learn to avoid obstacles in attending to whatever they are supposed to be thinking about. Where reasoning is concerned, their conceptual repertoire can expand and equip them for more sophisticated activity. They can telescope reasoning which once had to be more fully explicit into abbreviated chains of argumentation full of gaps, leaps, shortcuts. The judgements they make on particular occasions help them on future occasions to think more effectively, more powerfully, more deeply. In all these ways their thinking skills improve. If we like, we can speak of these things as improvements in their intelligence. But it may be better to back off from this for the reason suggested.

Is thinking *just* a skill, a form of know-how? In PE a child may learn how to climb a rope. She acquires this skill. But suppose – like most of us? – she then never uses it. For some time she may still *have* the skill, or a rusty version of it, even though she does not tap into it. When we encourage children to think, we can't be satisfied with this. We want them to use their skills on a more regular basis, to get into the *habit* of thinking clearly about what they are to do and to believe. We want to develop thinking *dispositions* in them.

Are there general thinking skills?

Very early in my teaching career – long before I became a father and got into the Milwaukee Maulers and the Chattanooga Cheetahs – I was already sold on the idea of general thinking skills. When I was a pupil myself, so much of my own school's curriculum had consisted of factual information or circumscribed skills. So did the History and French syllabuses I was expected to teach in my Ilford school.

What had the spat between Stephen and Matilda, or the use of the pluperfect, to do with the meaning of life? Learning could and should be more stimulating. The trouble was that schools were obsessed with easily examinable bits and pieces and had lost sight of fundamentals. They should be in the business of teaching pupils to think for themselves.

I had broached this, in fact, on my teaching practice – with a bright sixth-former whom I had been asked to prepare for the Oxford and Cambridge general papers. I began toughening up her mental powers with exercises from a book I was keen on called *Lines of Thought*. (I remember something about spotting the fallacy in the claim that if it takes one aspirin twenty minutes to clear a headache, two aspirins would cut the time in half.)

I do not know what became of Sasha or how tough her mind became in the end. But a few years later I was listening to a friend reading her paper to a conference of young teachers studying philosophy of education. 'We need radically to rethink the curriculum', she argued. 'Subjects have had their day. They obstruct the true task of education. Pupils must be encouraged to become critical and creative thinkers.'

My delight in her new vision of education was shattered by her respondent, one of the course tutors. He pointed out that there is no such thing as critical or creative thinking in general. It all depends on the subject matter. Someone who can think critically about a poem is not *ipso facto* able to think critically about a claim in history. A creative scientist – good at thinking up challenging hypotheses – is not necessarily good at composing music. You cannot get rid of school subjects as easily as that. Certainly, there is too much concentration on learning facts and not enough on thinking for oneself. Schools ought to spend more time fostering pupils' powers of reasoning and their capacity to generate original ideas. But these are not *general* traits which transcend timetable divisions. Each major discipline of thought – history, mathematics, science, literary studies, philosophy, etc. – has *its own* forms of reasoning, of critically assessing others' claims, of making imaginative leaps. To aim at improving thinking in general is a logical nonsense.

My faith in general thinking skills ended that day – until, that is, my lapse as a pedagogic parent. What I had not realised was how perennial the interest in them has been. In the late nineteenth century educationalists brought up on faculty psychology saw the aim of education as training various mental muscles, including understanding, reasoning and judgement (Selleck 1968, pp. 45–58). In the mid-twentieth, an influential US report distinguished three forms of effective thinking – logical, relational and imaginative – and claimed that these were respectively best promoted by the natural sciences, the social sciences and the humanities. Fifty years on again, the British government included thinking skills – information-processing, reasoning, enquiry, creative thinking, evaluation – in its revised National Curriculum for 2000 onwards.

What is the appeal of general thinking skills? Like 'key skills' in other areas, they are thought to be transferable, so that if we acquire them in one context we can apply them in others. Such messages are not lost on governments. Transferable skills deliver more educational goods than more specific forms of learning. They give students more intellectual power and use fewer resources. They are the educational policy-maker's magic key.

But it is highly unlikely that there are widely transferable thinking skills – for the reason put forward in that devastating conference session all those years ago. The reasoning and enquiring acquired in history classes is very different from the reasoning and enquiring involved in learning geometry or planning a family holiday. Each requires a knowledge of its particular subject matter, draws on its own kinds of evidence, and reasons according to its own standards. Imaginative (sometimes called 'lateral') thinking about how to get six people across a river using a piece of rope, a car tyre and five plastic bags looks very different from a speculation that human beings may have evolved through natural selection. There *may* be general skills that cover widely diverse fields, but it should not be assumed that they exist before evidence – and there is at present *no* good evidence – is provided for this. They may well prove to be a will-o'-the-wisp. No doubt there is likely to be some transfer in closely similar fields, but a belief in transferability *across the board* is (as yet) unfounded.

We can see the seductiveness of the idea. If we review the various curriculum subjects, we see that many of them involve children enquiring into things – the population explosion, photosynthesis, Keats's poems, volcanic eruption. So these all have something in common – enquiry. If we focus on this common element, abstracting from the particularities, we can – it seems – determine what enquiry is in general and then turn to finding how to teach it.

It is true enough that we can examine the concept of enquiry in general. But what follows from this about teaching and learning? There are cars, helicopters, motor bikes, speedboats, vans, trains and trams. All these have something in common. They are all vehicles of transport. But if we want to manufacture vehicles of transport, we do not make some abstract product that can go on roads, water, railtracks and across the sky.

Formal and informal logic have always attracted adherents of general thinking skills, especially the more philosophical ones. My work on fallacies with Sasha and later with Louise was in this mode. If you want people to think straight rather than crookedly, getting them to see what constitutes a good argument and what a defective one seems the most sensible way forward. Work on valid and invalid syllogisms is an obvious method of doing this.

Suppose a pupil is a whizz at sorting out the soundness of such arguments as 'Socrates is mortal. All men are mortal. So Socrates is a man.' What does that show about the quality of her thinking?

There are two points here. First, being good at spotting fallacies of this sort does not necessarily go with being good at criticising an argument in science or economics. Not all good arguments can be laid out in a tight logical form. If the historian's evidence is true, it does not yield the incontrovertible conclusion of the valid syllogism.

Second, an educationally important distinction is between the process and the product of thinking. The former is about what people are doing when engaged in the activity of thinking, the latter with what their thinking generates, if successful.

The distinction between product and activity is made harder for English speakers to see because they use the word 'thought' to cover both. Pascal's *Thoughts* were what he achieved through his thinking activity, that is his 'thought' in the procedural sense.

The whizz at syllogisms – or for that matter the whizz at degutting an argument in biochemistry or politics – operates on the *product* of thinking. She is good at separating premises from each other and from conclusions. Perhaps she is good at locating the presuppositions lying behind premises. All this makes her skilful at studying the relationships that exist between these various propositions.

But filleting the pinned-down products of thinking is only one kind of thinking activity, and a fairly rarified one at that – in the world at large that is, if not within the traditional secondary class or university seminar. You may be hopeless at the syllogism but excel at working out what is best to do in tricky problems of personal relationships or DIY. Logic puzzles may be good for sharpening your skill in solving logic puzzles, but they are not necessarily thinking-improvers across the board.

Whether in DIY or in scientific research, the thinking that the reasoner actually engages in – the process rather than the product – most likely exhibits none of the orderliness found in the logician's syllogisms. A sound argument is what the reasoner is *aiming at*, not what is already embodied in her thinking. On the way to attaining her aim, especially if the matter is at all complex, she may make all sorts of twists and turns, go down and extricate herself from all sorts of cul-de-sacs.

This is what is meant by learning to reason. The teacher helps this process by trying to keep the learner's attention both on the immediate object of thought and on the overall goal, pointing out irrelevancies, feeding in counter-suggestions, advising returning to the topic later, prompting deductions that can be made from evidence so far, encouraging fresh perspectives and hypotheses.

A plea for the practical

The quest for general thinking skills looks likely to come to nothing. If we want to improve children's thinking, it is more fruitful to revisit the distinction between theoretical and practical thinking.

Theoretical thinking aims at finding out the truth about something. Practical thinking aims at deciding what to do. Of the two, practical thinking is the wider notion. It draws on theoretical thinking. In order to decide what to do, we need to know relevant facts – and whoever discovers these engages in theoretical thinking. This is true whether we are dealing with the specialised thinking that goes into the building of a dam, or with everyday thinking about replacing worn curtains.

Although practical thinking – at different levels from the more cerebral to the more hands-on – is the central kind of thinking on which we all rely in private and public life, traditionally it has not been prominent in the school curriculum. Except, that is, at the hands-on end for so-called less academic children in such subjects as woodwork or cookery. Is there a case for giving it higher priority in schools?

The traditional school curriculum has been especially attached to subjects built around the pursuit of truth – mathematics, science, history, geography, the factual parts of religious education, literature and other arts. Among these, mathematics and the mathematical parts of the physical sciences have traditionally had a kudos that reasoning of other kinds, historical, for instance, has lacked.

There are all sorts of reasons why mathematics has this status. For one thing, it helps to deliver the goods – quite literally, in the shape of the transport systems, machine tools, computers and scientific farming, without which an industrial society could not exist. But it also owes its privileged position in the curriculum to the tenacious influence of the view, traditional since Plato, that the highest kind of thinking is that which yields the greatest certainty. (See also Chapter 1.) Historical thinking, for instance, seems to lag behind mathematical in its intellectual power because it does not issue in statements that can be *conclusively proved.* At best, with history, we can conclude that the evidence *strongly suggests* that, for instance, the agenda of the French Revolution was highjacked by groups of narrow-minded ideologues or that Hitler tried to the last to avoid a war with Britain.

Yet why should thinking that yields certainty and strict proof win out over thinking that leaves more room for the possibility of counter-vailing evidence? A traditional reason is that, given that theoretical reasoning is meant to give us *knowledge,* only a state of mind which leaves *no possibility of doubt* can qualify for this title.

This is a demanding requirement on the concept of knowledge. It would restrict what can be known to mathematical and logical truths. Even alleged knowledge of the world around us – that there are bookcases in this room, for instance – is not of certainties but of phenomena about which sceptical doubts could be raised.

We are skirting traditional epistemological debates about the nature of knowledge. Since these would require a book of their own, it would be inappropriate to go further into them here. The point to hold on to is that requiring what is known to exclude any possibility of doubt is part of a highly stringent definition of knowledge that we do not have to accept. Less demanding accounts allow the possibility of scientific, historical, everyday empirical and other forms of knowledge that fall short of certainty. Some of these hold that knowers must have *good grounds,* or *adequate evidence,* for propositions they claim to know to be true. (See Chapter 3.) There are problems in the epistemological literature about whether this condition is itself unduly restrictive; but at least we have some reason to think that geography and history can deliver knowledge proper and not something short of that.

This still leaves the question: are schools justified in placing the weight they do on theoretical rather than practical thinking? Why is the pursuit of truth held to be especially valuable?

To go much further into this would take us into ethical rather than psychological matters, better found in a book on the aims of education than one on the child's mind. But a signpost may be helpful.

There are two possible kinds of reason for involving pupils in thinking activity aimed at truth. First, it is desirable for its own sake. Second, it is important in the attainment of some further end outside itself.

There are problems about the first move. Just because *teachers* may attach high value to the untrammelled pursuit of scientific or geographical truth in its own right, that does not allow them to impose their own values on children, whose interests may turn out to be quite different. What they can legitimately do is *reveal* this kind of value to pupils, in case any of them choose at some point to adopt it.

The other alternative – the extrinsic justification – is found where students are taught to use their scientific knowledge to think about policy on pollution, or to think historically as an element in democratic citizenship. Here the rationale for theoretical thinking leads into these wider fields of practical thinking. We have seen that practical reasoning depends on theoretical reasoning, because thinking out what is to be done relies on thought about what is the case. Democratic citizens reflecting on whom to vote for need to think about past political achievements and evidence of trustworthiness. Young people deciding what kind of career to go for need to have done a good deal of theoretical thinking in a range of areas so as to understand available options.

This second justification reinforces the case for schools' encouraging practical thinking. In the world outside, this is an omnipresent feature of our lives. We need to reflect on what to do about our careers, our relationships, our moral obligations, our non-work activities, our holidays, running a home, tax arrangements, day-to-day time-management. As citizens we need to think about who to vote for, how far the privatisation of public services should go, how to tackle crime, and a host of other topics. If educational policies allowed it, schools could contribute massively to preparing us for this.

But they would have to be careful not to develop mere *cleverness*. This is a truncation of practical reasoning prized by finance houses and other commercial concerns. It is all about working out the most efficient means of attaining goals – without questioning the worth of the goals themselves. Sometimes it is also called 'intelligence'. (See Chapter 5.) Practical reasoning includes but goes beyond cleverness or intelligence into reflection on the worthwhileness of the goals themselves and what priority they should have when in conflict, as our goals so often are, with other valuable goals. Schools should not limit themselves to the more constrained, instrumental, type of practical reasoning but help their students to think about ends as well as means.

The claims of contemplation

Contemplative thinking also struggles for a place in the contemporary school. Its main curricular vehicles, at least in Britain, are religious studies and the arts, including literature. Even here, most work in both these areas is devoted to other things – to factual material on religions, and in literature and the other arts to critical assessment, making art works, performance.

Whether or not there needs to be more emphasis on contemplation takes us back, once again, to broader questions about the proper aims of education.

An earlier point is relevant here. Intentional objects may or may not exist. We can think about fairy cakes, which exist, or about fairies, which do not. Part of the parent's or teacher's task is to wean young children away from thought about non-existent phenomena such as evil spirits or werewolves. But this could not be the whole of the story, since it would discourage dwelling on the delights of *Thomas the Tank Engine* or *David Copperfield*.

How should the contemplative parts of religious education be conceived? If God does not exist, thinking about God in prayer, for instance, or meditation, is thinking about a fictional entity. Has the time come in our increasingly secular society to assimilate religious contemplation to thinking about other man-made characters such as Doctor Zhivago or Faust?

At least with the arts we are clearer about the phenomena. We do not doubt that there is *something there* for students to dwell on, even though what is there is sometimes, as in the case of Doctor Zhivago, a deliberate fiction. More generally, the object of contemplation is a work of art – a piece of music, a painting, a sculpture, a building, a dance, a poem, a play, a novel.

Part of the delight of engaging with art is the freedom to attend now to this or that detail, now to the whole of which all the parts are composed. Looking, listening and reflecting in this unhurried way takes time – a commodity in short supply in our time-rationed schools. Should schools create more room for such things – more room, not least, for students to read literature of their own choice, without having to produce some critical evaluation of it?

Contemplative thinking goes beyond the arts into absorption in the beauty and sublimity of the natural world. It includes, too, reflection on the uncanniness of existence in general, which for many secular people is their substitute for the contemplation of God. How best might schools promote such thinking?

Sign thinking and body language

Learning to think in sporting and other physical activities like cookery or carpentry is not confined to practical reasoning. Sign–cognition also comes into them – seeing the opposing forward as about to change direction, seeing the soup as about to boil, seeing the grain of a piece of wood as causing problems for a clean cut.

Its realm goes beyond these curriculum activities. Sign-cognition lies at the root of learning language. Before the infant understands the connotations of the word 'Daddy' – that Daddy is a man, a relative, the person whose daughter I am, etc. – she hears the sound 'Daddy' as a sign that someone she is attached to wants, for instance, to play with her or cuddle her. Unless we first heard words as sounds with signification, it is hard to see how we could ever learn language. Sign cognition is also central to our reactions to non-verbal 'body language'. We unrealisingly respond with anxiety to a frown or with sympathetic concern to a wince. Learning to perceive and respond appropriately to non-verbal signs of irritation, self-importance, insincerity, love or lust are at the heart of becoming a social creature, of learning to be human. For the most part this is picked up spontaneously in the course of our upbringing in the home and beyond it. But some people need more help than others over this and in more intractable cases deliberate teaching is required.

Conclusion

Teaching thinking goes much further than teaching how to think about arguments. It starts in the cradle with the shaping of sign-cognition, long before children become capable of assessing reasons. It covers not only reasoning, but also contemplation and the thinking required in physical skills. Where reasoning is concerned, teaching how to reason in some theoretical or practical area is not to be equated with teaching how to reason about reasons, important though this may be in some contexts.

Summary and key points

'Think' is an ambiguous term, covering belief (see Chapter 3) and thinking as an activity. Children's thinking in the activity sense is the topic of this chapter.

There are many types of thinking activity. Reasoning, whether theoretical or practical, is only one form. Contemplators are also thinkers; so is the child thinking what she is doing while playing tennis. Thinking is an intentional mental phenomenon (see Chapter 1), a goal-directed activity which involves the application of concepts (see Chapter 2). It can also be characterised as a skill, or family of skills, which can be developed through practice. (There are links here with Chapter 5 on intelligence.)

It is now fashionable – again – to claim that there are *general* thinking skills, and schools are being encouraged to teach them. These alleged skills are skills in reasoning, and are held to be transferable to widely differing domains. But the claim, though seductive, is questionable. So is the more specific claim that thinking skills are best promoted through formal logic.

A case is made for more attention to be paid in education to children's practical reasoning, given the weight now placed on theoretical reasoning, especially in its more abstract forms. (See Chapter 1 on the close association traditionally made between the mind and abstract thought.) Comments are also made on the cultivation of both contemplation and sign-cognition.

Further reading

Gilbert Ryle's essays on the concept of thinking are included in Ryle, G., (1979) *On Thinking* Towota, NJ: Roman and Littlefield. For more recent discussions, see McGinn, C., (1982) *The Character of Mind* Oxford: Oxford University Press, ch. 4; Kenny, A., (1989) *The Metaphysics of Mind* Oxford: Oxford University Press, ch. 9; and McGinn's entry on 'Thought' in Guttenplan, S., (1994) *A Companion to the Philosophy of Mind* Oxford: Blackwell.

On the educational side, there is a good full-length discussion of the role of thinking and general thinking skills in Schrag, F., (1988) *Thinking in School and Society* London: Routledge. A further critique of general thinking skills in education is to be found in Johnson, S., (2001) *The Teaching of Thinking Skills* Impact Pamphlet No. 9, Philosophy of Education Society of Great Britain. The subordination of theoretical reasoning to practical reasoning among educational priorities is a theme of White, J., (1990) *Education and the Good Life* London: Kogan Page, especially ch. 7. For a contrasting view, see Wringe, C., (1988) *Understanding Educational Aims* London: Unwin Hyman, especially Part IV. On practical reasoning see also MacIntyre, A., (1999) *Dependent Rational Animals* London: Duckworth, chs 8, 9. The inspiration for MacIntyre's and many other contemporary philosophers' interest in practical reasoning comes from Aristotle, *Nicomachean Ethics*, especially Bk VI, 12, 13.

Chapter 7

Imagination and creativity

I come to what for many parents and teachers is at the heart of education – the encouragement of children's imagination, their creative activity.

The first task is to get a clear view of what this involves. It is machete time. There is a mass of super-luxuriant writing about creativity and imagination, and we need a path through it.

Far from leading into the mysteries of the faculty of imagination and its place in education, this chapter will try to show there is *no such thing*.

The imagination

In the nineteenth century it was common among educators and psychologists to think of the imagination as a separate faculty of the mind, along with such things as memory, perception, reasoning, and the will. The task of education is to strengthen these powers. According to one source, it should 'chasten while it kindles the imagination'. Training the mental faculties is akin to training the body's muscles. The aim is to develop strength and prevent flabbiness.

People thought at that time that different parts of the curriculum build up different powers. While arithmetic develops reasoning and drawing from objects firms up 'the perceptive powers', history, art, science and mechanics all have a role in strengthening the imagination. As with other faculties, its power can then be applied to tasks beyond the schoolroom, 'to the affairs of life'. Its training is transferable (Selleck 1968, pp. 46–7).

This was the theory. Its echoes have been heard throughout the twentieth century and are still audible in places. But it fails to fit the facts. Not, however, in claiming that there are mental powers to do with the imagination, or that some curriculum activities are more closely bound up with these than others. There are such powers and there are such curricular applications.

Rather, the theory's problem lies in its simplicity, its monistic assumption that the imagination is *one thing*, a single faculty. On the contrary. There are many things at work here, many strands to disentangle.

In the mind's eye – and nose?

If you ask a child to imagine Buckingham Palace, he may well see it, as we say, 'in his mind's eye' – with its imposing facade, its courtyard, railings and soldiers in bearskin helmets standing guard outside. What he does here is form a *mental image*, in this case a visual one. Mental images need not be consciously formed as in this case; neither need they be visual.

Images may also just happen to him. For some reason Southend pier or David Beckham's face flashes through his mind, unbidden. Dropping off to sleep or dreaming, we often experience such things. At other times, as with Buckingham Palace, imaging is voluntary – something we do rather than something that happens to us.

When I hear Frank Sinatra singing *My Way* in my head, my imaging is not visual but aural. I can also have olfactory images, of the smell of furniture polish, or gustatory ones, of the taste of kiwi fruit. All this suggests some kind of connexion between imaging and perceiving.

What kind of connexion? When a child 'sees' in her mind a current popstar's face, is she really seeing some kind of mental picture of it? The features of the image and of a picture or photo of her are broadly the same – the eyes, the hair, the smile. But if the same child sees a photo, the object of her perception exists in its own right. It continues to exist when she is not looking at it. But the image seems to exist only in her mind.

Imaging is not really seeing a picture, but it has perception-like features. The girl could not imagine the popstar's face unless she had seen photos of it in the media. She could not have images of the taste of rhubarb without having eaten it. What if she dreamt up some image of an imaginary animal – a goose as big as a house with an alligator's head? She might not have seen such a creature in fact, but unless she had seen the elements from which she composed it, it is hard to think how she could have an image of it. Imaging does, indeed, seem to depend on previous perception.

If imaging is not a form of perception although it is linked to it in the ways described, how are we to think of it? Can we draw on any of the material from previous chapters?

It seems to require the power to conceptualise. The child could not visualise the singer's face unless she had the concept face, or imagine the smell of garlic unless she had *that* concept. So far, what we have said is also true of perception – of seeing and smelling these things. It seems that imaging depends on possessing certain concepts only because the original perceptions, on which our imaging is based, required them, too.

Imaging is in fact a form of thinking. Like other forms of thinking, it can be directed, as in the Buckingham Palace case, or undirected, as in dreaming. When we form an image of something in directed imaging, our thinking is focused on an object, that is to say an intentional object which may or may not exist – Buckingham Palace or a goose with an alligator's head. We think of this object under concepts like those just mentioned.

Of the various types of thinking outlined in Chapter 6, is imaging closer to contemplating than to reasoning? It may seem so, if we assimilate it to seeing pictures in the mind. Just as we gaze at a painting in a gallery for its own sake, does not the little girl do the same with the singer's imagined face?

We have already seen the difficulties here. What the child is contemplating is not the image, but the person herself. She is thinking of *her*. She does this *via* an image in this case, just as on another occasion she might dwell on her attractions *via* a photograph.

Now that an image seems to be more a *vehicle* of thinking than an *object* of thinking, there seems no particular reason to link it with contemplating rather than reasoning. Imaging may well come into the latter, too. If a child is thinking out how she is going to spend her pocket money, she may, on the way to this, conjure up pictures of comics or the taste of jelly beans. In theoretical rather than practical reasoning, a student working on a problem in geometry may have images of bisected triangles.

What if ... ?

A five-year-old dresses up in available bits of finery and imagines she is a princess. Is this a case of imaging?

It may be. She may see a fairytale princess in her mind's eye as she wanders elegantly along the garden path. But *need* she be having experiences like this?

We observers have good reason to think she is imagining herself to be a princess even if we have no evidence of what – if anything – she is seeing in her mind's eye. We know this from her behaviour – from how she conducts herself, what she wears, what she says about herself. We are dealing with a case of imagining that may have nothing to do with imaging.

What, then, is the little girl doing in imagining herself to be a princess? She is *supposing* that she is one. She does not, of course, really believe this. She is going beyond her beliefs into make-believe.

Another example. The actor Peter Falk plays the shambling sleuth Colombo in a TV series. To do this he has to use his imagination – to imagine what it would be like to be someone with this kind of personality. This again takes his thinking beyond belief.

We are dealing with a different kind of thinking from imaging – a kind where the agent is thinking that something is the case ('I am a princess', 'I am a shambolic detective'), and where this is not something he or she believes.

Both these examples have to do with acting a part. But take the thinking that historians or scientists engage in when framing hypotheses to explain their data. Suppose a historian lights on the thought that the British generals in the First World War may not have been inept 'donkeys' as usually portrayed, but did the best they could in difficult circumstances. This is at first a speculation, a supposition. It is not something she yet believes: belief only comes into the picture, if at all, once she has tested out the hypothesis and the evidence piles up in its favour.

All the examples drawn on so far are relevant to education – to early childhood play, to drama, to science, to history. I will come back to this later, as also to another educationally interesting case of this kind of imagining: what is often called 'sympathetic imagination'. This is the thinking we do when we 'put ourselves in the other person's shoes' in imagining what it would be like to lose a parent or be the victim of a hurricane disaster in the Caribbean. We do not believe we are the sufferer in these cases, but our thinking is directed to what we would be feeling or thinking if in the sufferer's place. (Although this is called 'sympathetic' imagination, a better name for it might be 'empathetic'. A torturer can imagine – only too well – the fear that his victim is feeling, but may not feel any sympathy.)

More generally, this kind of imagination – supposition – is important in human life because it takes us beyond actuality into the sphere of the possible. It allows us to speculate, to entertain alternative scenarios, to escape from our own concerns and identify with other people's. These abilities are especially important in an open, rapidly changing, pluralistic society.

Imagination in this sense is not to be conflated with imaging. We may or may not form images when we suppose or speculate. If a boy is unavoidably separated from a sick friend, he may well visualise him lying in his hospital bed at the same time as he runs through in his mind how he must be feeling. But if he is actually with him he almost certainly will not be framing images of him, even though he is still imagining what he must be going through.

Similarly, there can be imaging without supposing. If I visualise the cheeseboard on the buffet table I am planning, I am not normally supposing at the same time that I am looking at it. I am part of the object of my thinking in the latter case, but the imaging's object is just the cheeseboard, not myself.

Breaking new ground

Scientists hypothesise. Sometimes their hypotheses break really new ground – like Darwin's theory of evolution through natural selection. We then call their work 'imaginative'. Poets and other artists can be imaginative, too, in so far as their work too manifests originality. So can more ordinary people – in working out an unusual solution to a household problem or seeing their way around some glitch in personal relationships.

Being imaginative requires going beyond the expected or conventional in some way. This might be in a remarkable way, as with Darwin or Goethe; or in a more homely fashion, as in our last two examples. Imaginativeness can be a matter of degree. But it is not *just* a matter of going beyond usual expectations. People who are very rude, or mad, can do that, but that does not make them imaginative. We have to add the requirement that what they produce – the original idea they come up with, their theory, concerto, sonnet – remains within the bounds of what is appropriate in the context. To merit the label, Darwin's theory had to fit the known facts and provide a possible explanation of them. The inventor of the mobile phone had to devise something that enabled communication to take place.

The notion of imaginativeness is different from the other two main concepts of the imagination. Imaging need not be imaginative. Visualising a singer's face is something millions of people have done and demands no originality. Supposing need not be imaginative. An uninspired amateur actor can imagine himself into the role of Sky Masterson in *Guys and Dolls*. When we put ourself as a moral agent into another person's shoes, it is not originality that is required but fidelity to how the other feels.

Unlike the other two concepts, too, being imaginative is not a form of thinking. It has to do not with the activity of thinking but with its product (see Chapter 6). It is Darwin's theory that is imaginative, Beethoven's music, Pushkin's poetry, a brilliant move at chess, the invention of email. We also call the people who produce such things imaginative. This is sometimes for a particular imaginative achievement, and sometimes if they tend often to produce original things.

Teachers and parents rightly think it important to encourage imaginativeness. We shall be looking at its educational significance in the next section.

Developing imagination(s)

How can parents and teachers foster children's imagination? Not as a unitary faculty, if the untangling of strands in the last section is on the right lines. Indeed, it is hard to see how we could answer the question without starting from the three notions we have just separated from each other. We can now reintroduce them via their more usual names.

Imaging

Imaging is a natural power. Children do not have to be taught to do it. Yet educators call on it and can develop it in various ways.

This happens in the daily life of the classroom as well as at home. Both teachers and parents have to motivate children, get them to do things. Presenting concrete sensuous material to them is a good way of engaging their attention and their inclinations. Telling a little boy 'When we get to grandma's, we'll all go to the park and feed the birds' is effective if the child hears and sees in his mind all that squawking and beating of great wings from his last visit and just wants to be there again. Teachers of any curriculum subject can use image-evoking triggers.

Imaging also features more substantively in some subjects. In literature it is a must. Without this ability, we are cut off from most poetry and fiction. If pupils cannot visualise the Ancient Mariner in the heat of the ocean or Pierre Bezukhov at the battle of Borodino, it is hard to know what sense they would make of them. Teachers of literature do not teach imaging. They leave it to the skill of the writer to evoke it.

Imaging requires both previous sense-experience of the relevant kind and also concept-application. A student need not have sailed tropical seas without drinking water to picture Coleridge's mariner, but she needs experience of heat, expanses of water and thirst. The full imaginal impact of some literature may be at present beyond pupils because they lack the requisite understanding. One way in which parents or teachers cannot only evoke but also develop a child's powers of imagery is by equipping them with this. Only when the student has some grasp of the notions of aristocracy, war between two nations, officers and other ranks, artillery fire, musketry, and the use of bayonets can Pierre's experience at Borodino be brought home to her.

For a student of literature imaging is essential, not a replaceable means to other ends. In some other school subjects the power to image is obviously *useful*, but is it indispensable? Someone working through a problem in geometry may visualise operations on triangles, but suppose for some reason her powers of imagery are poor. How far can she get by propositional reasoning alone, backed up by diagrams in textbooks and constructions of her own? Need geographers rely on anything more than maps, photographs, films and verbal reasoning?

Supposing

Supposing goes beyond belief. Unlike imaging, it is not a power with which we are born. What *is* innate in us, as it is in some other animals, is a disposition to believe things (see Chapter 3). This is apparent among non-human animals in their capacity for sign-cognition – for example in a deer's seeing a tiger as a sign of danger and running away. Learned beliefs can be built up on the back of innate believings, as when a cat sees a tin-opener being taken from a drawer as a sign of food to come.

Much the same can be said about human beings. We, too, come hard-wired with emotions and desires that bring beliefs with them – fear of loud noises associated with the thought that these are threatening, desire for the breast associated with relief from hunger. (For more on the connexion between emotions and belief, see Chapter 9.) Sign-cognition and very quickly the concept-acquisition that comes *via* language put human children in possession of a vast network of beliefs about the world they live in.

We are born as believers, but need to learn how to imagine in the supposal sense. Unless we are inducted into supposing, we remain imprisoned within actuality, unable to detach ourselves from it. We cannot think about what might be rather than what is. Human beings are, as far as we know, unique among animals in being able to think in this way. This power has enabled them to plan for the future, interact with insight into others' thoughts and feelings, build up intellectual edifices such as science and history. It is the source of civilisation.

The secret of our ability must lie in our powers of conceptualising. We are able to see or think about the same phenomenon under more than one concept. This does not in itself detach us from the actual, since the plural concepts could all apply correctly. We see an object as a Red Admiral, a butterfly, an insect. But sometimes our concepts do not fit reality. For one thing we might be mistaken. We call something a Red Admiral when it is in fact a Peacock. But sometimes we make use of our ability to apply multiple concepts by invoking one that, without our making any mistake, fails to match what is really the case. We may do this for various reasons.

Young children are early initiated into this kind of thinking activity. Their parents consciously draw their attention to the plurality of concepts applicable to the same thing, reinforcing first of all the distinction between correct and mistaken application. 'What a lovely elephant!' you might say, holding up a toy bear. The child quickly cottons on to the fact that you are teasing her. She sees, perhaps dimly at first, that it is not that you have made a silly mistake, but that you have deliberately said something which is not true. She is beginning to see that people can have a certain freedom in calling things by all sorts of names that do not properly fit – and soon begins to exercise the same freedom herself.

Experiences like this are a seed-bed not only for the development of a power of the imagination but also for a sense of humour, much of which trades on different ways of taking the same thing.

They also help to shape the child's perception of authority. If parents and teachers restricted themselves to passing on beliefs – hopefully true beliefs, but this is not always so – children would always be in a position of epistemic subordination, learning from authority figures. A parent who calls a teddy bear an elephant is, perhaps unconsciously, making the child think that perhaps Mummy does not always know best. The daughter becomes aware of an area in her life where, as she learns to play the game, too, she can be on all fours with grown-ups. The origins of supposing are also the origins of liberation from tutelage, perhaps even of equality of respect and the democratic disposition itself.

Thinking in general, as we have seen, is about intentional objects that may or may not exist. It is this latter feature which is at the root of supposing. Once the child becomes used to entertaining such thoughts as 'This is an elephant', she can go on to a whole range of other kinds of imagining. Among other things, she can begin to apply non-actual concepts to *herself*. Just as she is free to call a bear an elephant, she is equally free to think of herself as a princess or a spaceperson. Encouraged by her parents to put herself in other people's shoes, she can also think what it would be like if *she* were pushed over roughly, or if *she* lost a favourite toy. All this also puts her in a good position to enjoy stories and films, since she can now begin to identify with Cinderella and with Bambi.

As she grows older she will imagine things about herself of a different and more realistic sort. She will develop a conception of herself as she might indeed become – as a teacher, a scientist, a kinder person, a successful one. But even when she is still very young, she will be exercising this same kind of thinking about her own future, although the more immediate future. Her mother gives her a choice: 'What should we do this afternoon? Shall we go to the swings or feed the ducks on the common?' The child has to consider these two pieces of non-actuality, supposing now that she is whizzing round on the roundabout, now watching the ducks racing towards her as she holds out the bread.

Imagining in the supposal sense is becoming a pervasive feature of her life. Her parents shape it towards desirable ends. The child is allowed, perhaps encouraged, to think of herself as a princess, but not as a machine-gunner. She learns, too, that there is a time and a place for imagining herself a princess. She is praised for placing herself in other people's shoes, chivvied for failing to do so. She is introduced to stories, but not those which frighten her out of her wits. If she free-wheels too often into fantasy in inappropriate situations, her parents tease her out of it.

Many of her experiences of supposing will be inextricably inter-twined with experiences of imaging. Both these powers of the imagination are likely to be present when she listens to the story of Cinderella, or wonders whether she should go to the park or the duck-pond, or feels sorry for her doll because she has hurt her head. It is important, when philosophising about the mind, to keep the two phenomena analytically separate, but we should remember that psychologically speaking they are often found together.

Once at primary and later secondary school, further demands on her powers of supposal are made of her. As her understanding grows, she becomes capable of a deeper and more extensive empathy with other people and with characters in literature. Her drama lessons and work she does in art lessons on understanding works of art will call on and develop these same powers. So will many of her attempts at creative writing in lessons in her native language. In science, mathematics, geography and history, she will be gradually introduced to the notion and practice of hypothesising.

Indeed, in history and social sciences such as human geography she will meet the supposal form of imagining twice over. Not only will she be introduced to others' hypotheses and encouraged to hypothesise herself, but since the object of her enquiry is human beings rather than molecules or genes, she will need to call on her empathetic imagination also.

Her personal and social education (PSE) and career education, both formal and informal, will encourage her to dwell on alternative futures for herself, her society and the world. In much of her learning that entails supposing, this kind of thinking will be part of a larger process of reasoning – theoretical in the case of history and science, practical-cum-theoretical in PSE – in which different scenarios, hypotheses and possibilities are rigorously examined to see if they pass muster. In other parts of her curriculum, in the literary and visual arts most notably, supposing will be embodied in contemplative activity for its own sake.

Needless to say, the above brief sketch of a school education is an ideal. There are still many schools around the world whose Gradgrind pedagogues and Gradgrind policy-makers have patience only for facts and none for the imagination.

As an ideal, though, the call, supported by Dickens not least, for imagination to be given more prominence in school education stands in need of justification. This takes us, yet again, into the domain of educational aims and ethical values. Bypassing a full treatment of this, we can at least say that if staple curriculum activities like those just mentioned – literature, drama, art, creative writing, science, mathematics, history, geography, PSE, careers education and civics – are themselves justified in terms of wider desirable aims and values, the exercising and nurturing of the imagination in the present sense that they all require are justified for the same reasons.

Imaginativeness

Unlike imaging and supposing, being imaginative is not engaging in a kind of thinking. It *depends* on kinds of thinking, of course, sometimes including the two kinds just mentioned, but that is a different matter. The term 'imaginative' is applied to products of thought, not to the activity of thinking. Where we call people, rather than theories, proposals or works of art 'imaginative', this is because of their success in having produced imaginative things, and possibly because they are expected to do the same in future.

A product – and this could include an idea – is imaginative if it transcends conventional expectations while remaining within bounds of appropriateness. The merely unconventional, or odd, or novel, is not necessarily imaginative: it might be the production of a lunatic, a show-off or a charlatan. What counts as appropriate depends on the field in question. An imaginative scientific theory has to be original, but in a way that provides an alternative explanation of the known facts from that provided by current theories. Imaginativeness in copywriting is partly a matter of devising an advertisement that seizes the attention of the spectator.

Imaginativeness also comes in different degrees. Some deviations from the conventional are earth-shaking, others slight. Darwin, Cezanne and Freud were imaginative; but so, perhaps, is someone who comes up with a new idea for where to go for the weekend.

These reminders help us to locate the place of imaginativeness in education. To start at the earth-shaking end. There are obvious reasons for acquainting students at some point in their education with the work of past groundbreakers – Newton and Galileo, Giotto and Turner, Shakespeare and Dostoevsky. And with achievements not just in the arts and the sciences, but also in invention (the steam engine, television, the computer), town-planning (Peter the Great's St Petersburg), political ideas (liberal democracy), political systems (the regimes of Hitler and Stalin, Mao's Cultural Revolution). As the last examples show, imaginativeness is not always to be welcomed. It can be harnessed to undesirable ends.

Reasons for introducing students to exemplars of imaginativeness are various. Sometimes this is an intrinsic part of initiation into an academic discipline or art form. How could one learn physical science properly without having heard of Newton, or know English literature without having read Wordsworth, or understand twentieth-century history and not be familiar with Gandhi? A deeper reason has to do with an understanding of human nature itself, especially its highpoints of possible achievement, but also its lows.

Education can also make students aware of more ordinary imaginativeness. If it is a good thing that they gain some understanding of the way their society works, this must include understanding the activities of advertising copy writers. Again, whether being imaginative is always to be applauded is not something they should take as read. They learn discrimination about when it is desirable and when not.

Still closer to home – more the province of family than school education – is becoming acquainted with little examples of imaginative thought and behaviour in everyday life. Take the talent grandpa has for seeing solutions to problems of personal relationships that no one else sees. Or mum's ability to knock up an unusual and tasty meal from what seem uninspiring ingredients. Children can come to see how some people are particularly productive in this way, while others seem locked for ever into conventionality. Not that young children are introduced in any analytic or philosophical way to these things. That can come later, if at all.

In what ways should students' *own* imaginativeness be developed? (We can take it for granted that this is to be in a desirable direction.) A traditional view favours education in the arts. But this is misguided. Imaginativeness is a feature of many academic and non-academic pursuits and has no particular connexion with aesthetic matters. Only by running together the different senses of 'imagination' can the case for singling out the arts seem plausible. I am thinking of the connexion between at least some of the arts – poetry for instance – and imaging. There is also a connexion between some of the arts, for instance fiction and drama, and the empathetic imagination. Neither of these types of imagination *has to be* present in science or many other fields.

There are different kinds of imaginativeness depending on the domain. Einstein has in common with Peter the Great that he broke free from conventional ways of viewing things, but there the likeness stops. If students are to become imaginative physicists rather than town planners on marshland, they need a thorough grounding in contemporary physics. In order to break free from conventional expectations and see things in an original way, they must at least know what those conventional expectations *are*. If Einstein had been unacquainted with Newton he could not have gone beyond him.

A thorough grounding in an area is essential for imaginativeness. But it is not sufficient for it. There are many competent philosophers and mathematicians who know their field well but are weak on originality. What more must teachers do to make pupils imaginative?

Imaginativeness differs in degree. If we are talking about the earth-shaking variety, this seems way outside a teacher's powers. How could mere pedagogy *guarantee* a Mozart or a Pushkin? Could *anything* guarantee this?

Can teachers at least *make it more likely* that pupils will be imaginative on the grand scale? There are difficulties about this, too. For as soon as we believed we had discovered some kind of formula for doing this, this would be acquirable in principle by many students. Suppose 100,000 successful science students per annum pass out of the Originality Academy. Why should we think them all likely to make astounding breakthroughs or discoveries?

Not everything original — not yet thought of in the history of the world — is of the earth-shattering variety. Think of the first person who dreamed up the potato-peeler or cornflakes coated with honey. Or of a historian who produces a plausible hypothesis about why some little known nineteenth-century cabinet minister left office. Or of any PhD student breaking new ground in a yet more minimal sense.

Can teachers encourage such lower-key imaginativeness? They can at the very least draw pupils' attention to imaginative work others have done in the field, praise their more original ideas. There may also be psychological blockages to imaginativeness which teachers and psychological specialists can help to remove. If someone persistently sees himself as utterly conventional, his chances of transcending this without help may be low.

So far the kinds of originality we have been dealing with have been all about products that are new *in the history of the world*. This is one reason why there is little that educators can do here. Yet there is a sense in which younger children, too, can be original — in producing work which, in going beyond the conventional, is *new for them*, even if not new in the more absolute sense.

A child who has only ever written about things in his daily life suddenly takes off into stories about some deserted island. Someone else has bright ideas about a family outing or a class assembly. What can parents and teachers do to encourage this kind of imaginativeness? The earlier suggestions make sense here, too: exemplars, encouragement, removing psychological obstacles.

Creativity and education: a note

Creativity is an iconic ingredient of our culture. Prized in art, business, advertising, science, it has been especially valued in the world of education. Here it came to prominence in the US after the shock launching of the first Soviet space-ship, Sputnik, in 1957. If the US was to catch up, the creative potential of young scientists and engineers had to be released.

But even before Sputnik, the unlocking of a child's creativity had been a staple of child-centred, or progressive, thinking. This had some-times been associated with notions of psychological impediments, especially unconscious ones, to the development of children's potentialities. Once these are removed, people believed, children's full creativity will be released.

Interest in creativity is still strong at the beginning of the twenty-first century. In 1999 a British government-appointed national committee reported on *Creativity, Culture and Education*. Creative thinking skills feature in the post-2000 National Curriculum for England and Wales.

But what *is* creativity?

There is no need, after the section on imagination, to labour the point that it may not be one thing. Creativity has long been associated with the arts. 'Creative activities' have often to do with the aesthetic parts of the curriculum – especially visual art, but also 'creative writing' and music as well. But how does this square with the reaction to Sputnik? For in that case the connection was not with the arts, but with science and technology.

We seem to have been here before – in looking at imagination. Once again, the same popular association with the arts. Once again, the same counter-proposal that science and other non-aesthetic fields also be included.

We need to disentangle a couple of strands. In one sense of the term, to create something is basically to *make* something. God, some say, created the world. Artists are creators because they, too, are makers. They are makers of objects – paintings, symphonies, poems – for our contemplation.

The other sense is that in which we speak of 'creative' scientists, or mathematicians, or admen, or managers. What makes people like these creative is not that they have *made* something, but that they have had *original ideas*. They have broken beyond conventional perspectives and seen things in a new way. We have already met this sense of creativity in this chapter. It is a synonym for imaginativeness. On the teaching and learning of creativity in this sense, see the previous section above.

Sometimes people or their products are creative in both senses. The ancient Egyptians expected their (creative) artists to work within a rigid framework of convention. But increasingly over the last two hundred years our own culture has expected *its* artists, visual and other, to be innovators – and thus doubly creative.

There is much to say about the place of creativity in education in both its senses. As this is a work about the mind rather than educational aims, here is not the place for that. There is also much work that could be done in revealing the confusedness in writings in the field, but I am restricting myself to the barest, plainest of strand-partings.

Just one more point on the psychological side. Creativity in both its main senses is an attribute of a thought-*product* – of an idea/hypothesis, or of something made. It is not some kind of mental process. A creative person is not to be identified as someone in whose mind certain things are happening, consciously or unconsciously, and whether or not the result of his own volition. We know that Shakespeare was a creative genius, but not because we know what was going on in his mind when he created. About this we know nothing. We know about his creativity from the qualities of his public works.

I inject this sceptical comment about creativity as a process because of the persistent temptation among educationists to see it in that way.

Summary and key points

Imagination is not a unitary faculty of the child's mind. It cannot, therefore be an aim of education to cultivate the imagination *tout court*. There are three main concepts in this area, which need to be distinguished from each other. First, mental images. Second, imagining or supposing something to be the case. Third, imaginativeness. The first two are forms of thinking (see Chapter 6) and as such conceptualisation plays an important part in both (see Chapter 2). The third has to do with breaking free from conventional perspectives and producing something original.

'Educating the imagination' needs to be discussed under these three headings. In formal education, imaging is a *sine qua non* of enjoying literature, but it may not have the same role in other areas. Developing children's powers to imagine is crucial if they are ever to diverge from their default state of belief (see Chapter 3). It is important not only in the growth of the children's intellectual autonomy, sense of humour, and self-understanding, but also in their empathetic understanding of others' points of view, as well as in learning to frame hypotheses in, for instance, science and history. As for imaginativeness, while there is a case for acquainting children with the imaginative works of others, in developing their own imaginativeness there are, from a theoretical point of view, more problems about doing this the higher the criteria for originality are pitched.

Developing children's creativity is often seen as an important educational goal. But the term is ambiguous. Creativity in one of its senses is the same as imaginativeness. In another it has to do with making objects for contemplation. Both kinds have their place in education.

Further reading

There are brief philosophical accounts of imagination in Kenny, A., (1989) *The Metaphysics of Mind* Oxford: Oxford University Press, ch. 8; Scruton, R., (1994) *Modern Philosophy* London: Sinclair-Stevenson, ch. 24; Hamlyn, D.W., 'Imagination', in Guttenplan, S., (ed.) (1994) *A Companion to the Philosophy of Mind* Oxford: Blackwell. The best somewhat longer treatment of the concept is still Scruton, R., (1974) *Art and Imagination* London: Methuen, chs 7, 8. On the notion of creativity, see the entry by White, J., in Cooper, D.E., (ed.) (1992) *A Companion to Aesthetics* Oxford: Blackwell.

The best philosophical essays on imagination and creativity in an educational context remain Elliott, R.K., (1971) 'Versions of Creativity' *Proceedings of the Philosophy of Education Society of Great Britain* Vol. V, No 2; and Passmore, J., (1980) *The Philosophy of Teaching*, ch. 8 'Cultivating Imagination' London: Duckworth. Both are included in Hirst P.H., and White, P., (eds) (1998) *Philosophy of Education: Major Themes in the Analytic Tradition* (4 vols) London: Routledge, Vol. 2. On creativity in the arts, see Best, D., (1990) *The Rationality of Feeling: The Arts in Education* London: Falmer. Official interest in developing creativity is reflected in the Report of the National Advisory Committee on Creative and Cultural Education (1999) *All Our Futures: Creativity, Culture and Education* London: Department for Education and Employment.

Chapter 8

Motivating children

What is motivation?

Children are active creatures, often surprisingly so. Tobias Lindseth Melsbu, for instance. In August 2001, when he was aged three, he was reported to have driven the family minibus back home after nursery school. Tobias, from Ramsund, a Norwegian town 125 miles north of the Arctic Circle, took the keys, turned on the ignition and cruised home. He took in a slope, two 90-degree turns, a creek and a sharp swing into the family driveway. He crashed into the garage door but was unhurt. He had developed his driving skills while sitting in his mother's lap as she drove.

Tobias, I guess you could say, was highly motivated to drive the minibus. He also steers us neatly into an area of mental life about which this book has so far said nothing directly.

This territory covers action, activity, desire, motivation. So much of the work parents and teachers do with children revolves around activities they engage in – not often bus driving, it is true, but things like dressing, eating, playing games, drawing, and thinking about problems in science.

In very early childhood parents have to help children to understand the notion of agency itself – not in any philosophical sense, but as built into the correct use of words such as 'dressing', 'drawing', 'lifting', 'being cruel'. Children have to learn to use such words about both their own behaviour and others'.

They also need to know how actions are to be explained. 'Why did Daddy laugh like that?', asks the five-year-old; 'Why did Hitler invade Poland?', asks the sixteen-year-old history student. On occasion parents and teachers, too, need to find out why children act as they do. 'Why does Hannah keep disappearing off upstairs?' 'Why is Neil so aggressive today?'

One context, then, in which educators must deal with motivation is thinking about what makes children behave as they do. Another is encouraging or getting them to do something – sometimes when they do not want to. These two things – explaining children's actions, and motivating them – are closely connected. Grasping the factors involved in why children act as they do gives you a lever you can use in urging them to do what you would like them to do.

It is tempting to think of this lever in the causal terms we are used to in the physical world. If you know why someone's headache was cured – through aspirin – you can use this knowledge if someone else gets a headache in the future. Some discussions of motivation in educational psychology see it after a causal pattern like this. Whether this makes good sense we shall have to see.

Before looking at motivation, something more basic. This is the notion of human agency itself. Children have to grasp this concept in their early years. What is it they come to understand about it?

Human agency

Suppose a young child – say between two and three – sees her mother writing a letter. How does she understand what is going on? We adults would say, as I have just said, 'She is writing a letter'. We know what writing is and what letters are. The little girl does not yet have this understanding, or only the first beginnings of it. She sees her mother doing something – making marks on paper – but cannot bring to this the understanding we have as adults. Perhaps she sees her as drawing little shapes. Or perhaps her mother has told her she is 'writing a letter' or 'inviting Laura to your party' and the child makes what sense she can of what she is told.

Is there one correct answer to the question 'What is the mother doing?' – in the way that there is one correct answer, in primary school arithmetic, to 'What is 7 + 8?'? Is the correct answer 'writing a letter'? This might seem the most natural way to answer, but it is also true that she is making marks on paper and that she is inviting someone to a party.

Human actions are capable of many true descriptions. This is also true of other things. What I see when I look out into the garden is 'a tree', 'an apple tree', 'a mature specimen', 'a dark shape'. The peculiar feature of human actions is that the descriptions have to be in terms of what the agent *has in mind* in doing what she is doing. People can make marks on paper for all sorts of reasons. In the present case, the mother is making them with the intention of communicating with someone, more specifically with the intention of inviting someone to a party.

Inducting children into what agency is involves bringing them – gradually – to understand people's intentions in acting as they do. Human actions typically have a structure. They do not exist as isolated events, but are undertaken for *reasons*. Reasons are not isolated phenomena either. They are connected with a host of other aspects of the agent's life. (See also Chapter 6 on practical reasoning.)

The mother is writing a letter. Why? She wants to invite a child to a birthday party. The reason is not self-standing. Behind it are her unspelt-out reasons for wanting a party and for wanting this particular child to come to it. All this takes us into a web of further considerations – her caring attitudes towards her own child, the place of children's birthday parties in the culture, her child's relationship with the other child.

So far the focus has been on the mother's wants or desires. But these do not give a full account of her reasons for writing the letter. They do not explain why she chose *this* way of trying to get the child to come to the party. She could have gone round to her house, telephoned or e-mailed her mother, put a notice in the local paper. What were her reasons for writing a letter? She believed it is the proper thing to do on such occasions. There is also her belief, almost too obvious to spell out, that sending a letter is an effective means of letting someone know something. She also has further background beliefs – that the postal service is generally reliable, for instance.

Her beliefs as well as her wants enter into her reasons for action. Together they form a structure. In this case, she understands what she is doing (writing the letter) as a means to an end (inviting the child). Behind this goal lie further things that she wants – to please her child, to do what is expected of her in the community. She wants the end and believes that writing the letter is an effective and appropriate means. There are also background beliefs she has about both the means and the end. She believes that Britain has a postal service; that people in her community expect her to organise a party.

This everyday example helps in seeing what goes into the notion of human agency. Some of its features, as we shall see, are not found across the board, but the involvement of our beliefs and desires in what we are doing is of central importance.

This last point shows that human agency, like most other mental phenomena, brings with it intentional objects. Beliefs, as we have seen, are always beliefs *that* something is the case. Desires are also desires *that*, even though language sometimes hides this, as in English. The mother who wants to write a letter desires that she write one. As with all intentional objects, this state of affairs need not exist. She may want to write it, but is then prevented.

There is more to human action than believing and wanting. I may want an ice-cream and believe I can get one by going out to the man in the ice-cream van. But I may not actually go out because I also want to do something else for which I have a stronger preference – lie in bed, finish watching a TV programme. Action also requires something else. I must also at least *intend* to buy the ice-cream. Not merely that, for intentions too can come to grief.

In uncovering the mother's web of beliefs and desires I am not implying she has any of this consciously before her mind when doing what she does. Some of these things – wanting the child to come to the party – may be more present to her than others, like believing that Britain has a postal service. But quite possibly she has none of them directly in mind. The invitation may be the fourteenth she has written that morning.

Even wholly habitual actions like tying your shoelaces still bring with them beliefs and desires. The shoelace-tier wants to be properly dressed and believes that tying his laces is a part of this. Although he is not conscious of these things at the time, at least he must know them. If asked why he is tying the laces, these are the kinds of thing he mentions. The mother similarly knows her reasons for writing the letter and can articulate them if required. Human agency depends on the possession of language.

All this, once we begin to think about it, is very familiar. But very young children are still largely outside these thought-structures. They have to be inducted into the whole business of tying laces and writing letters, so as to understand the reasons people have in general for doing these things and what intentions particular individuals have in doing them. They need to get inside the structures of desires and beliefs that make such actions intelligible.

The examples given so far have been of intentional actions – things that people have intended to bring about (even though they may not have formulated such intentions to themselves). I said earlier that human actions typically have a certain structure. We have now seen how this is built around reasons, and how beliefs and desires enter into these. But there are exceptions.

If a child *unintentionally* knocks over a bottle of sauce, he has no reason for doing this. Hence he has no wants that may be satisfied by doing so or beliefs about this being a means to a desired end. In cottoning on to the notion of human agency, the young child has to learn the difference between intentional and unintentional behaviour – and with it differences in blame and responsibility which each of these brings with it.

I have talked about the young learner coming to understand *human* agency. Non-human animals are agents, too. As with human beings, we can make a broad distinction in their case between the things they do and the things that simply happen to them. If a dog gets kicked, feels toothache, finds himself wedged in a hole, he is not an agent – unlike when he bounds across a field, eats his food, chases an intruder. How, if at all, is non-human agency different from human?

There is a traditional answer that has come down to us from Descartes. Animals are mindless machines. A dog's running after someone is to be understood as a chain of causal connexions at the physical level. Human beings, on the other hand, are capable of action brought under the control of reason. What happens when someone runs for a bus is this. As soon as he rationally decides to do this, an act of willing in his mind operates on the brain in such a way as to cause muscle movements to his legs.

This will not do. It is just not true that some kind of mental act – deciding or willing – always initiates our rational actions. We often do things out of habit – change gear while driving, spread butter on our bread – where we are not on each occasion *making decisions* to do these things, let alone willing that they come about.

To come back to the difference between human and non-human agency. If we are willing to ascribe to non-human animals something of a mental life – to talk of dogs and cats feeling pain, seeing, hearing and smelling things, being afraid of things – then there should be no problem about seeing their active states – their running, digging for bones, coming up to be stroked – as also manifestations of their mentality. Non-human animals – some of them, at least – have wants. Hungry cats want to eat, sleepy dogs to sleep. We explain animals' behaviour by their wants. Why is my cat standing by the back door? Because he wants to be let out into the garden. Why is he rubbing against my leg? Because he wants to be fed. *So far*, the pattern of explanation is similar to explanations in human cases: we explain why agents do the things they do in terms of their desires.

But only so far. Lacking language, animals cannot *express their reasons* for doing what they do – if indeed they can be said to have reasons. My cat wants to go out into the garden. Perhaps in some embryonic sense he believes (see Chapter 3) that standing by the door is an effective means of getting me to open it for him. Do his desire plus his belief add up to his having a reason for action? Or can we not speak this way of cats or dogs because they are not language-using creatures? Must having a reason require being able to express that reason?

Whatever the answer, at least we know that *human beings* can normally give a linguistic account of the reasons they have for acting as they do. If asked why she was writing a letter the mother can reply that she wants to invite a child to a party. She is able to formulate her wants (and, if need be, her relevant beliefs) in language and thus explain her behaviour.

Not, of course, that human beings always *do* express what they have in mind. For the most part we do not. The crucial point is that we *can* do so. If asked, we can give an account of why we are doing what we are doing. A man puts ground coffee into the filter on the coffee machine. He does this every morning, never thinks about it. But if someone – from another culture, perhaps – were to ask him why he is going through this operation, he would have no difficulty in answering 'Because I want a cup of coffee' or in spelling out his belief that the operation was part of a process whereby coffee could be made.

Motives as explanations

I have looked, very briefly, at what human actions are. Now I shall move on to how we explain them.

Although these may look like two separate topics, they are inseparable. To show this, I go back to the point that the same action can be described in many ways:

(i)   She is making marks on paper
(ii) She is writing a letter
(iii) She is inviting someone to a party.

If we want to explain (ii) we can invoke (iii). This gives the reason why she is writing the letter. Here the explanation of the action is another description of it. It is not always like this. Another explanation of why she is writing the letter is that she wants her child to be happy. This is *not* another description of what she is doing. The important fact remains, however, that explanations *are* often redescriptions ('Why is he drinking that coffee? He is slaking his thirst.').

In this respect, explaining human actions is *quite unlike* explaining events in the physical world. When asked why gases expand when heated, our answer cannot be a further description of the event. It has to go beyond this, into underlying laws of nature.

Asking why a child acted in such and such a way is normally to ask for her *motive*. Her motive is her reason for acting as she does. Sometimes the motive may take the form of a redescription ('Why is he writing in that book? He is doing his GCSE coursework.'). At other times it may go beyond this ('Why has she put her hand up? Because she wants to attract the teacher's attention.').

We have already seen how beliefs and desires enter into people's motives. Motives can be of different sorts, and the way beliefs and desires occur in them differ accordingly.

Very often the explanation of a child's behaviour will be in terms of some future end to which he sees his action as a means. 'Why is Steve showing off? Because he wants to impress the girls.' His desire to impress and his belief that making funny remarks is a good way of impressing both come into the explanation – as well as further beliefs and desires that may be in the background.

Why did Tobias Lindseth Melsbu drive the minibus home? Perhaps because he wanted to get there quickly, or to impress his mother. Again, his beliefs also come into the frame: that he knows how to steer, that Mummy will be pleased with him.

But not all motives are instrumental. No doubt Tobias's were not wholly so by any means. Driving the minibus would also be good fun. 'Why is Julia singing at the top of her voice? No reason, she's just enjoying herself, that's all.' Although we say 'no reason', we really mean 'no further reason'. She *has* a reason, all right, for such lusty singing, but the reason is intrinsic: she just wants to do it for its own sake. In this case there are no additional reasons to do with beliefs about appropriate means to ends.

All this is beginning to unravel some of the complexities of the concept of motivation. More will become evident as we go on. A distinction just made was between instrumental and intrinsic motivation. Are these two categories together exhaustive? Could there be non-intrinsic motives which are not instrumental? As I shall try to show later, this is a key question for teachers and parents.

The folk-psychology of motivation

Before coming to this, a warning against too reductive an account of motivation. Some philosophers have suggested that explanations of human actions are resolvable into combinations of desires and beliefs, full stop. Why do people act as they do? Because they want Y, believe that X is a means to Y, and so do X. We have already seen that this account falls down when applied to intrinsic motivation. More generally, it fails to do justice to the complexities of the situations that people often find themselves in when they do things. All sorts of factors come into the motivational story.

A teenager goes berserk in a classroom, lashing out at everyone, throwing chairs around, shouting abuse. Why did he do this? We find out that a fellow student had just touched him on a raw spot. He was feeling low in any case, partly because of domestic circumstances, partly because he never gets on well in this particular class. There is much more to the story than that – more, indeed, that we would need to refer to in giving a comprehensive explanation. These things would all come into his reason for acting as he did. It is because motives are many-faceted and complex rather than able to be regimented into a few basic components that novelists often cast more light on them than philosophers or psychologists of reductionist inclination.

Classroom teachers are as well placed as parents to see the force of these remarks. In non-routine cases such as the one described, only someone like themselves, *au fait* with the whole situation in which the out-of-the-way behaviour occurs, is able to provide anything like a full explanation of it.

If any of them think there are people better placed than themselves – academic psychologists? – they should have more confidence in their own powers. Understanding motivation is not a recondite matter, the province of behavioural science or some other specialism. It has to do with sensitively applying everyday psychological concepts – beliefs, wants, perceptions, emotional responses, means-to-ends, doing something for its own sake – to capture all the complexities.

Although we only use the word 'motive' in English when asking for people's reasons in cases that are untoward in some way ('What was his motive for killing his wife?'), it still remains true that other, quite ordinary, actions can have motives – even though we do not refer to them as such. Although we would normally never *ask about* a child's motive in switching on a light, that does not mean that she does not *have* a motive. (See also Chapter 5 for a similar point about intelligence.) Perhaps it is so banal that it is taken for granted: she wants to do something in the room and it is too dark. Motives have to do with reasons for action. Her reasons involve her desires – to look for the cordless phone, go to bed, feed the gerbil – as well as her belief that switching on the light will enable her to see such objects; and perhaps other considerations, too.

In everyday cases like these teachers and parents do not need experts in motivation to help them make sense of children's behaviour. Their own immersion in a culture where moving a piece of plastic on a wall provides illumination means that they can take the child's reasons for doing this as read.

This is not at all to say that experts have nothing to offer. Teachers have, for instance, found work on children's self-perception helpful – studies suggesting that pupils' low opinion of their own intelligence, or their low self-esteem in general, lie behind their poor performance in the classroom. Whether this psychological research has told them something they found brand-new is a further question. The chances are that they know a good deal about these things from their own experience. What psychology can do is to take them beyond this experience and show them that their own beliefs or half-beliefs are confirmed in other settings where there are greater controls on idiosyncratic perceptions. A large part of psychological work of this sort has to do with reinforcing and clarifying ideas that educators have already. It is partly in the business of confidence-building and self-understanding.

In this respect it has much in common with a book like this one. Both take it for granted that practitioners already have the psychological equipment they need in order to carry out their work. This is drawn from the psychological concepts we use in everyday language, from immersion in their culture, from reading fiction, and from their day-to-day transactions with children, partners, friends and colleagues. Philosophers help them to become more explicitly aware of their conceptual apparatus. Psychologists focus on specific kinds of belief or attitude (children's beliefs about their own inadequacy, for instance). Neither discipline uncovers facts previously wholly unknown to the reader – as a chemist does or a historian. Both help to make the implicit more explicit, the confused less tangled.

Other psychologists of motivation move in more scientific realms. A motto for parents or teachers turning to psychology texts for guidance on motivation could be 'beware of chapter headings'. Some textbooks fill most of their chapter on the topic with physiological data on hunger, thirst, sex and aggression. These desires, shared at their root with some non–human animals, do indeed generate reasons for action. How far teachers and parents need to go into their biology or physiology is another question. Most human motives, including those by which children are guided, go far beyond these biological drives. The reasons why we all do what we do are often highly complex and reflect values and beliefs acquired from many sources, not least the culture in which we live.

Sometimes, admittedly, children's behaviour can only be explained by factors requiring scientific investigation. It might be caused by epilepsy or other physical diseases. In these cases we are beyond the realm of motives, for children do not have reasons for going into fits. This is not to say there are not reasons why they have them. But here reasons are simply causes – in the same sense that there is a reason why water turns into ice at a certain temperature. Even though there *is* a reason for this, the water does not *have* a reason.

It is also true that, where children do indeed have motives, these may be too complex for educators relying only on their own psychological resources. In some cases of sexual abuse, for instance, they need expert psychological help to sort out the twisted array of factors in their students' background. Specialists also come in where motives proper have to be separated from physiological or other causes where these are closely intertwined – as where a child's behaviour can be partly, but not wholly, attributed to taking drugs.

The only other point to make about the psychology of motivation is to issue a safety warning, if such is needed, about textbooks that obscure far more than they illuminate. No names, no packdrill. But if readers should find themselves getting horribly lost among lists of 'internal processes' such as instincts, hierarchies of needs, drives, and cognitive dissonance, or among diagrams with arrows of causation leading from 'need reduction' to 'drive' to 'activity' to 'satisfaction' and back to 'drive', they can be reassured that the problem does not lie with them.

Types of motivation: intrinsic and extrinsic

There are many ways of classifying motives. I mentioned above the division between biological and non-biological ones. Here, with education in mind, I want to focus on another kind of classification, expanding on what I was saying earlier about instrumental motives and intrinsic ones. I asked whether these two categories exhausted the field or whether there could be extrinsic reasons that are not instrumental.

I think there can be. An extrinsic reason is one that is not intrinsic – where intrinsic motives have to do with what is done for its own sake, not for the sake of something else. A child may play the piano simply out of enjoyment and not because he is preparing for a music lesson or for a concert performance. Enjoying playing the piano is here an end in itself. Extrinsic reasons are reasons which refer to ends outside the activity itself.

There are three importantly different types of extrinsic reason. The first is involved where the action or activity undertaken is a *replaceable* means to an end. A teacher is planning a group trip to the Science Museum. How will he go? By train and tube or by minibus? He thinks it through and chooses the train. If asked 'Why are you catching this train?', his answer is that he wants to get to London. This is an example of a straightforward means–end reason where the means selected is replaceable by another. But not all extrinsic reasons are of this sort. Sometimes the means is irreplaceable. Someone is filling in the answer to a crossword clue. Why? Because she wants to complete the crossword. Here the means − answering clue number 7 across − is an integral *part* of the end − answering all the clues. Nothing can substitute for it.

The distinction between these first two types of extrinsic reasons is between those which are (purely) *instrumental,* i.e. where one means can take the place of another, and those referring to *wholes* of which the action or activity is an integral part. This is of great importance educationally, as will become clear.

The role of whole–part reasons in our lives goes way beyond crossword puzzles. Suppose the answer to the question 'Why did that woman kiss her daughter as she left for school?' is that she was expressing her affection for her. This is a reason for her kissing, but what kind of a reason is it? 'Expressing affection' does not refer to a goal to attain to which kissing is one particular means, replaceable by other ways of showing affection such as hugging or gentle words. It is a reason that serves to locate the kissing as part of a larger picture, to do with a certain kind of relationship.

Whole–part reasons are found, unsurprisingly enough, where there are whole–part features in our lives. Two examples of wholes have been given: doing crossword puzzles and being in a loving relationship. Other examples would be: creating, performing or attending to a work of art; belonging to a flourishing enterprise or social group − a school or firm, for instance, or a football club or a nation; playing a game of chess or snooker.

We come to the third kind of extrinsic reason. This one is wholly or chiefly orientated to *the past.* A teacher intervenes in a physical attack of one pupil on another. 'Why did you lash out at him?' 'I was in a blinding rage: he was reading my private diary.' Here the lashing out is an immediate response to a perceived hurt. It is not undertaken primarily with a view to bringing about some future end, as would be, for instance, a calculated design to teach someone a lesson so that he would think twice before doing the same thing again.

Among the emotions, some are future-orientated, like fear or hope, others look to the past, like anger, grief, remorse or shame, while yet others dwell in the present, like joy, or straddle past, present and future like certain kinds of love (see Chapter 9). Insofar as emotions motivate people to do things – as distinct from affecting them more passively – they fit into the categorisation of motives given so far. They provide us with intrinsic reasons (like joy) and among extrinsic reasons instrumental ones (like fear), whole–part ones (like love of one's family or country), and backward-looking ones (like shame or anger).

I have mentioned so far a number of different kinds of motive: intrinsic reasons and three types of extrinsic, i.e. instrumental, whole–part, and past-orientated. Will this categorisation do? Is there not a sense in which all our motives come down to whole–part reasons? Consider playing the piano for its own sake. Is 'for enjoyment' the last reason that can be given in a chain of reasons? After all, playing the piano for enjoyment is not wholly detached from other areas of life. It has its part in a wider canvas filled with other intrinsic as well as extrinsic goals. Similarly with travelling by train to get to London. There are larger considerations behind this ultimately connected in some way with the whole of a person's life

It is tempting but mistaken to take this as showing all motivation to be part–whole. Some people may treat their lives like works of art, of which they are the (self-) creators. Just as in a painting or poem, so in the unfolding story of their life the parts have to be crafted together to make a harmonious whole. For them piano playing for enjoyment is not, or not only, an end in itself, but has its place in a greater totality. Usually, though, people are not self-creators in this way. The things they enjoy for their own sake are parts of their lives, certainly, but they do not see in them a contribution to a totality. For most of us, 'Because it is enjoyable' is a reason which stands in no need of further reasons behind it.

One last remark. Although I have analytically separated various types of intrinsic and extrinsic motive, these do not usually occur separately from each other. A child may be playing the piano *partly* for enjoyment and *partly* because she is practising for a music exam. We often have mixed motives for what we do.

Motivation in education

Understanding motives

The intrinsic and extrinsic reasons that pupils and teachers have for acting as they do are often immediately intelligible from the context. We know why children collect trays and cutlery in the canteen, why Jonathan asked those silly questions in class, why the head of history sits in that chair in the staff room. Strangers to the school or strangers to British or modern Western culture might find some of these things puzzling and would need to ferret out the agents' relevant desires and beliefs.

Sometimes we participants are also puzzled. We do not know why that child is behaving out of character, or suspect that the reason she gives us may not be her real reason. We, too, may need to find out about her beliefs and/or desires. Why did Ellie surreptitiously eat those grapes in class? If we discover that she has just come to believe that eating fruit every hour throughout the day is a good recipe for slimming, we have a possible belief–desire pair to help explain her odd behaviour. There may be more severe cases of unintelligibility where the school needs professional psychological help. Yet even here the pattern of attempted explanation is the same – penetrating the bizarre belief-system of a schizophrenic person's mind, trying to find out what he really wants.

There are also ethical issues falling under this section about when it is right to try to find out what pupils' or colleagues' motives are and when doing so would invade their privacy. I will leave these on one side.

Motivating children

More problematic for many teachers is how to motivate their pupils to engage in learning activities. Some of their problems are more intractable than others. Every teacher has to find some way of involving children in schoolwork and good lesson planning provides part of the answer. But how can they cope with students who are apathetic, or just do not want to know, or find anything to do with school a turn-off?

These are all practical matters and practitioners are the ones who can give most help. But philosophical considerations may be useful in establishing a conceptual framework for these more specific suggestions. I have four of them in mind.

Preliminaries

Motivating pupils is getting them to engage in activities by furnishing them with reasons for doing so that are meaningful to them. I phrase this with deliberate care. If you want a child to work at algebraic equations, it is not helpful to tell him he will need to understand algebra in order to become a maths teacher, true though this might well be, if he has no desire to become one. The reasons you give must be such as to make him want to do the algebra: they must be meaningful to him in this sense.

Motivating pupils is not always or only a matter of linking the activity to some desire, intrinsic or extrinsic, to which it was not linked before: it sometimes involves working on their beliefs. A girl at secondary school would like a well-paid job and sees doing well at science as a route to one; but she has given up on science because she thinks of it as a boys' subject. Challenging this last belief may be all that is necessary for her to be able to throw herself into it.

Being motivated has to do with having reasons for some action or activity. Strictly, you cannot motivate children to *learn* something, because learning is not an activity but an *achievement* – usually, coming to know something one did not know before. Teachers want pupils to learn, say, German word order and they do this by setting them various tasks. Children have to be motivated to engage *in these tasks*.

A point about goals. During the liquidation of the kulaks Soviet children were incited to denounce their parents. One of them, Pavlik Morozov, became hero-worshipped for doing so. Being able to motivate pupils may or may not be a good thing. It depends on the desirability of what is learnt. This is a point where the philosophical psychology of education abuts onto the philosophy of educational aims.

How to motivate

Motivating pupils is getting them to engage in activities by furnishing them with reasons for doing so that are meaningful to them. These reasons are largely compounds of desires and beliefs. All this implies an active stance on the part of the teacher or parent, who has to hook up an activity with desires and beliefs that children have already, or change these desires or beliefs where appropriate. It also implies some understanding of the desires and beliefs that weigh with particular learners, rather than operating in some more global way which ignores individual differences.

This way of looking at motivation – as an active and nuanced inter-vention into particular pupils' mental structures – is poles apart from theories that leave more to nature and less to culture. It may suit some child-centred thinkers to believe that children will become interested in deepening their understanding or their aesthetic experience all in good time, once their needs for love or self-esteem are adequately met. Or that you cannot expect young children to be other than egoistic in their outlook because they are not yet at a stage of development where altruism becomes possible. But education is not a standing-back and letting benign nature take its course. It is necessarily a shaping, an intervention, an initiation into cultural practices. We met this point in the discussion of developmentalism in Chapter 4.

Pupils can be motivated via attention to their beliefs; or by attention to their desires.

What children think

Normally, when people engage in activity A to fulfil a desire B – mowing the lawn, for instance, to keep the garden tidy – certain beliefs on their part are taken for granted. They must think that A is a way of bringing about B, that they have the ability to do A (they have the strength to cut the grass, they know how to operate the mower), that they can muster the effort required to do A (they are not too tired), that A is an appropriate activity for them to engage in (it is their own lawn they are cutting, not their neighbour's), that there are no insuperable external impediments (the lawn is not waterlogged).

Beliefs like these are so obvious that they hardly seem worth mentioning. This is why talk of motives often bypasses agents' beliefs in favour of their desires.

Where one or other of these commonplace beliefs is missing, however, motivation may fail. However strong the agent's desire to do A (in order to bring about B, or whatever), if he thinks that doing A is not in within his power, that A is unachievable by anyone, or that it is wrong to do A, he will not have a sufficient reason for doing A and may end up not doing it. If he is to come to do it, his beliefs must alter appropriately.

This is true, not least, of learning tasks. Perhaps a pupil would really like to learn to swim – so that he could go off with his friends to the outdoor pool and bathe in the sea in the summer. Suitable desires are in place, but he shies away from swimming lessons because he thinks he is hopeless at anything physical, and in addition he will sink and possibly drown once he gets out of his depth. Motivating a pupil like this is a matter first of understanding the beliefs that impede him and then of encouraging him to see they are baseless.

What children want

Pupils also need appropriate desires. We can now apply our earlier, desire-based, typology of motives to issues of motivating pupils. We discussed extrinsic and intrinsic motives. Among extrinsic motives we distinguished purely instrumental from part–whole and from backward-looking motives. Backward-looking motives are unlikely to be used to motivate students. I cannot imagine a teacher trying to get a pupil to do a piece of work out of revenge, anger or grief. But all the other types of motive are of great importance in education.

PURELY INSTRUMENTAL MOTIVES

Not long ago, Latin was a requirement for admission to certain British universities. What motivated many young people to study it was their desire to get into Oxford or Cambridge. If Sanskrit had been prescribed in Latin's place, they would have probably buckled down to this instead. Doing Latin was a replaceable activity.

These days Latin is less in evidence, but some students at school or university choose subjects because they think they are most likely to lead to a well-paid job. They are not interested in accountancy courses in themselves but grind through them for the sake of the rewards. If doing sociology or media studies were guaranteed to net them a huge income in their first year and accountancy graduates were two a penny, their choices would be quite different.

Purely instrumental motives are also used to motivate much younger pupils. A primary child works hard at spelling because her teacher is keen on this and praises children for good work. If the teacher had thought correct spelling a bourgeois fetish and gave recognition for creative writing, she would have thrown herself into this.

If expectation of reward or punishment are used as motivators, those who use them should realise that, as far as the learner is concerned, the learning activity is replaceable by any other that is more likely to produce the reward or prevent the punishment.

One thing at issue here is the commitment the learner has towards the learning activity. Some of the things pupils learn are intended as permanent and irreplaceable pieces of mental equipment on which they will draw throughout their lives. Being able to read, write and count are obvious examples. So, too, you might argue, would be treating others with respect, having an understanding of how your society works, being responsive to aesthetic qualities in art or nature. (I am moving into controversial territory, to do, once again, with the philosophy of educational aims. But the examples are less important than the general point that much educational learning is meant to be permanent and irreplaceable.)

The point I am driving at is this. If we want pupils to come to have a proper attitude to these permanent and irreplaceable kinds of learning (whatever they are), that is, to *come to see them as permanent and irreplaceable*, it seems a bad bet to rely on motivation that treats them as replaceable. If other forms of motivation are available it would seem more sensible to resort to those.

But sometimes this objection is overridable. Very young children love doing what brings parents' and, later, teachers' approval. There is no harm in capitalising on this motivation − quite the contrary − provided (i) that the activity in question has to do with permanent and irreplaceable equipment, and (ii) that as soon as possible the child is encouraged to engage it for other than instrumental reasons. For example, children can begin to decipher letters and words because they get good parental feedback and then come to enjoy doing this for its own sake or because they begin to see the whole business of reading as part of what it is to become like other people.

A danger in relying on purely instrumental motivation in young children is that it encourages authoritarian behaviour in them. The reason why they are doing what they are doing is that someone wants them to do this − and if this person wanted them to do something else, they would do that instead. This, too, points towards replacing instrumental by other forms of motivation.

INTRINSIC MOTIVES

Pupils can also be brought to engage in an activity because they find it interesting or enjoyable for its own sake. Young children like listening to stories, drawing, playing games. Some older students throw themselves into mathematics or history because they find these things fascinating in themselves.

Intrinsic motivation is understandably what many teachers value. It is worth cultivating for more than one reason. Most obviously, it helps to generate committed absorption in the learning activity. Children learning to write can get great pleasure from copying the shapes of letters if they are in the hands of a teacher who associates them with pigs' tails, step ladders and other objects. Yet forming letters is not something in which the teacher wants them to develop an intrinsic interest throughout their lives. From the child's point of view the activity may be delightful in itself, but from the teacher's its value is as a skill to be harnessed to other ends. At some point the children's interest must shift in this direction.

A second reason for encouraging intrinsic motivation has to do with the aims of education in a liberal society. These are many-sided, of course. Among them is the aim of introducing pupils to a range of intrinsically interesting activities from among which to choose those they wish to follow as major concerns in their lives. These could include all sorts of things, from playing or following sport to craft activities to studying history to gardening or the arts. An important component in a flourishing life is the whole-heartedness of a person's engagement in activities of major importance to them. Acquiring such a sense of total absorption in one or more activities as a child can, with luck, give that child the taste for it in other areas. Education has much to do with the proliferation of enthusiasms.

Some people leave school with little in the way of any. To prevent this, a first task of school education is to ensure that the delights of intrinsically motivated activity are experienced throughout a person's school career – not allowed to grow thin as the child becomes an adolescent. A second task is to extend experience of intrinsic motivation across a widening range of activities from which the self-directed adults whom the pupils will become can choose their preferences.

Whether all the staples of the secondary curriculum are best suited to promote these aims is another question. Some are all but irrelevant. There is, it is true, an intrinsic aspect to learning to speak or read a foreign language, but this is of small account as compared to its practical uses. Mathematics is pleasurable in itself for some people, adults included, but they tend to be few. Given this limited appeal, there is no good reason I can see why we should expect every student to get intrinsic buzzes from it. This is not to say that teachers should not aim at such a reaction, only that if they do not succeed with many pupils they should not lose sleep over it. As long as every pupil is equipped with experience or understanding of a *broad range* of intrinsically interesting activities, the liberal aim I mentioned is met. This is compatible with some possibilities, such as mathematical pleasures, remaining outside their ken. Artistic activities are different in that virtually everybody – again, I am thinking mainly of adults – finds some intrinsic interest in something in this broad field. I am assuming here we are not making too tight a ring round 'artistic activities' and restricting these to the more arcane reaches of serious art: there is no sharp borderline between the latter and entertainment art.

Would it be enough for teachers to rely on intrinsic motivation? I do not think so. Suppose a secondary school student came to love not only mathematics for its own sake, but also history, literature, music, and science. She might keep all these activities in discrete compartments, turning with delight from one to another. This could be a good outcome as far as it went, but would it be good enough?

What it leaves out is the element of evaluation, of learning to weigh the relative importance to oneself of this project or that. Evaluation is a condition of becoming a relatively integrated person rather than a being whose life fractures into a collection of unconnected enterprises. It is not enough to immerse yourself in many things for their own sake: at some point, your reasons for being involved must also include some reference to the part that the activity plays in your psychic constitution as a whole. (This need not go so far as seeing your life on the model of a work of art.) This leads us to another kind of motive.

LEGO TRUCKS AND ANIMAL FRIEZES: PART–WHOLE MOTIVES

In his fine essay on 'The fragmentation of value', Thomas Nagel writes:

> If you have set out to climb Everest, or translate Aristotle's *Metaphysics*, or master the *Well-Tempered Clavier*, or synthesise an amino acid, then the further pursuit of that project, once begun, acquires remarkable importance. It is partly a matter of justifying earlier investment of time and energy, and not allowing it to have been in vain. It is partly a desire to be the sort of person who finishes what he begins. But whatever the reason, our projects make autonomous claims on us, once undertaken, which they need not have made in advance.
>
> (1979, p. 130)

Nagel's examples are all of part–whole motivation. The process of climbing Everest is no doubt rewarding in itself, but this is not the only, and certainly not the main, reason that a climber will give for doing what she is doing. She has in mind the final achievement, reaching the summit. What she is doing now is a part of that whole enterprise.

Nagel's examples are also all rather grand and out of the ordinary. But parents and teachers know the force of what he is saying from more mundane situations. Wanting to finish a Lego truck, reading a novel, a history project, a piece of writing, an experiment in science – all these things can be powerful motives for children.

They are perhaps at their most powerful when the wholes in question are most archetypically wholes. Created objects, including aesthetic objects, best fit this bill. A Lego truck is complete in itself, and so is *Animal Farm*. A history project is also a bounded entity, but there is always a certain arbitrariness about its borders, the product of practical requirements. In this it is like a set of problems given out for maths homework. Completing the latter, too, can be a motivator, but there need be no intrinsic unity about the set.

If pupils are motivated in this part–whole way, the assumption is that they have started on the activity in the first place. What has motivated them to do this? Perhaps a reason drawn from one of our first two categories: (i) purely instrumental and (ii) intrinsic. A teacher may persuade a reluctant child to read the first few pages of a story by relying on desire for praise or recognition, knowing that, once hooked, the child will need no further prompting to finish the whole thing. Or a learner may simply be fascinated by the subject matter in general – science, music, or whatever – and *that* is why she has embarked on the particular project.

But sometimes this third category (iii) of part–whole motives can also spark off an activity in the first place. Building the Lego truck could be part of a larger enterprise of making a toy village. What makes some children want to learn to read may be some inchoate sense that doing so – and they may only have the dimmest of apprehensions of what it is all about – will make them more like all those people around them for whom it is obviously important to be able to do whatever it is they are doing with these strange shapes. They want to read so as to become – as we might put it – part of this community of initiates.

Social part–whole motives, of which this is an example, are of especial interest to educators. So many curriculum activities can be approached from this direction. A primary class is busy painting animals to go in a frieze around the classroom. The children are not only enjoying creating their bears and zebras for its own sake: they are doing this, too, as part of a communal enterprise.

Communities or groups can differ in size. Secondary school children can be encouraged to see their history lessons – indeed their science or mathematics lessons – as equipping them as citizens of Britain or Portugal. There are also communities centred on different kinds of social practice. Young footballers can see themselves as belonging to Spurs or Newcastle United or a wider confraternity of enthusiasts. Young poetry lovers can grow into an awareness of an unseen community of creators and responders, spread out across centuries and continents. They can read their Keats or their Yeats not only for intrinsic enjoyment but also as proto-members of this group.

These social motives cannot get off the ground unless the students *care* about belonging to these collectives or communities. Again, we come back to underlying aims of education. There is a strong case, which must be argued elsewhere, for children being brought up concerned for the well-being of others whose communal life they share, whether at the level of family, friends, local community, national community, humanity as a whole.

Parents and teachers who think this way will wish to develop the attitudes, emotions and beliefs that enhance this altruistic concern – for instance sympathy, love, loyalty, trust, a belief in the equal intrinsic importance of every person. It is these that provide the fundamental motivation at issue. The more it is in place, the greater the motivational scope open to the educator when it comes to particular activities. He or she is not driven back, as is the parent or teacher of more individualistic temper, more narrowly attentive to the worldly success, happiness or well-being of the child, towards the purely instrumental or the intrinsic. Here, perhaps, is part of the explanation of the sheer enthusiasm for learning so noticeable in a country like Taiwan, with its strong communal traditions.

Like earlier categories discussed, social part–whole motives can be put to bad as well as good uses. Red Nose Day is one thing; the Red Guards were another. Pavlik Morozov, mentioned above, was motivated to shop his own parents by his vision of himself as part of the Communist cause. In present-day Britain, motivation can arise from the demands of your gang or from the expectations of public opinion as worked on by the mass media. It should be a part of every student-teacher's training to reflect on when social motivation is desirable and when it goes too far.

In this section I have looked at part–whole motives and their place in education. Although I have concentrated on social motives, I also noted the motivation that comes from wanting to finish an uncompleted task. This leads me to another type of part-whole motivation.

Self-creation is an uncompleted task, not least for young adolescents only recently embarked on it. As pointed out earlier, being moved for wholly intrinsic reasons to engage in a range of activities, from athletics, say, to rock music and science, is not enough. Persons are not compartmentalisable. If students themselves are not self-motivated to relate their discrete commitments to a more global picture of what they might become, their mentors have some responsibility to help them to do so. This again takes the argument back to the aims of education. For students to be able to respond to such promptings, they have to have some care for themselves as whole persons in the first place.

As always, reliance on this type of motivation can go too far. Human lives do not share all the features of works of art, even though they share some. Someone's love of scuba-diving has a high value in itself for the diver: its significance does not lie chiefly in the part it plays in his overall structure of desires. In this way it is unlike a patch of colour in the corner of a painting. Here, as elsewhere, teachers and other guides of young people need delicacy of judgement in the motivational appeals they make. They should be wary of imprisoning their charges in compartmentalised activities, but cautious, too, about encouraging a Hamlet-like over-reflectiveness about the unity of their selves.

'ONE DAY YOU'LL SEE WHY'

Before leaving this section, a word about a way of motivating that is ancient history among schoolteachers but which does not fit neatly under any of the other headings.

Teachers trying to put over some recondite material in mathematics, say, or science sometimes say 'You may not understand at the moment why you have to learn this, but one day you'll see why and be glad of it'. If a child is swayed by some such appeal, how does this happen?

Belief is central here. She believes 'teacher knows best'. But desire must come into the story, too. What does she believe teacher knows best *about*? Well, she may not be very clear about this, but it must have something to do with what will be good for her or right for her to do. The child wants what is good for her in the future and believes that her teacher knows what this is. Being only ten or twelve years old she has only the dimmest of pictures of what her future well-being might consist in. It is understandable that she falls in with what an apparent authority on this urges her to do.

The basic issue here is whether the teacher *does* know what is best for her. There are not, so far as I know, experts on the good life. In *some* contexts, true, teachers may well be on fairly firm ground in making this sort of motivational appeal. If it is a question of literacy, for instance, or of everyday arithmetic, it is a fair bet that the child will be glad he or she has learnt these things.

But schools and teachers have sometimes trodden more uncertain territory: in the past, Latin and Greek or the rote-learning of Bible passages; in the present, parts of the secondary curriculum. Not by any means that pupils' trust in their teachers' wisdom always depends on things these teachers say explicitly. Sometimes the very ethos of the school reinforces it. I remember in my own case how it seemed to be taken as read at the age of twelve that I would do best to drop science for ever; and later – on entry to the sixth form – that two years of medieval history were the ideal prospect for me. How wrong the school was on both counts!

Developing children's reasons for action

Motivation also belongs to educational content in its own right. Parents and teachers have a responsibility to induct children into an understanding of what count as good reasons for action.

At first the very youngest children operate much in the way that animals do. They have certain (innate) wants and act in accordance with these. Gradually, as they develop the necessary language and conceptual ability, they come to act for reasons. They can tell you why they are looking in the cupboard, thereby revealing their implicit grasp of the desire- and belief-structures we rely on in explaining human behaviour (they are looking in the cupboard for biscuits; and they believe that this is where the biscuits are kept).

As they grow older, their upbringers can help them to expand these structures into more complex and sometimes more appropriate forms. Existing desires become more determinate: enjoying physical exercise becomes specified into playing volleyball or rollerblading; while brand-new desires – to play a musical instrument, to construct mathematical proofs, to flirt – become grafted onto old. Undesirable desires get sifted out. Acceptable ones get chained together in complicated, hierarchical structures of means–end and part–whole relationships.

Beliefs undergo similar transformations. Children acquire more and more information in different domains, much of which can be incorporated into reasons for action. False or unfounded beliefs are winnowed away. (Older children may smoke so as to gain the approval of their peer group. Is the belief correct? If smoking is a means of gaining approval, is it on balance a good means? Why is it important to gain the approval of the group?) Those beliefs that pass muster are bound by logical links within increasingly sophisticated thought-structures. Or such, at least, is the ideal, however much some children fall short of this in practice.

More than just this work on expanding desire- and belief-structures is required. Pupils have to learn to choose between desires when they conflict, make one rather than another the motivating desire from which they will act. They want to smoke and they want to be healthy. They need to acquire *second-order* desires of desiring their health-desire to trump the smoking-desire. As they grow older and their desires multiply, they are likely to face more, and more intractable, conflicts between them. In their earlier years, their parents and teachers were on hand to help them resolve them. Now, gradually, they will take over this office themselves and make their own autonomous judgements as to what to do.

Developing children's understanding of their own and others' motives

There is an asymmetry between our understanding of our own motives and our understanding of others'. By and large our own motives are open to us. We know why we are writing this letter to the tax office or buying a bus ticket to Wood Green. If we saw a stranger doing these things, we would not immediately know why. We would have to have recourse to evidence, in the shape of what he or she said their reasons were, for instance.

This claim needs to be qualified in two ways. We do not always know our own motives. A man may tell himself he is interested in a woman only because of her intellect, wanting for whatever reason to repress his awareness of being sexually attracted to her. Also, others' motives are by no means always as opaque as in the examples given. If I see my neighbour watering her garden during dry weather, I need no detective work to tell me she wants her plants not to suffer.

These remarks open up new directions for motivational education. The watering example reminds us of the significance of cultural background. We all know – at least in broad terms – what people have in mind when they spray water from a can, or when they tap numbers into a mobile phone, or pull a trolley out from a rack in the super-market. There is a taken-for-granted background here that we all share, but which for a tribesperson from a totally different culture would be unintelligible.

Very young children are something like the tribesperson. I heard a little girl in an art gallery recently asking of a Degas nude why they put up rude pictures like this. As I walked past, her mother was carefully explaining about the patches of light on the skin. She was initiating her daughter into what will become for her a taken-as-read horizon shared with all lovers of Western art.

Children need to be inducted into their own culture's motivational structures. They will soon become second nature to them. But their education needs more than this. There are at least three kinds of opacities which they will require extra guidance to dispel. The first has to do with their own unconscious motives. I am not thinking of the deeply embedded forms of repression associated with psycho-pathology, but of more commonplace examples of self-deception that affect us all. In pupils' own interests they should be made aware that they may have motives which they are reluctant to admit to them-selves. Literature is one resource for this.

Second, a shrinking and increasingly multicultural world brings with it greater demands on being able to interpret the behaviour of people from other cultures. This is a matter partly of learning about other taken-for-granted backgrounds, partly of avoiding stereotypes or refusing to step outside your own cultural horizons so as to make the exotic more familiar.

Third, the motives of those who share your own cultural horizons are not always as patent as those of the gardener or the mobile-phone user. Sometimes they may *seem* patent, as in the case of a bogus police officer I recently encountered as a member of a jury, who called at a flat claiming to be investigating robberies in the area while his accomplice was busy stealing an engagement ring from another room. Pupils need to be intellectually equipped against the con artist, the deceptively friendly salesman or advertiser.

At other times motives are from the outset more indiscernible. We just cannot understand why a friend should be so uncharacteristically blunt with us, or why the Prime Minister should timetable the prorogation of Parliament as he did. Here, too, pupils need to acquire appropriate intellectual resources – a general, nuanced understanding of human nature in the first case, insight into British party politics in the second.

All these points indicate the sophistication which pupils need to attain in their understanding of their own and others' motives. Modern society contains plenty of institutions ready, each for its own reasons, to present a simplified, stereotyped picture of the motivational scene. Soap operas, tabloid newspapers, advertisements show people dominated by – usually short-term – desires for money, sex, power, recognition, comfort, security. Political movements can pin crude low motives on undesirable groups, as the Nazis did on the Jews or Stalin on his political enemies. Pupils need to be armoured against such reductionisms through initiation into the subtleties and complexities of the world of motives.

I have argued for this initiation on the grounds of the extrinsic benefits it produces for our own well-being or in our role as citizens. But there is an intrinsic aspect as well. For most of us, other people's motives are objects of fascination in their own right. Gossip trades on this. So do history books, plays, novels, films, detective stories. Parents and teachers should, and do, see to it that children are equipped to enjoy all these delights.

Summary and key points

Philosophical perspectives on motivating children are best approached via the more general notion of human agency. Inducting children into what agency is involves bringing them – gradually – to understand people's reasons for acting as they do. (See also Chapter 6 on practical thinking.) These reasons include both beliefs (see Chapter 3) and desires. Reasons for action are not always consciously before the agent's mind. Non-human animals are agents, too, although whether they can be said to have reasons for their behaviour is unclear. Motives as reasons for action can be either intrinsic or extrinsic. Extrinsic motives can be either purely instrumental, or part–whole, or past-orientated.

Motivating children to learn is a practical task on which philosophy can give no specific advice. It can, however, provide a helpful framework. Attention can be paid both to children's beliefs and to their desires. The chapter discusses the advantages and drawbacks of relying on purely instrumental, intrinsic and part–whole motivation. Education is also partly a matter of expanding children's reasons for action in desirable directions. Teachers and parents also have the task of helping children to understand motives in other people and in themselves.

Further reading

There are several good philosophical accounts of human agency, motives and related concepts. Brief discussions are in McGinn, C., (1982) *The Character of Mind* Oxford: Oxford University Press, ch. 5; Searle, J., (1984) *Minds, Brains and Science* London: British Broadcasting Corporation, ch. 4; Kenny, A., (1989) *The Metaphysics of Mind* Oxford: Oxford University Press, ch. 3; Hamlyn, D. W., 'Motivation', in Cooper, D. E., (ed.) (1986) *Education, Values and Mind: Essays for R.S. Peters* London: Routledge and Kegan Paul.

Strangely, as far as I know, the general topic of motivation has not previously been discussed at any length in the philosophy of education literature. The essay by Hamlyn, just referred to, is basically in general philosophy. But see MacIntyre, A., (1999) *Dependent Rational Animals* London: Duckworth, chs 8, 9 on how young children learn to become independent practical reasoners. Chapter 6 of the same book argues against Kenny (op. cit.) that non-human animals *can* have reasons for action.

Chapter 9

Educating the emotions

What emotions are

Are they feelings?

From motivation in the last chapter we move now to the closely related topic of emotion. As I write, I can hear Jamie having a tantrum in next door's garden. Jamie is three and three-quarters. Four months ago his mother gave birth to a second child, Catherine. Until that time Jamie and his mother had spent nearly all their time together. 'I feel I never want to see another park', she told us once. Jamie's wall-to-wall sunny nature has now clouded over. When I see him or hear him he is often cross, rude, miserable. What does he feel towards Catherine? A mixture, perhaps, of hatred, anger, envy, jealousy. What does he feel towards his mother? Hatred and anger again? Disappointment? Hope that things may return to the way they were?

All these are emotions. So are fear, shame, guilt, embarrassment, anxiety, contempt, joy, sympathy, pride, depression, love, surprise. I imagine everyone would all agree about those. But what about lust? Is that an emotion? If lust, what about hunger or thirst? Are physical drives like these emotions? If not, why not?

I will leave this last question hanging for the moment and turn back to the uncontroversial items on the list. One thing these share is that they can all be *felt*. Emotions are feelings. If there is such a thing as the education of the emotions, it must be the education of feelings.

So far so good? Not quite. Lust is bubbling up again. So are hunger and thirst. For feelings come into all these things, too. Is there any significant difference between feeling frightened and feeling ravenous?

I will start with fear. What is the feeling associated with this emotion?

Could the story go something like this? Suppose the fear a child feels is evoked by a man with a knife ahead of him in the street. He sees the man. This causes a feeling of fear inside his mind. This in turn causes him to take to his heels.

This account both begins in the physical world – with light waves from the man striking the boy's eye – and also ends there – in the shape of the muscle movements in his legs that remove him from the scene. In between lie events in the mental world. Nervous transmission from the eye to the brain causes a feeling of fear within the mind. This feeling in its turn affects other parts of the brain, causing it to send signals to the muscles in the legs and other places.

In this – Cartesian – story, emotions come out as feelings in much the same way as pains or hunger pangs are feelings. The same kind of causal story can be given of a girl playing in her back garden who is pricked by a thorn on a rose bush. This causes her to feel a painful sensation, which in turn causes her to pull out the thorn. Just as thorn pricks, bee stings, toothaches and headaches are each a distinct kind of sensation, so, too, are fear, shame, embarrassment and anger. Of course, there are pleasurable emotions, too, like joy, love and pride. In this story these are distinct kinds of pleasurable sensation, just like pleasurable experiences of being stroked, or lying in the warm sun, or being tickled.

So there would be no difficulty about lumping feelings of hunger, thirst and lust in with those of joy, contempt or indignation.

Are they educable?

Or would there be? Remember the claim in Chapter 1 that all areas of mental life are educable *except* pains and other sensations. Toothaches cannot be modified by learning or teaching, as can beliefs or perceptions. Treating pains is a job for medics, not for educators. It seems to follow that if emotions are another kind of sensation, developing them turns out to be impossible.

Many educationists would be happy enough with this verdict. Education, they would say, is an intellectual enterprise. It has to do with shaping pupils' powers of thought, deepening and extending their understanding, making them self-critical about their beliefs. Feelings of all sorts lie beyond its province.

Someone might object that even where intellectualist conceptions of education have taken most hold – in, say, the British public schools – *some* attention has been paid to the emotions, if only to keep them under firm control. From Korea to Caracas the notion of the 'stiff upper lip' is associated with the education of the emotions found in top British private schools.

But this objection is unlikely to faze our intellectualists. 'It is still not the emotions themselves that are being modified,' they will reply. 'The phrase "the education of the emotions" is a misnomer. What the house-masters of Eton or Winchester have taught their timorous charges is to *control the expression*, including the facial expression, of their fears and other feelings. This is indeed a kind of skill that can be taught and learned. But it leaves the emotion itself – the private, invisible inner feeling – wholly untouched.'

Is there any answer to be made to them? Can they be shown that they are simply wrong about the undevelopability of the emotions? Can parents and teachers be shown that they *can* modify, pedagogically rather than medically, the anxieties, the sympathies, the embarrassments that children feel – that they can change *the emotions themselves*, not merely their outward manifestations?

Emotions and objects

I want to go back to the man with the knife and the boy's fear. A feature of this situation is that the boy is afraid *of the man*. This may seem hardly worth mentioning, since it is so obviously true. Yet it is really important. For it brings out the point that fear is fear *of* something. We cannot simply be afraid, full stop. We are always afraid of something – a mugger, other people's opinions about us, the Unknown, aliens, slugs. In the language of Chapter 1, fear takes an intentional object.

The example of aliens reminds us that intentional objects need not exist in reality. A young child can be afraid of gremlins, demons, or the Controller of Alpha Centaurus even though there are no such things. We will come back to this.

Just as children cannot be afraid without being afraid *of* something, so they cannot feel relieved without feeling relieved *about* something, or feel sympathy without feeling sympathy *with* or *for* someone. Similarly, love is love for, and anger is anger at, someone or something. How far is this general point also true of shame, guilt, pity, pride and resentment?

Are *all* cases of emotion directed onto objects? Suppose a teenager wakes up one morning and everything looks black. He find himself in a depressed state and cannot shake himself out of it. It is not that he is depressed about anything in particular – his relationships, his exam results, his prospects. He is just depressed, full stop.

Is this a counter-example to the claim that emotion is an intentional phenomenon? Not really, I think. What it may show is that emotion is not a tidy notion with sharp edges to it. It may have a fuzzy border, which shades off into other things. Somewhere in this border one may find objectless emotions, like the depression just mentioned. Whether to call it an emotion or just a mood is not clear-cut.

On this view, leaving aside the fuzzy area we can still hang onto the claim that emotions take objects. Indeed, this is true of feeling depressed. It is only in certain circumstances, where, perhaps, some physiological cause is at work, that a person's depression is about nothing in particular. Often it is about something more than obvious to them – bad news about a friend's health, a poor showing in a Diploma course, splitting up with a boyfriend.

If all this is true, emotions are not at all the same kind of thing as sensations. Joy, pride, love and anger are importantly different from toothache, butterflies in the stomach or the feeling of being stroked. They are different from the painful sensations experienced with hunger or thirst or the bittersweet sensations of lust. None of these are directed towards an intentional object. For this reason they are insusceptible of modification through education. Emotions are educable because they are intentional.

To go back to the the man with the knife. On the earlier account given of this, when the child feels afraid of him, the man causes in him a physiological-cum-mental chain of events which gives rise to a sensation – i.e. emotion – of fear. On this view, the emotion is describable without reference to the man. But if, as we now see, fear is not fear full stop but fear *of* something, the emotion the boy feels must refer to its object, i.e. the man with the knife. So it seems that the earlier account must be defective.

What might make it hard to see this at first is that in this case the man is both the *object* of the boy's fear and its *cause*. In other cases, cause and object come apart. Suppose I am at present filled with hope that soon I will be the outright winner of the National Lottery. The *object* of my hope is being the Lottery winner. But is this also its *cause*? Hardly. For my being a Lottery winner is an event that may well never happen and only an event which *has* happened can cause the feelings of hope I am now experiencing. Whatever the cause of my hope is, it cannot be a highly improbable future event. We should rather look to things like my ridiculously optimistic temperament or the seven black cats I saw on the way to the station.

Again, the fact that intentional objects do not necessarily exist in reality is relevant here. Just as I can be afraid of non-existent objects like evil spirits, so I can hope for (almost certainly) non-existent objects like winning the National Lottery or an afterlife in paradise. Other emotions follow the same pattern. I can feel guilty about a sin I never committed, be angry at an imaginary slight, love the God of Christianity.

Emotions and thoughts

How does all this bear on the education of the emotions? Chapter 1 argued that mental states directed towards intentional objects also bring with them the application of concepts. If a child is afraid of something, there must be some way he characterises this something to himself. He must be aware of it in a certain light, *as* something or other. In the example given, he is afraid of . . . a man with a knife. This is how he characterises the object to himself. There are many other ways in which the man might be described – as a bald man, a person wearing an anorak, a football fan . . . . But these are not the ways in which the person who is afraid would describe the object of his fear. It is significant that the boy sees him as a man *with a knife*. Why is this?

Fear, like other emotions, brings with it characteristic *thoughts* about the object towards which it is directed. Being afraid of the man with the knife brings with it the thought that he might do the boy an injury. If a child is afraid of a teacher, she sees him as someone who might harm her in some way – by ridiculing her, for instance. Generalising, fear of X involves thinking of X as likely to *cause one harm*.

What about other emotions? I was discussing hope just now. If we hope for something, what thoughts must we have about it? If an examinee hopes to pass in French, he obviously thinks this would be *a good thing for him*. More fully and more generally, when someone hopes for X, they see X as something desirable from their point of view, and as something that may – but may not – happen in the future.

In the same way, feeling angry about something (your brother's spilling juice on your comic, not being able to go out and play) is among other things to see it as in some way *frustrating*. Children feel proud about things they see as *their own achievement* (the collage they've brought home from school, not crying when pricked by a thorn) or the achievement of someone or something with whom or which they have an intimate connexion (the new family people-mover, Manchester United). When they experience guilt, they think that *they have done something wrong*, or perhaps sinful: they have overstepped a moral mark. Shame is different. In feeling ashamed of what they have done, they think of themselves as *having fallen below some personal or communally expected standard*.

There is perhaps no need to spell out the thoughts similarly associated with sympathy, pity, contempt, love, sadness, joy, and other emotions. Once the principle is clear, these are not too difficult to work out.

What differentiates one emotion from another is its characteristic thought. There are, of course, other ways in which emotions are unlike each other. Compare fear and anger. These are associated, in their more extreme form, with very different bodily feelings – with shivering or butterflies in the stomach in the one case and with hot, 'boiling over', sensations in the other. Arising from this, the way fear and anger manifest themselves in children's facial expression, bodily stance and behaviour are also different. On the one hand, looking pale, shrinking away, running from danger; on the other, looking red, frowning, hunching forwards, striking back. At the physiological level there are also detectable differences between some emotions, including these two, in chemical secretions.

But all these modes of differentiation – bodily feeling, expression, behaviour, physiological events – are too gross to be reliable across the board. Some emotional states are not intense enough to bring with them discernible physical sensations. Imagine hoping in a mild way that the weather will be better next week, but not pinning too much on it. Not all emotions are revealed in outward expression or action: we can keep our shame or joy to ourselves. Physiology does not begin to tell the difference between contempt and disgust, or between pity and sympathy.

Thought is the key to identifying an emotion. The closer emotions are to each other, the more evident this becomes. What distinguishes anger from indignation? On all the other indices just mentioned there is nothing to choose between them. In both, people tend to look the same, act in the same way and have similar sensations. Yet the angry person is not necessarily the indignant person. If going home on a crowded tube train someone treads on a pupil's foot, she may well feel angry, but scarcely indignant. Indignation goes beyond the frustration of our purposes. It carries, too, a certain *moral* charge. A secondary school student feels indignant with his teacher because she has, in his eyes, falsely accused him of causing trouble. He sees her as having *wronged* him.

Emotions can be classified in different ways according to the thoughts that enter into them. There are moral emotions, whose thought includes some moral concept, and non-moral emotions, where this is not so. Guilt as well as indignation is a moral emotion. It has to do with what is considered *wrong*. Unlike indignation, though, guilt brings with it the thought that one has done something wrong *oneself*. Non-moral emotions include fear, hope, grief, and pride. These do not necessarily refer to what is morally wrong.

Time also divides emotions. Some are directed towards the past. To feel anger is to see someone or something as *having* frustrated us, just as we feel guilt about something we think we have done wrong. Hope, on the other hand, is future-directed. Other examples of past-oriented emotions are shame, embarrassment and grief, and of future-oriented ones, fear and anxiety. Not all emotions are as clear-cut as these. Joy or delight can be directed towards the present – in listening to an album – as well as towards the past – in hearing some good news. Pride always looks back to past achievement. But not only the past. A student may feel pride in her moral uprightness, which she sees as a trait she has possessed and will continue to possess. Feelings of revenge carry with them thoughts about what we *will* or might do because of an event that *has* already happened.

Some emotions carry an essential reference to oneself. If a child feels guilty, he must believe that *he* has done something wrong. If proud, that *he* (or *those closely connected with him*) has or have done something good. Shame, embarrassment and remorse also fall into this category of self-referring emotions – unlike, say, disgust. Someone may feel disgust at their own unsavoury action, but equally they may feel it about someone else's.

The thoughts associated with emotions divide without remainder into the pleasurable, where a state of affairs is seen as good or desirable, and the distressing, where we think of it as bad. Love, joy, hope, pride are on the one side; anger, pity, grief, fear, anxiety, shame, contempt, on the other. A pair of emotions can be divided in this way even though they each share part of the same thought. *Schadenfreude* and sympathy each bring with them the thought that someone is in distress, but while the sympathetic person thinks of this as undesirable, *schadenfreude* makes one revel in it.

Can magpies feel shame?

Emotions are not confined to our species. Other animals, too, can feel at least some of them. Fear is innately built into cats, rabbits, vicuña and other species. This is not surprising given the biological advantages of mechanisms to deal with impending danger. There need be no problem here about the connexion suggested between emotion and thought. If certain animals are capable of sign-cognition, as suggested in Chapter 2, they may be capable of seeing a predator as likely to harm them.

At the same time, fear in other animals cannot carry the richness of connotation that we find in human lives. Non-humans' conception of their future must be minimal, confined to the immediate future at most. Unlike other animals, we can be afraid of things – perhaps death itself – that may happen in years to come. Equally, our notion of danger is far more sophisticated than theirs. We can be afraid not only of physical damage but also of psychological, each of these categories being capable of innumerable subdivisions. In addition, we relate particular types of damage to wider pictures of our well-being.

Our emotional life is rooted, genetically, in our nature shared with other animals; but it far transcends this. Whole classes of emotion are inapplicable to non-humans because non-humans lack the concepts on which the characteristic thought depends. If we assume greyhounds and magpies have no conception of themselves, they cannot feel self-referring emotions like shame or pride. Without the concept of others they are cut off from love, contempt, sympathy; without the idea of morality, from guilt or indignation.

Occurrent and continuant emotion

On a particular occasion a child may glow with pride at something he sees himself as having achieved – such as a prize in a school painting competition. Here the emotion he feels is a present experience. But his pride may be longer-lasting, not in the sense that the glow goes on for hours rather than minutes, but in that he is still proud of his achievements, his looks or his character, even when not currently experiencing any such feeling. He is *a proud person* – at all times, even when asleep.

We can make a similar distinction with other emotions – between the mugger's victim who feels afraid when attacked and the person constantly fearful of being mugged, between feeling contempt towards someone for something they have just said, and holding them in contempt over many years.

All this brings us back to the distinction made in Chapter 1, between occurrent and continuant mental phenomena. It applies to the emotions, too – to emotional experiences on the one hand, and dispositions to love or hate, be joyful, sympathetic or morose on the other.

The distinction is also relevant to the type of thought connected with emotion. A child's constant fear of being attacked may incorporate the continuing *belief* that he may be threatened by men with weapons, even though he is not always calling this consciously to mind. When he actually sees a man with a knife, his (occurrent) fear brings with it the (equally occurrent) *judgement* that this person is a threat to him. Of course, if he judges in this way, he must also *believe* that he is a threat. Judgements depend on beliefs; but we may have beliefs even though not at the time making any judgements.

Emotion, sensation, desire, action

Emotion cannot consist *just* in thought. If it did, it would be a purely cerebral phenomenon – which it plainly is not. Feeling remorse is not equatable with judging in a dispassionate way that we have done something morally wrong. It also stirs us up, makes us go hot or feel stabs of anguish. Emotions are typically accompanied by bodily sensations.

Typically, though not invariably. A *slight* feeling of remorse may still pull us down, but otherwise we feel no stabs. At the margin, some emotions may be so free of bodily sensation as to be virtually mere thoughts.

Bodily sensations *happen* to us: we are passive vis-à-vis them. Some writers, with such sensations in mind, urge that emotions are *wholly* passive things. But is this so? Many, if not all, are associated with action and desire. Children (and non-human animals) who are afraid of something often want to *run away* from it or otherwise try to avoid it. If they are angry, they may want to *strike back* ; if feeling sympathy, to *comfort and support*. One indication of the link between emotion and action is the fact that emotions can also be motives. Children can act out of fear, revenge, gratitude, love, hatred – just as they can act out of non-emotions like hunger and thirst (see Chapter 8).

Not every case of feeling emotion brings with it either a desire – to do something in response – or an action itself. Actions can be inhibited. A soldier on the field of battle may be petrified with fear but stand his ground. In this case, he may still *want* to run away yet manages to control this. In other cases even the desire to do something may be absent – in a state of grief so intense, for instance, as to be completely overwhelming.

Emotional learning

One thing should be plain from the preceding discussion. The idea that the emotions are ineducable is a nonsense. Only if they were assimilated to sensations would this be credible, since sensations – pains, or glows of physical good health – cannot be modified by learning and teaching. The most that parents and teachers could do about pupils' emotional lives would be to help them control bodily manifestations in action or in facial or other expression. Students could be trained to stand their ground in situations where fear sensations cause a tendency to flee from danger. They could be trained not to show the sensations of contempt or anger they feel inside.

But we have seen that although emotions typically *incorporate* sensations, they are not reducible to them. Emotions involve thoughts about their objects. That is the main reason why the education of the emotions is a possibility. Thoughts – whether occurrent like judgements or continuant like beliefs – can be changed through learning and teaching. I will say more about this in a moment. But remember that emotion includes more than thought. At its core it is also connected with sensation, bodily expression, desire and action.

Although there is nothing that educators can do about sensations, these other things do fall within their remit. Facial and other signs of sadness or joy can be inhibited, allowed to be manifested, or simulated when the emotion itself is absent. So can actions. Expressions, actions and desires can be subtly shaped as part of character education.

Thoughts as the key

To begin, then, with what education can do about thought. Imagine a very young child who is afraid of the dark. She sees darkness, perhaps the darkness of her bedroom, as in some way threatening. She carries the belief about with her – even when not consciously thinking about it. When she goes to bed, the belief is activated into all-too-present particular trains of thought or judgements – that something may be moving behind the curtain, that the blackness is filled with hundreds of evil goblins.

Emotion, as I said earlier, is an intentional phenomenon. It is directed towards an object. This, being an intentional object, *may or may not* exist. What is the object in the present case? To say the child is afraid of the dark is shorthand for saying that she is afraid of the dark *as she understands it*, that is, as a space filled with invisible beings who may do her harm. This fuller specification of the object introduces the thought relevant to her fear – the belief, sometimes crystallising into a judgement, that there are invisible spirits lurking there that could spell danger.

The object of her fear does not exist. There is no such thing as goblin-filled darkness. Put another way, the belief she has that there is such a thing is just false. What the parent-educator will do is bring her to see this, change her perception of the situation so that her thought comes to match reality.

In one way, this aspect of the education of the emotions resembles the replacement of false or unfounded beliefs a child may have about the natural world, mathematics or human affairs by beliefs that are more adequate in being true and well-grounded in evidence. Educational theorists with no time for anything but the teaching of facts put emotional development beyond the educational pale. Dickens's Thomas Gradgrind, for instance, had no time for it. But the fear of darkness case shows how crude such thinking is. For it shows that it is towards Fact above all that the educator of the emotions steers the child.

How she does this is another matter. It may be enough simply to reassure the child that there is nothing there, that darkness is just darkness. Or changing the perception may take time. The girl may half-realise that what her mother tells her is true, but her habit of dwelling, petrified, on what might be happening may be difficult to erode. But however the learning comes about, it will be a matter of replacing illusion with reality.

One aspect, then, of the education of the emotions is helping to remove the feelings that children have towards certain objects by ridding them of the false or unfounded beliefs on which they rest. Anti-racist education sometimes takes this form – where, for instance, the hatred or contempt that some children pick up towards other groups is based on untrue beliefs about their lack of intelligence, criminal tendencies, or greed.

Unlike eroding fear of the dark, this can often be a task for teachers rather than parents. As children grow older and used to the idea that beliefs should not be uncritically accepted, they become better able to pay explicit attention to the beliefs embedded in emotional attitudes and to check out their credentials, e.g. through class discussion. They will thus be less likely to be led astray in their personal life or, on the civic dimension, emotionally swayed by politicians, demagogues and admen.

But how far will this take them?

They may or may not become better able than Othello to check their jealousies for unfoundedness. They may be equipped to see through rabble-rousing adorations and hatreds. But the emotional manipulation they are more likely to face on a day-to-day basis will be more subtle.

Consider the appeal to *envy* that so many TV commercials and newspaper advertisements make. If I wish I possessed the social ease, the wealth and the lovely companion of the man in the Peugeot ad, there is nothing – so far – false or unsupported about the underlying belief that it would be good for me if I had these things. It is not irrational in that sense.

Of course, the admen also suggest that if, like him, I bought a Peugeot, I would be in the same league as him as far as his other advantages go. *This* almost certainly false belief certainly needs challenging, but it does not have the same relationship to envying the man as the false belief that darkness is alive with goblins has to fear of the dark. It is a belief about what is instrumentally effective to possessing wealth and women. Schools can and do help students to unpick and evaluate beliefs of this instrumental sort as well as false beliefs about the objects of emotions.

Here, then are some of the complexities involved in educating the emotions. In this respect, before leaving the Peugeot example, a further comment on its appeal to envy. Envying the man with the car is, as we have seen, not a patently *irrational* emotion. It is unlike fear of the dark in that way. And yet, we may want to say, there is something about envy of this sort that makes it at least open to question. For what is at issue here is the underlying picture of a flourishing, or successful, life that accompanies it – the suggestion that success depends on money and attractiveness.

What this is pointing to is that emotions are assessable not only in terms of their truth or well-foundedness, but also ethically, in terms of the worthwhileness of the values which they embody. This, too, is an aspect of their place in education.

This section has concentrated so far on what educators can do about the thoughts – both beliefs and judgements – that enter into emotions, on how they can help children to question and revise them when they go adrift. But the education of the emotions goes wider than this. It is concerned with the formation of boys and girls as persons of a certain sort, not only with their capacities as reasoners, important though this is.

Expression, desires, actions, virtues

Emotions include, but transcend, thought. They typically also incorporate desires. Because they do so, emotions can be motives for action. Feeling anger, for instance, often brings with it the desire to retaliate; sexual love, wanting to be with the beloved.

Emotions also involve expression. Sadness typically goes with an unsmiling face, downturned mouth, slowness of movement, shame with blushing or hiding our head. We may feel these things without showing them, but it could not always be like that.

In emotional education parents and teachers can help to shape children's desires, actions and expressions. Although all these have biological roots, they are massively dependent on cultural norms. In any kind of upbringing biologically implanted desires – to run away in fear, to strike back in anger – are always strictly regulated. Children are taught to withstand many of the fears they feel and not always to give in to them. The particular forms this may take will vary from culture to culture, but every culture will have its way of building up appropriate dispositions in children to have or not have certain desires and to act or not act in different situations. In time the reactions they learn become extremely sensitive to specific circumstances.

In British, and more broadly Western, culture children are brought up not to run away from frogs or beetles, the dark, or men with beards, because these things are not in themselves fearworthy. They are taught not even to *feel* fear towards such things and so not to want to avoid them. Bees near their hive, dogs off the leash, buses and cars, cruel acquaintances – these are quite other matters. Children have to learn that it is perfectly appropriate to be afraid of such things and to keep out of their way. *How* to do this varies from case to case. Bees are often a threat – unless one is trained and equipped to handle them. Buses and cars are not usually dangerous if we take care when crossing roads. Dogs off leads are likely to be less fearsome if they are your pets rather than unknown to you, spaniels rather than Rottweilers, old rather than young.

The fine-tuning is greater than this, of course. I am not suggesting that children learn clear-cut rules about what to want and what action to take in all these areas. Their learning is more responsive to differences in circumstances. With respect to our physical fears, we all learn from an early age what to feel, desire and do, on what occasions and in what ways.

This said, young children do need definite directions about what to do and think. 'Face your fears, Carl!' says a mother to her seven-year-old, upset by a spider on the blackberry bush from which he is picking. What is he to do? *How* does he face his fears? What does the injunction mean?

Could it mean 'Although you're afraid of spiders, overcome this fear by not backing away, standing your ground, even picking the spider off the bush!' There would be something stiff-upper-lippish and English about this – and it does not seem very good advice. If, unlike tarantulas, the spiders children find on blackberry bushes are not harmful, it would seem more sensible to bring this home to them. Only some fears have to be faced in the tough-minded, front-line way suggested. Others, like those to do with spiders, have to be *evaporated*.

Our fears are not only to do with possible *physical* damage. We can also be afraid of what we might say, of what others think of us, of hurting someone's feelings. We need to learn here, too, how appropriately to behave in different contexts.

The education of the emotions overlaps character education, or education in the virtues. Virtues are desirable qualities of character that are sensitive to different situations in the way just described. Examples are fairness, generosity, benevolence, kindness, judiciousness, self-confidence.

Some virtues – like courage, for instance – regulate the way we feel and handle our emotions – our fears and despairs in this case.

Others regulate not our *emotions* but our *bodily desires*. The most general name for this last group is 'temperance', the virtue that helps us to manage our innately-based desires for food, drink and sex. Acquiring temperance in relation to food is, again, learning what is appropriate to eat, on what occasions, in what quantities, at what times.

Temperance apart, most virtues help us to manage our *emotional* life. Courageous people are those who keep their physical or non-physical fears in proper bounds. Good-temperedness regulates our anger, guiding us to where and when it is appropriate to feel or act on it. We all also need to possess a similarly sensitive management of our sympathies, sorrows, delights, revilings.

In what directions our emotional lives should be shaped in this way is an ethical matter largely outside the scope of this book. Once again, this would lead to a discussion of what the aims of education should be and away from the main topic.

I have not said much so far about the education of expression. Situation-responsiveness comes in again. Sometimes – perhaps in the family – it is perfectly acceptable, indeed the expected thing, to show our sadness about a friend's misfortune. In other contexts it may be inappropriate to do so. All this has to be learnt. In the same way, the appropriate *degree* of sadness as registered on our face and in our posture has to be assimilated – not in any formal, rule-impregnated way, but insensibly and by example, as part of our everyday experience of life.

A further ingredient is learning to express emotions that we do *not feel* in situations where this is fitting – in jokes, games, giving accounts of incidents, story-telling. It is also the core of education in drama.

I have dealt with several aspects of educating the emotions: thoughts, desires/action and expression. In any actual upbringing these all interact with each other in complex ways. What holds them together is that they are all part of coming to acquire certain desirable qualities of character. Depending partly on culture, these qualities could include such things as a sense of honour (which builds on shame); various forms of altruistic concern from sexual love, intimacy and friendship to civic sympathy and respect for future generations; a measured optimism; sweet-temperedness; the appropriate handling of grief. Such emotion-related dispositions are *themselves* not isolable phenomena, but are complicatedly interrelated. What binds them together is their participation in a person's (ideal) character taken as a whole.

Understanding emotions

I have looked at different aspects of educating the emotions, but there are more to come. Understanding others' feelings, for instance. Children have to come to know when people are sad, feeling low in self-esteem, ecstatically happy, nostalgic or aggrieved.

How do they do this?

At first they have to go by the emotion language that others use in the context of people's behaviour – the looks on their faces, the things they do. They also have to learn to pay attention to the situation people are in and what they can know of their values – the insult just hurled that gives rise to indignation, Lottery numbers having come up leading to uncontrollable joy.

Once children can anchor their understanding of others' emotions in first-hand experience in this way, they are in a position to extend and refine it imaginatively via conversation and literature.

They also need to learn about – and from – their *own* emotions. They initially recognise what they are feeling via interaction with others. Their parents, seeing their situation and reactions to it, tell them there is no need to be afraid or ask them what is making them sad. This helps young children to grasp the meaning of emotion concepts and learn to apply them in similar circumstances.

As they grow older, emotions present them with a key to *self-knowledge*. This is possible because of connexions between what they feel and what they value. Reflecting on the pity they tend to feel towards people in all sorts of desperate circumstances – as seen in television news programmes – can give young people insight into their own self-satisfaction at being lucky enough to live in comfort and relative affluence.

Feeling surprised by the pleasure they feel when someone they know gets into trouble may make them realise there are darker values in themselves, which they are normally reluctant to admit. (In this example, what triggers off the new self-knowledge is a double emotion: *schadenfreude*, and the feeling of surprise at being affected by this. The example also reveals a further complexity in the world of the emotions – that emotions can take as objects other emotions. I can be proud of the compassion I have shown someone or ashamed of feeling slighted.)

Being surprised by our emotions happens when we are not aware, or not fully aware, that we have them. Emotions can be to different degrees unconscious. This is especially true of negative emotions, particularly those which it might be thought morally wrong to possess. In extremer cases, we might take steps – of a kind that interested Freud – to repress, that is, try to forget, our bitter hatred of, say, our father. Values in which young people have been brought up can steer them, unknown to themselves, towards envy of those more fortunate than themselves. It is not surprising that there are aspects of our character of which we are unaware, or only partially aware. Others' reactions to us can often help us to become conscious of these. So can our own reflections on our emotional responses and associated thoughts.

Because of their connexion with values, *all* our emotions may play a part in self-understanding in the way described. (See Chapter 10.) Some of them, however, have a more *direct* role. These are the ones referred to earlier as the 'emotions of self-reference' – guilt, shame and pride. They are so called because the thoughts which identify them contain an essential reference to the agent. They are necessarily thoughts about ourselves, unlike the thoughts involved in sorrow, say, or joy. Reflection on occasions when they have felt ashamed can lead youngsters straight to the personal standards from which they have seen themselves as falling short.

Learning the language of emotions

Children also need an understanding of emotion concepts themselves. They have to come to know what grief, hope, resentment, sympathy and so on *are*. They are taught to use and learn to use the words which stand for these concepts in the context of their own and others' behaviour and expression, the situations in which emotion-talk is used, and their own experience of accompanying sensations.

Because we cannot have an emotion without being capable of the thought it brings with it, and because we cannot have this thought without some understanding of the concepts it employs, it follows that some children will be incapable of having or feeling certain emotions where they lack the appropriate conceptual equipment. A child who as yet knows nothing about morality is cut off from experiencing moral guilt or indignation. A child who has not yet acquired a concept of herself will not be able to feel ashamed or proud.

Not that concept-learning is an all-or-nothing matter. A very young child may have *something* of a concept of herself, and this may be enough, along with some grasp of the notion of achievement, to give her the first rudiments of feeling pride.

Mainly about love

This chapter has tried to present a picture of what emotions are and of how the education of the emotions might be conceived. Like the rest of the book, it has been schematic and analytical – very much a bare bones account. It needs to be fleshed out – and in several directions.

It is psychologists who take us from such generalities into the complexities of the emotional life in different individuals. Not only academic psychologists. Novelists, dramatists and biographers are psychologists, too. They can go further into the richness of it all than many professional psychologists, unfettered by the demands of scientific research methodology that constrain the latter.

The bare account that constitutes this chapter also needs supplementing when it comes to education. More has to be said about love. I am not thinking here mainly about sex education lessons – although the role of love in lessons on sexual relationships often needs more attention. I am thinking more broadly about the role of teachers and parents in developing *attachments* to whatever subject-matter is being learnt. In this way children come to love the science or physical education or history they are made to learn – to want to do more of it and, as they grow more expert in it, to care for the field in question and want it to prosper.

Love transcends school subjects. As well as love of science, there is love of the world that science helps us to understand. As well as love of landscape painting, there is love of landscape itself. Beyond absorption in novels and poems there is fascination by our human nature. Joy as an emotion is akin to love. One of the overarching aims of the new National Curriculum for England and Wales is that pupils come to enjoy and be committed to learning. But how seriously will this aim be taken, given the emotion-parched content of so much of this curriculum, so wedded to the acquisition of factual knowledge and skills?

There could be more flesh, too, on the role of the arts, especially literature, in *refining* pupils' feelings. They can help to take them beyond conventional reactions, challenge stereotypic emotions towards other groups and individual, penetrate subtleties of pride, love, envy as displayed in fictional characters. How far, though, is the influence of the arts on pupils' feelings wholly positive? Can novels, films, plays, paintings not *reinforce* shallow conventional attitudes and feelings as well as break them down?

Summary and key points

Are the fear, joy, rage, sympathy that children experience feelings in the way that their headaches and toothaches are feelings? If so, how could they then be educable?

Emotions are in fact different from sensations of pain in taking intentional objects (see Chapter 1). Kinds of emotion are differentiated from each other in that each brings with it a specific thought about its object. In the case of continuant emotions this is a belief (see Chapter 3), while occurrent feelings of anger, sadness, etc. embody (occurrent) judgements. The key role of thoughts makes possible various classifications of emotions – with regard to time, for instance, self-reference, and pleasure/distress. It also helps to explain how emotions can be ascribed to non-human animals. But emotions are not *just* thoughts, since they also typically involve sensations and are intimately connected with desire and action (see Chapter 8). The key to educating children's emotions is their intentionality and the thought embedded in them. Sometimes the thought is wanting – as in fear of ghosts, or racial hatred – and needs to be corrected. This can be either because it is untrue and/or because it is ethically questionable. More broadly, the education of the emotions is the shaping of character. This involves attending to other things than thought – to the control of emotional expression and the regulation of emotion in our conduct. Children also need induction into understanding their own and others' emotions. The former plays a major role in children's self-understanding (see Chapter 10). The chapter concludes with remarks on the nature of love and its place in education.

Further reading

On the emotions in general, see Kenny, A., (1989) *The Metaphysics of Mind* Oxford: Oxford University Press, ch. 4; Budd, M., (1985) *Music and the Emotions* London: Routledge and Kegan Paul, ch. 1; the entry on 'Emotion' in Guttenplan, S., (ed.) (1994) *A Companion to the Philosophy of Mind* Oxford: Blackwell. For a recent book-length discussion, see Goldie, P., (2000) *The Emotions* Oxford: Clarendon Press.

On self-referring emotions, see Taylor, G., (1985) *Pride, Shame and Guilt* Oxford: Oxford University Press; and on love, Fisher, M., (1990) *Personal Love* London: Duckworth.

The education of the emotions is discussed in essays all with this title by Peters, R.S., in Dearden, R.F., Hirst, P.H., and Peters, R.S., (1972) *Education and the Development of Reason* London: Routledge and Kegan Paul; White, J., (1984) in *Journal of Philosophy of Education*, Vol. 8, No. 2; and Warnock, M., in Cooper, D.E., (ed.) (1986) *Education, Values and Mind* London: Routledge and Kegan Paul. All three are included in Hirst, P.H. and White, P., (eds) (1998) *Philosophy of Education: Major Themes in the Analytic Tradition* (4 vols) London: Routledge, Vol. 2. See also Elliott, R., (1974) 'Education, love of one's subject and the love of truth', in *Proceedings of the Philosophy of Education Society of Great Britain*, Vol. 8, No. 1. Aristotle's *Nicomachean Ethics* has been enormously influential in general philosophy and in the philosophy of education since the mid-1980s. In it he discusses, among other things, the place of the emotions and their fine-tuning in the cultivation of the virtues. On the civic education of the virtues of hope, friendship and courage (which is related to the emotion of fear), see White, P., (1996) *Civic Virtues and Public Schooling* New York: Teachers College Press. On the role of literature and other arts in education in refining human feelings, see Hepburn, R.W., 'The arts in the education of feeling and emotion', in Dearden, R.F., Hirst, P.H. and Peters, R.S., (1972) *Education and the Development of Reason* London: Routledge and Kegan Paul. This is included in Hirst, P.H. and White, P.A., (eds) (1998) (see above), Vol. 4.

Chapter 10

The whole child

Tracking down the self

I have looked at *particular* aspects of mental life and their place in education – concepts, thinking, intelligence, imagination, motivation, emotion. These are interconnected in many ways. But what holds them together as parts of a whole? True, they are all *mental* phenomena. But this does not get us very far.

From a parent's or a teacher's point of view, this may be particularly unsatisfactory. What is missing is what is *so often* missing in educational arrangements and debates – reference to 'the whole child'. Just as a traditional, subject-based curriculum is built round History and Mathematics and Music and Science and PE and RE but can lose sight of the pupil as a whole, the same complaint of piecemealism can be made about this book.

It is time to put that right. But where to begin? How to characterise the holistic unit that keeps all the parts together? The mind? The soul? The self? The person? The whole child?

From a Cartesian perspective all these boil down to the same thing. The integrating factor is a non-material entity, a substantive mind or soul, harnessed to a material body during this life but – on the religious version of the theory – outlasting its death. It is within this substance that mental activity – that is, rational thinking – occurs. And it is this substance that is to be identified with the self or person, with the child as learner.

I have already looked at several problems with Descartes's account. Here is another. If there are supposed to be such things as substantive selves, what grounds do we have for their existence? According to Descartes, we each possess – or, more accurately, consist in – such an entity. But what happens when we look into ourselves for evidence that it is there? As Hume argued, we do not find it. All that introspection reveals is particular experiences – this snatch of thought about the World Cup, that olfactory image of a bacon sandwich, that shivery feeling or rush of anger. However diligently I search, I do not discover any *container* that holds all these things.

What then *is* the self? Does it evaporate, as Hume thought, into the succession of experiences themselves? Is what a child means by 'myself' nothing more than a colligation of experiences? When one probes at what educators mean by 'the whole child', does this reduce to a collection of specific mental items?

Surely not, I want to say. But if not, why not? What else is there for a self to be if it is not container or contained, neither framework nor filling?

One reason why people might be reluctant to follow Hume is that the particular experiences which, he claimed, are all there is to discover cannot be treated as independent entities. They are not self-subsistent. For when I review the contents of my mind (as we say), I do not light on thoughts, images, sensations and so on as though these had some autonomous existence of their own.

Take a particular feeling of pain – a stab of toothache in the left bottom jaw. I do not discover this as I discover a clump of kidney vetch on a Cornish cliff. It comes with owner attached in a way the clump does not. It is not just *any* stab of toothache I pick out. It could not be yours, for instance, or Jenghiz Khan's. It is mine. My thoughts, feelings, memories and so on come with my personal name-tag attached to them. What I reflect on is that *I* am filled with remorse, *I* have been thinking about my mother, *I* have been looking at the five-day weather forecast.

I began this chapter by searching for the unifying, integrative factor that holds together particular mental phenomena such as acts of thought, desires, sensations or images. Since these cannot occur self-subsistently, have we now found it in this 'I'?

But does this really get us any further? Moving, as we have done, from periphery to centre seems to have brought us back from Hume to Descartes. Have we not returned to his immaterial Ego?

Not necessarily. The point we have reached is that experiences are all experiences of *someone*. They are mine, yours, hers, somebody else's. The same is true not only of occurrent mental phenomena but also of continuants. My own beliefs, capacities and dispositions also figure as possible objects of my reflection. When I dwell on the lack of confidence I see in myself, it is, once again, not just anyone's but my own.

Whatever mental phenomenon we take, occurrent or continuant, if we possess it then it must always be possible for each one of us to reflect on the fact that we do so — in other words, it must always be possible for us to frame the thought 'I . . .', where the dots stand for the mental attribute in question: 'I want my rights', 'I think snooker is dead boring', 'I feel queasy'.

The point now reached is that mental phenomena require a *subject*. We refer to this subject in English by the word 'I', in other languages by words like 'je', 'ich', 'ego', 'ya', 'io'. Although Descartes's Ego is an entity, a mental substance, there is no reason to think there must be some *entity* to which the ordinary word 'I' refers. To do so would be to confuse subject with substance.

But can this be right? If I am not something, does this mean I am nothing?

There is surely something wrong with this line of thought. To myself I seem real enough. How can mere philosophical argument destroy this conviction, persuade me I am nothing more than a presupposition of the possibility of experience?

One reason I feel so sure I am more substantial than this is that as well as attributing thoughts, feelings and desires to myself, I can also ascribe weights, numbers of limbs, hairiness. I can think not only the thought 'I feel happy', but also 'I am eleven stone two', 'I have two legs', 'I am bald'.

If I can possess physical properties of these sorts, could I not just be *my body*? An apparent obstacle to this is that, as we have seen, *non*-physical phenomena can also be attributed to me. If I am a body, what sense does it make to say that a body, which is a non-mental thing, is capable of such mental phenomena as imagining, recalling, believing?

Whichever way we turn there are insuperable difficulties. Perhaps this is one reason why the topic of the self has always seemed so mysterious — not only to philosophers, but to all of us. The very words we use appear to point to intellectual abysses. Take the question I put above: 'could I not just be my body?' Talk of 'my body' suggests that the body in question is something which I possess. But if I possess it, must I not be something distinguishable from it, its owner? How, then, could I just *be* my body? For if I *am* my body, I can hardly also be what owns it.

Or take the expression 'myself'. When I say 'I see myself in the mirror', what is this self that is the object of my gaze? Is the self the same thing as the I that does the looking?

This is all very exasperating. No wonder people fight shy of philosophy. Why tangle with a so-called discipline that, far from helping you to order your thoughts, simply makes your head spin?

But we should not give up quite yet. Especially because, as I see it, a possible solution may be close at hand. Let us go back to the view that what we are is bodies. The problem on which this got stuck was that if we are indeed bodies, and so non-mental things, how can it be that non-mental things are capable of mental activity?

Materialists would find no difficulty with this. They hold that thinking, for instance, is reducible to, or otherwise identical with a series of events at the physiological level, and ultimately at the level of physical particles and processes, so they would be happy enough with the idea that thought can occur in bodies.

But suppose we are *not* materialists — perhaps for reasons mentioned in Chapter 1 and in the Appendix. Is it still possible to accept the thought that a body might think? This is a problem on the assumption that *mental phenomena cannot be ascribed to physical objects*. This is an assumption taken over from Descartes. Is it true?

Why should it be assumed that bodies are incapable of possessing mental properties? If we start, like Descartes, with a dualist metaphysics that divides all reality into the two mutually exclusive areas of the material and the mental, it is easy to see how we could conclude that bodies, which plainly have material characteristics, cannot also have mental ones.

Descartes lived before Darwin and Mendel. He also had his own religious reasons, which reflected the Christian culture in which he lived, for advocating the existence of purely mental substances. An age like our own, used to thinking of human life in evolutionary terms and freer from religious preconceptions, may be able to see things differently.

We know there are things which are *purely* material, in that a comprehensive account of their nature can be provided, in theory, by the physical sciences. Rocks, for instance, fire, thunderstorms, clouds. But what shall we say of biological organisms — plants and animals? Shall we assimilate them all to stones and sunshine as things that are wholly physical? Or are we dealing, at least with some of them, with a different kind of entity?

We know that plants and animals are teleological phenomena, in that, unlike stones, they develop from seeds towards mature end-states. This in itself may not make them anything over and above purely physical entities. But we also have good reason to think that in some —

fuzzy – area of the phylogenetic chain, organisms became not only teleological creatures, but also creatures capable of some or other forms of consciousness put to the service of teleological ends. At some unclear point in the evolutionary story, animal organisms began, perhaps, to feel pain when the living tissue of which they were composed was in mortal danger and avoiding action had to be taken; or began to see and hear things in their environment such as food or predators.

A natural way of putting this is that organisms which were not conscious, and whose nature is describable in theory in purely physical terms, evolved gradually into organisms capable first of rudimentary and later of more sophisticated forms of consciousness. These organisms into which they evolved were still physical entities, but they were no longer *merely* physical entities, but physical entities capable also of sensation, perception, desire. Given the gradual nature of these evolutionary changes, there is no room here for sharp metaphysical divisions between physical and non-physical things – such as the line Descartes drew between non-physical animals on the one hand and human beings as immortal souls on the other.

In stating all this, I am not claiming that this account of our evolutionary pre-history is *correct*. On the basis of what we now know, it seems to be roughly on the right lines. But that is not the main point. The main point is conceptual, not empirical. It is to show how sense may be attached to the notion of a physical thing that is not only physical but is also capable of possessing mental characteristics.

This clears the way for a wholly unmysterious notion of the self. What I am, what you are, what a child is, is basically a biological organism – a human being. Like some other animals, human beings are capable of various forms of consciousness. In animals of this sort, there is in one sense a subject of consciousness. The cat, Zeus, who both feels pain when bloodied by a rival and also hears you when you call his name, is the organism to whom both experiences belong. The whole of his mental life, like the whole mental life of each human being, is unified by its belonging to the same subject.

With rare exceptions, human beings become subjects in a richer sense than this. Not only do they feel the pain of lacerated skin, they become aware that they feel it. They become capable of the thought 'I am in pain'. The same is true of every other experience or type of continuant. Human beings can frame such thoughts as: 'I want to go to bed', 'I'm still upset by what she told me', 'I just think you're wrong'.

Human beings, in other words, are not only unifying subjects of experience, they know that they are. They know that it is they who not only dream and worry, but also hear and taste things, remember, conjecture, plan. Other animals may be capable of some of these things, but they lack the understanding that it is *they* to whom they are to be ascribed.

How is it that human beings transcend other animals in this way? Zeus *feels* pain, but, it is safe to say, he has no *concept* of pain. Human beings acquire this concept – generally via its more determinate forms like tummy-aches and hurting fingers – as they learn their native language. In the same way they learn to use the other mental concepts. By three or four years of age they generally have no difficulty in using expressions like 'wanting to', 'touching', 'dreaming', 'thinking about', 'sad' – both about their own experiences and about other people's.

As the last phrase indicates, at the same time as they acquire these mental concepts they learn to ascribe them to themselves and to others. We have seen that pains and perceptions do not exist as autonomous, self-standing phenomena, but only as the pains and perceptions of *someone*. The learning of the mental concepts must go hand in hand with learning the concepts of subjects of experience, the concepts I, you, she, etc.

Whether we say that non-human animals like cats and dogs have, or are, selves depends on how this term is taken. If we are using it to mean subjects of experience in the thin sense that brings with it no awareness that they are such, there seems to be no problem. For just the same reason, I would be relaxed if someone wanted to call such creatures 'persons'.

But the use of 'self' or 'person' more usually requires the additional element of self-awareness. It is normally only creatures able to ascribe mental attributes to themselves and others through using linguistic expressions like 'I don't want to go', or 'What do you think?' who are held to be persons. (We do not so often use the word 'self'.)

On this view, babies and very young children *learn* to become persons. Although refinements – becoming deeper, more many-sided, persons – may continue through the rest of their lives, a watershed is crossed when they become adept at handling simple expressions like the ones mentioned. New-born babies are not yet persons in *this* sense. They are potential persons, no doubt, and for this reason are treated with many of the same rights – not to be physically abused, for instance – that we ascribe to persons proper. In the thin, non-human animal, sense of 'person', babies clearly qualify – simply by virtue of the desires, pains and so on which they experience, but of which they as yet have no awareness.

The place of the self in education

Educational thinking has long been, and is still, dominated by the Cartesian concept of the self. Not that this should be attributed only to Descartes. Plato, too, held that we are essentially immortal souls whose characteristic activity is to engage in rational thinking about the nature of reality. But since this view was given its clearest expression and rationale by Descartes, I will use the term 'Cartesian' to label this wider flow of thought.

As we have seen in Chapters 1 and 6, the Cartesian conception of the self is etched into school arrangements today. The association with personal immortality has largely gone, except in some religious schools; but the idea that education is basically about the development of theoretical rationality structures school curricula across the world. The child's mind is often viewed as a receptacle to be filled with facts and theories, at worst an empty box into which all these are heaped, but in more enlightened institutions something more like a machine – a psychical dishwasher, perhaps, or a washing machine – into which facts and ideas are continually fed for the mind's internal engines of rationality to get to work on them. In this way they are connected together and transformed into more general structures.

The Platonic-Cartesian assumption that the highest exercises of mind are also the most abstract, the most removed from our embodied existence, is powerful. It is seen in the greater curricular prestige accorded to the physics over biology among the sciences, to natural science in general over history and literature, to mathematics as the subject in no circumstances to be dropped from the later stages of the compulsory curriculum, however meaningless its abstractions have by then become for some students.

The Cartesian conception, finally, informs the school's greater attachment to theoretical reasoning than practical – to engaging pupils in the pursuit of truth as distinct from helping them to live good lives.

What alternative account of the development of the self might replace Cartesianism? What follows is structured around three stages. I should emphasise that the phrase 'the development of the self' should be understood in its transitive rather than intransitive sense. Selves do not develop from seeds into mature specimens analogously to the growth of plants or animal bodies (see Chapter 4). It is parents and teachers who, at least in the early stages, do the developing. The changes they bring about in children are the product of teaching and learning. As children grow older there is increasing room for their being the agents of their own learning.

Stages

From birth to first-person personhood

I start with the new born child. She comes into the world with various capacities. She can feel painful and pleasurable sensations. She has certain desires – for food and drink, for instance. She has the capacity, as yet still dormant, to acquire conceptual capacities (see Chapter 5). She can hear, see and taste. She has, or soon will have, rudimentary emotional reactions – of fear and rage. She can move her limbs and other parts of her body.

Her parents shape these primitive abilities in such a way that – at the first of our stages – she grows into a little person. Building on her ability to see things as signs of other things (see Chapter 2), they encourage her understanding of and, soon, use of language. Once she can operate with 'I' and other personal pronouns and with an array of psychological terms, she attains the specifically human form of personhood already described. She will be acquiring at the same time a further range of concepts to do with features of the world around her, good behaviour, and other things.

She thus gradually becomes capable of her own point of view on the world and on the things, events, people within it. This comes with her ability to use mental concepts. For the most part, as we saw in Chapter 1, these include the notion of intentionality. In learning to use words such as 'see', 'afraid', 'wanting to . . .', 'dreaming', she learns to attach intentional objects to them. She can say things like 'I don't want to go to bed', 'I heard the doorbell'. She conceptualises these objects with what resources are so far available to her within her growing conceptual schemes. Sometimes her characterisations are defective and need to be corrected. She uses the wrong name for something, beliefs she has are misguided.

To a large extent her early upbringing is an initiation into ways of perceiving and thinking which bring her in closer touch with how things actually are, or at least are publicly agreed to be, as distinct from how she takes them to be. Depending on cultural background, some of this social consensus may – or may not – itself be challenged in due course, especially when formal education is added to that provided in the home. Traditional beliefs about the world are deepened by scientific understanding, stereotypes of other people replaced by more sensitive portrayals. The child gains an increasingly objective picture of how things are.

But this could not be the whole of her early education. It would be practically – and I think conceptually – impossible to regiment all her intentional states and experiences so that they tallied with public perceptions of reality, leaving no room for anything else. Take attitudes to food and drink. Children develop different preferences. Some adore parsnips, others hate them. Not all likes and dislikes are as acute as this but range towards these from the mildest predilections and aversions.

Or take the different visual perceptions children have of the same objects. The same alsatian will carry with it different associations for the child who has been brought up with dogs, the child from a pet-less home who was once attacked by a dog, or the child who has just read Andersen's *The Tinder Box*. How we see the world is partly a function of our previous experience. The only way in which subjective differences of perspective could be eliminated would be by making everyone's background experience identical. But children live in different places, vary in age, position in family, religious and cultural background. Subjectivity of viewpoint is ineradicable.

Who, indeed, would ever want to eradicate it? Only an ideologised enthusiast for a wholly homogeneous society. For most of us in a liberal society the fact that human beings, unlike other animals, have and articulate different perceptions of the world, or different beliefs about the same subject matter, is a plus, not a minus. We value the different viewpoints that others bring, both intrinsically, and for their bearing on our own beliefs and judgements.

This lies behind the encouragement we also give in this connexion to children's imaginative powers. Differences of view can stem not only from the passive influence of past experience, but also from children's voluntary entertainings and seeings-as. Think of such things as their seeing a fishing cove as the haunt of smugglers, a toad as a prince transformed by a spell, clouds as a range of mountains. (See Chapter 7.)

Learning to become a person has thus both objective and subjective aspects. Children's thinking must to an extent be brought closer and closer to reality; but space must also exist for their own idiosyncratic responses.

Before moving on to the second of our stages, let me add something about the social nature of the self. Descartes's self, as we saw in

Chapter 2, is an a-social atom – certain of his own existence, but initially sceptical of the existence of other people. The new-born infant is a biological organism, as yet culturally untouched. By the end of stage one, however, when she is able to use mental concepts and concepts of herself and others, she has become inducted into the social world.

As we saw in Chapters 3 and 4, these and other concepts are public phenomena. They do not develop within her in some quasi-biological way as some psychologists and educationists would have us believe. On the contrary, she has to learn the publicly agreed rules and criteria that govern their sense and application, and submit to correction when she gets things wrong. It is because being a person – in the stage one sense – brings with it possession of basic conceptual schemes that sociality enters into its essence. In time the child comes to see herself as a member of a community all of whose participants, in sharing a language, have been brought up within the same basic conceptual structures.

Self-understanding

The second stage of learning to be a self, or person, is conceptually separate from the first, even though temporally they may well overlap. So far in our story, although the child can use the word 'I' correctly with psychological predicates such as 'want to . . .' or 'see . . .', her consciousness is directed outwards, on to the objects of her desires and perceptions. It is not yet reflexive, directed backwards onto herself. It is this reflexivity which identifies the second stage. The child becomes able – and her parents and teachers encourage her in this – to *think about* her actions, her perceptions, her imaginings, her beliefs.

How in detail this encouragement takes place is an empirical matter going beyond the present framework. But we know from everyday experience that *mistakes* can be a trigger. It is when a child has done something naughty – jumped off a wall with her shoelaces tied together, been horrid to a friend – that parents call her to account. They focus her attention on what she has done, getting her to see its wrongness. At other times it is not so much definite mistakes but as yet unjustified remarks that prompt a similar response. The child says she does not like her teacher, because he thinks she is stupid. 'Really?' replies her father. 'Why do you think so?'

The need to modify or justify her actions or beliefs helps the young learner to direct her attention to these. This in itself may or may not produce much by way of self-reflection, since although the action or belief is indeed her action or belief, she may put the weight of her attention not on the fact that it is hers, but on other features. She no longer behaves horridly to her friends, because she wants to do what is right as her parents see it. She thus changes her behaviour without much, if anything, in the way of the thought 'How awful of *me* to be a person who treats a friend like that!'

Even so, occasions like this can prepare the ground for such self-assessments as she grows older. In the way they handle such incidents, parents, too, can help to steer children in that direction. By causing them to be *ashamed* of what they have done, parents induce in them what we saw in Chapter 9 to be a *self-referring* emotion. The child's attention is directed to herself, to the gap between what she has just done and ideal standards to which she knows she should live up.

Reflection on beliefs, like reflection on actions, may or may not lead a child to self-reflection. Very often it does not – where the subject matter does not lend itself to this. 'Why do you say the tide has turned?' a child may be asked. 'Because that pile of seaweed . . .'. But thinking about our beliefs can also involve ourselves more personally. A child comes to be aware of his racist attitudes and is, again, ashamed. 'How could I have ever thought that . . . ?' Where thinking about our beliefs promotes self-reflection, the beliefs are typically associated with our conduct, values, desires or attitudes, rather than with more impersonal matters.

Self-reflection is not only about specific actions or beliefs. It is also more global, stretching from the present far back into our past and forward into the future. As the child grows older, and as she passes into adulthood, she acquires an ever-increasing number of recollections about her past life. These do not come back to her as an unorganised mass – although this is not to deny that the odd recollection can arrive unbidden. As we saw in Chapter 8, our actions are not atomic phenomena, but intimately intermeshed in patterns of means–ends relationships and describable in narrower and wider ways. These threads of interconnexion make possible this enduring and developing sense of self.

The child imposes her own structure on her past life. She puts what has happened to her within a chronological narrative. Like any narrative, the story she tells herself about herself is bound to be selective. Like them it must also have an inner coherence. Its parts must hang together in an intelligible way.

None of this is to say that it must be wholly true. We can and do embroider the facts so as to put ourselves in a good light, or sometimes merely for dramatic or humorous effect. We can and do leave out of our account events we would rather forget.

How far one of the aims of education should be to encourage people to be as objective as they can about their own past is a question – once again – belonging to the ethical rather than the psychological side of philosophy of education. For that reason I will not deal with it here. What I *do* want to underline, though, is the close connexion between memory and selfhood (in this second stage of its development). We take it wholly for granted that to be a human person we must have a picture of our past – objective or embroidered – on the lines described. This is why Alzheimer's is such a horrifying disease, since as the illness progresses and more memories are blotted out the patient comes to lose all sense of who they are. They are no longer persons in the full sense of that word.

If one is a self, one must be a rememberer. And a rememberer of a particular sort. Testees and examinees have to remember the dates of the Stuart kings, the chemical formula for ammonia, how to use a footbrake. One can be a self having forgotten such things. But one cannot be a self having forgotten everything about one's own life, whether these memories are of facts (or supposed facts) – such as remembering that I was brought up in a certain town – or of events (or supposed events) – such as remembering a look on a teacher's face. And although I have stressed that some of our memories may in fact be *mis*-rememberings, it is hard to imagine that they *all* may be.

Being a self also brings with it thoughts about the future – again, one's personal future. Since that future is bounded by our death, awareness of the latter must enter into the notion of selfhood. I cannot be a person in this third sense without being conscious of my own mortality. I think of my life as stretching out in front of me towards my death. Some people – life-planners – try to map out their future in as much detail as possible. Others are more laid back, take things as they come. But even the most laid back must have *some* goals which they seek to attain.

Part of bringing up young human beings to be persons is to make them aware of this temporal dimension of their existence, past and future. Just how this is to be done confronts us again with ethical questions about what educational aims in this area are desirable.

How far should we try to discourage people from going through life with fanciful episodes in their self-narrated stories about their past? If we insist on maximum veridicality, what reasons might we have? Would we be weighting things against embroiderers like Coleridge, or the less noted tale-spinners all of us know and whose liberties with the facts we – within reason – not only tolerate, but enjoy? Again, should we discourage people from trying to forget disturbing episodes in their lives, urge them to face up to them and learn to cope with them? Or can repression be sometimes beneficial?

With regard to the future, should we, as we often do in our career-minded culture, turn out our students as life-planners? That aside, what *kinds* of goals, if any, should we direct them to? To what extent should we equip them to choose their own goals?

These questions about personal futures have been well worked over in contemporary philosophical discussions of the aims of education. There has been less written about aims connected with the pupil's personal past.

All this connects with what was said in Chapter 9 on the education of the emotions. We saw there that emotions are time-related. Some of them, anger and pride and remorse for instance, look towards the past; others like hope and fear, towards the future. Given the time-relatedness of being a person, it would not be surprising to find the education of the emotions playing an especially intimate role in the overall development of the self. And so it does.

The events that fill out our past are not included in our self-narrative in a bloodless way. We remember them as coloured by the emotional attitudes we had towards them at the time – the shames we felt, the indignations, the feelings of abhorrence. We also remember our past feelings towards the future – anxieties about a career, hopes we had for a socialist new world. Reminding students of the emotion-impregnated nature of self-pictures – through literature or in their own experience – can help them towards a truer and richer self-understanding.

The emotions of self-reference – shame, pride, guilt, remorse – are all past-orientated. As we have seen, reflection on incidents in their lives which have provoked them can help students towards a clearer understanding of their values and hence towards deeper self-knowledge. Teachers and parents can also encourage them to become more attentive to their hopes, their fears, their unarticulated anxieties about the uncertainties of the future.

In this we can see, once again, how work on the education of the emotions cannot be conceived in an atomistic way, as developing just this or that perception, set of beliefs, attitude. In focussing on hope and despair, feelings of foreboding, existential anxieties, educators can help their pupils to throw light on their conception of their future – and thus, again, aid them in knowing themselves.

Joy is an emotion directed neither to past nor future, but to the present. Persons, being time-related in their essence, can also become absorbed in present experience. Whether they have to is another question. Of course, they *dwell* in the present, in that their imaginings, recollectings, feelings of pain and other occurrent experiences take place then. But their attention can be on their past or future. For many of us in our busy and radically uncertain world the future would preoccupy us entirely unless we took deliberate steps to stop it doing so.

There are ethical questions here about the good life. They are relevant to philosophical thought about educational aims – about what balance to strike between absorption in the present and preoccupation with the future or the past. For the reason spelt out in the Introduction, in this book I can do no more than raise these questions.

Human being

We have looked at two stages in the development of the self:

- The new-born child begins life, mentally speaking, as a centre of consciousness but without a conception of herself as such. This she acquires in learning language, including the use of 'I' and other personal pronouns in conjunction with words for mental phenomena.
- She uses 'I' at first unselfconsciously but this gives her the conceptual equipment necessary, at the second stage, to reflect on herself – on her actions, beliefs, emotions and also, more broadly, on her past and on her future.

There is yet another level of self-reflectiveness. This involves a more abstract, higher-order kind of thinking. So far, her thoughts have been about matters peculiar to her. At the higher-order stage, she thinks about what she is in a way that puts her on all fours with other people. Her topic now becomes the nature of human beings in general, she herself being only one instance of this. She can now share in that peculiar emotion familiar to most of us and springboard for so much deeper involvement in art and philosophy – the feeling of strangeness that human beings are the only part of the as yet known universe aware of their own existence and the existence of their world.

More generally, her reflection on human nature – in its multi-fariousness as well as its common features – will take different forms, drawing on everyday practices – conversation, not least – as well as academic study. Literature, history and psychology will furnish her with imagined exemplars of human variety for her contemplation. All these disciplines, and philosophy, too, will give her a clearer under-standing of what we all have in common – including, in the case of philosophy, the interconnected structure of mental concepts we have been examining in this book.

To what extent the ability to engage in this higher-order level of thought should be an educational aim for all pupils takes us back into the ethics of education. How far does focussing on what we all have in common link up with attachment to political equality, a value at the heart of education for democratic citizenship? Should the contemplation of what it is to be human be fostered as an intrinsically valuable aim? Should philosophical thinking about this be part of every older child's curriculum, or only for those inclined towards it?

Summary and key points

This last chapter turns from specific areas of the child's mind to the whole child. What is this unity in which these various phenomena are held together? What is the self?

We have already looked (in Chapter 1) at the Cartesian equation of the mind with the soul, with the self. For Hume the substantial self dissolves into a series of experiences – which is all we can discover when we search for our self through introspection. But these experiences are unified in that they are all *mine*: they belong to the same subject of experience. Can the child's self be identified, then, with the subject of his or her experience?

But children possess bodily characteristics, too, as well as mental. Is there a case for saying that selves or persons are basically physical entities, capable, like some other biological entities, of various experi-ences? Some non-human animals may be subjects of experience, but, lacking language, including personal pronouns and terms for mental phenomena that come with it, cannot be aware that they are. In this sense of personhood, which involves self-awareness, children have to *learn* to become persons.

As broached in Chapter 1, the problematic Cartesian concept of the self has deeply affected educational thinking. As an alternative to it, we can discern three stages in learning to become a person.

At birth human babies are, like some non-human animals, unifying subjects of experience. The first stage is reached when they begin to learn language and can operate with the word 'I' and other personal pronouns. This makes it possible for them to begin to have their own point of view on the world. As implied in Chapter 2, young persons at this stage cannot be the atomic entities of the Cartesian tradition, but must be social beings living in a social world.

A second stage is reached when children become reflectively aware of themselves as creatures with feelings, thoughts, desires, etc. They learn to see their past lives in terms of a narrative structure. Memory of their past is crucial here (see Chapter 3 on memory and Chapter 8 on the interconnectedness of actions). More generally, children become more aware of the temporal structure of their lives, of future possibilities as well as of their past. Their emotions – not least emotions of self-reference – can play a central role in developing their self-awareness (see Chapter 9).

The third stage of personhood is reached when young persons come to reflect on the nature of human beings in general, seeing themselves as one instance of this more general kind.

Further reading

A very readable short philosophical book on the self and the whole person is Glover, J., (1988) *I: the Philosophy and Psychology of Personal Identity* London: The Penguin Press. McGinn, C., (1982) *The Character of Mind* Oxford: Oxford University Press, ch. 6 and Kenny, A., (1989) *The Metaphysics of Mind* Oxford: Oxford University Press, ch. 6 are both about the notion of the self, as is the entry on this topic in Guttenplan, S., (ed.) (1994) *A Companion to the Philosophy of Mind* Oxford: Blackwell. For Descartes's notion of the self, see his *Meditations* 1, 2, 6. The reference in the text to Hume's inability to light on the self when he reviews the content of his mind comes from Hume, D., *Treatise of Human Nature* Book I, Part iv, Section vi. On the narrative structure of human lives, see MacIntyre, A., (1981) *After Virtue* London: Duckworth ch. 15. The role of emotions in self-understanding is discussed in Taylor, C., (1985) 'Self-interpreting animals' in his *Human Agency and Language: Philosophical Papers 1* Cambridge: Cambridge University Press. See also his 'The Concept of a Person' in the same volume. All the texts mentioned are in general philosophy. A relevant essay from the philosophy of education is Smith, R., (1983) 'The use of memory', *Journal of Philosophy of Education*, Vol. 17, No. 1. On ethical issues to do with the place of life-planning among aims of education, see White, J., (1997) *Education and the End of Work* London: Cassell, pp. 94–5.

Appendix: More about minds

How are minds related to bodies?

From the educator's point of view, the account given of the child's mind in Chapter 1 was perhaps all that was needed – at least in a brief book like this one. But I am more than aware that there are questions about the nature of mind that I did not raise there and about which you may have been expecting some discussion.

How is the mind related to the body? To the brain? Are minds identical with brains? Can minds be modelled in some way on computers?

These are important questions. They are central to philosophy of mind as a branch of general philosophy. Texts in this area typically go deep into these metaphysical underpinnings. So prominent, indeed, are they that most works are devoted to them *alone*, without, that is, including a discussion of specific mental phenomena such as emotion, imagination, other types of thinking, motivation or concept-possession. There are exceptions to this. Anthony Kenny's *The Metaphysics of Mind* (Kenny 1989) deliberately follows Gilbert Ryle's post-war classic *The Concept of Mind* (Ryle 1949) in providing a comprehensive review of all the major departments of the mind and their interconnexions. Colin McGinn's *The Character of Mind* (McGinn 1982) also moves from a general account of the mind into more specific topics such as perception, thought, action and the self, but is less all-inclusive than the other two texts, not dealing, for instance, with emotion or imagination.

Such exceptions apart, most recent philosophy of mind has been directed almost exclusively to fundamental questions about the relationship between the mental and the physical. The issues here are fascinating, mysterious, unresolved and perhaps unresolvable. This appendix will provide an introduction to them.

Yet despite or, more accurately, *because of* the fundamental nature of these issues, the discussion of them will be brief. This book is written for teachers and parents. Its aim is to provide them with a broad understanding of children's minds as background for their more practical concerns.

Lying behind this is a deeper level of philosophical enquiry to do with how the mental is related to the physical. It is more remote from educators' practical interests than the discussions in this book. Philosophical debates at this deeper level can seem less relevant, cut less ice. Whereas parents' and teachers' work can be sharply illuminated by, say, discussions of the nature of emotion, it is harder to see how it might be significantly affected by, say, the increasingly complex debates about the reducibility or irreducibility of the mental to the physical that have so preoccupied the leading scholars in the subject over the past half century. Perhaps the truth of this claim will become more apparent as we turn, as we do now, to some of the deeper issues.

Is there interaction between the mind and the body?

One approach to the mind–body problem lies in Descartes's theory, which has come our way briefly already in Chapter 1. This holds that minds and bodies are radically different kinds of substance, or entity, which causally interact. The interaction is two-way. It runs from body to mind in the case of sense-perception – when changes in the optic nerve, for instance, cause us to see things. It runs from mind to body when our deciding to write a letter causes neural transmission to our finger muscles. Descartes believes that this interaction takes place at the pineal gland in the brain.

If we give up the Cartesian notion of mind as non-physical substance, we can ignore the problem of how an entity without physical characteristics can be in a causal relationship with one which possesses them. But perhaps interactionism, in any case, is not necessarily between entities. We could ask how mental occurrences – such as seeing something or desiring something – are connected with states of the body. Could one answer to this question still be that they causally interact?

I have a bad tooth which gives me toothache. What causes my pain? The obvious answer is the rotten state of my tooth. Here we seem to have a pretty uncontroversial example of a one-way causal relationship, from body to mind. Can we complete the picture of two-way interaction, by identifying a mental cause of a physical event or state?

What about this? I decide to pick up a pencil and do indeed pick it up. Whatever the action of picking it up comprehensively consists in, it at least involves some kind of change at the physical level: my fingers move to grasp the pencil, muscles move in my arm, neurones fire. What causes these movements? Some can be traced causally back to others: micro-events at the neural level cause gross movements observable of the body. But what causes the micro-movements? An obvious answer seems to be my decision to pick up the pencil. It was this that set the chain of physical events in motion, culminating in my picking up the pencil. If it had not been for my decision, these movements would not have occurred. We seem to have found what we were looking for – a mental event causing physical events. More generally, we seem to have located an example of two-way interaction that has no dependence on a Cartesian entity theory of mind.

But have we? Can decisions really cause physical movements? One source of difficulty here is that the notion of causal agency with which we are most familiar is firmly attached to the physical. This is why, I suggest, we are happier with the idea of a bad tooth causing pain than with that of a decision causing changes in the neurones. How can a mere mental event such as a decision bring about changes in the physical world? We find it hard to conceptualise to ourselves how this could happen. Second, and in line with this objection, we take it for granted, when dealing with purely physical causation, that whenever one physical event or state A causes another B, event A must in its turn have been caused by some other physical event or state. The idea of some physical event or state happening without being traceable back to something else at the physical level that brought it about, is something we find hard to conceive. If so, what are we to say about the neural change the decision was supposed to bring about? What really caused it? Was it indeed something mental – the decision? Or, in line with the second objection, was it some other physical event or state? If it was the latter, what place is there still for mental causation?

Considerations like these have led some philosophers to adopt a one-way, rather than two-way, version of interactionism. According to this view, there is no mental causation of physical events, but there can be physical causes of mental events: bad teeth can cause toothache. The general name for one-way interactionism is epiphenomenalism. Its attraction is clear, given the difficulties over mental causation. When we have a toothache, something must have caused it: it is not an uncaused event. What else could this be but something happening in the tooth? The difficulty with epiphenomenalism, however, is that it leaves mentality simply as a by-product of the physical world and powerless to affect it. This is counter-intuitive. Think of the way human beings have transformed the world in recent industrial and post-industrial times, creating factories, cities, aeroplanes, space rockets and the rest. All this represents the action of mind on matter. How can our thoughts and decisions be mere by-products rather than causal agencies in their own right?

Are we anything more than physical entities?

We are going round in circles. Problems with two-way interactionism lead towards epiphenomenalism and vice-versa. Is there any alternative? One that has found favour with very many philosophers in recent decades is some form of physicalism or materialism. Basically this claims that only physical phenomena exist and that causal relationships can only occur between such phenomena.

How do physicalists deal with what we have been calling the realm of the mental?

In many different ways. Philosophical behaviourists have held that Descartes's conception of mental phenomena as events observable only to ourselves in a private, immaterial world will not do. Mentality is observable from without, by other people. They can see your intelligence, your wit, your depression in the actions you take, the things you say, your body language. Gilbert Ryle argues this, for instance, in his *The Concept of Mind*, especially Chapter 2. Although he is not unambiguously either a physicalist or a behaviourist, the attractiveness to him of a behaviourist alternative to Descartes is clear enough.

One difficulty – among others – with behaviourism has been its apparent inability to cope with passive phenomena, such as painful experiences. When I have a toothache, I may wince or hold my jaw. But although these publicly observable events may in some sense be expressions of my pain, they are not the pain itself. Sometimes, indeed, I may experience pains without manifesting them publicly in any way: I may, for instance, want to pretend that I am not in distress. Such experiences are not, it seems, redescribable in behavioural terms.

In the light of this, a second physicalist move has been to argue that, while experiences like pains certainly exist, they are in fact identical with brain processes such as firings of C-fibres in the neurones. What we have here are two alternative ways of describing the same happening. Given that the planet Venus can be called 'the Morning

Star' or 'the Evening Star' according to when it is seen, it is true that the Morning Star is (i.e. is identical with) the Evening Star. In the same way it is true that a particular feeling of pain is identical with a particular firing of C-fibres. On this view, often called 'central state materialism', mental discourse is otiose. There is no independent realm of mental states and events. Reality is wholly and only physical. Psychology is eliminable in favour of brain physiology. Minds are brains.

Identity theorists have found it difficult to rebut the objection that they have not properly taken on board what it feels like to be in pain. If pains and brain processes are in fact identical, then what is true of one is true of the other. If a brain process is wholly physical and has no characteristics which invoke consciousness, then this must be true, too, of my toothache. But to leave out of account the quality of my experience when my tooth aches, the sharp stabs of pain I suffer, is quite to misrepresent it. Consciousness, it seems, is not so easily eliminable.

A further problem with central state materialism is that in identifying mental phenomena with brain processes, it has no room for the possibility that mentality might exist in creatures structured differently from human beings and perhaps some other animals – creatures from another planet, for instance, who do not have brains but are equipped with some organ made of a metal unknown to us that functions broadly in the way that human brains do. Considerations like this tie in with what has been called the 'functionalist' account of the mind and its relation to matter. According to most functionalists, mental phenomena do not belong to a different order of reality from physical, but are to be understood as ways in which certain kinds of physical matter – for instance human bodies, Martian bodies, machines – function. Mental states are understood in terms of their place in a pattern of causal relations between input and output. Belief, for example. If I believe that it is raining, this state is brought about by, say, visual and tactile input to my brain. It leads in turn to the unfurling of my umbrella or my standing in a shop doorway. Given that it is this pattern of relationships which is important, it could in principle be replicated in other material than brains and human bodies.

A particularly influential form of functionalism has come into being with the computer revolution of recent years. If mind is to be under-stood in terms of input–output relationships not necessarily dependent on human brains and bodies, perhaps the way to conceive it is as 'software' that can belong to various sorts of computer hardware, brains included. Theories of 'artificial intelligence' have grown up on these lines. Just as human minds have been assimilated to computer software, so the notion that computers may themselves be capable of thought has become widely-canvassed.

How acceptable are functionalism in general and theories of artificial intelligence in particular? We saw with behaviourism and the identity theory that they do not capture the subjective feel of conscious mental phenomena, like the experience of pain. The same is true of functionalism. On this account, a pain such as toothache mediates between some damage to the 'hardware' on the input side and some reaction such as holding my jaw or seeking relief on the output side. But if pain is to be understood in terms of patterns of causal relationships in this way, the analysis seems to leave out something of ineliminable importance, namely the subjective experience of toothache, its peculiar feel. Functionalism gives an account of mind which appears to leave out its most central characteristic, consciousness.

The same is true, *a fortiori*, for the version of functionalism represented by artificial intelligence theory. We are invited to imagine what might go on in a computer – perhaps not those we know today, but more advanced machines of the future – between input (keyed-in instructions) and output (e.g. the product on the screen) as functionally equivalent to human thinking. But could it be like this? John Searle has produced a vivid refutation of the idea in his 'Chinese Room' argument (Searle 1992, p. 45).

Imagine a person in a room producing answers to questions posed in Chinese, say on a screen. She knows no Chinese herself but uses a manual of instructions indicating both the incoming symbols and the appropriate symbols she has to find that constitute the answer in each case. She is able to produce these answers without any understanding of what any of the Chinese symbols mean. In this she is operating like a computer producing output in response to input. Like herself, the computer mechanically follows its programmed instructions without any understanding of meanings.

What it lacks is the intentionality present in ordinary human responses to questions – assuming, that is, that the agent understands the meaning of the questions and of his or her replies. If asked 'What is the time?' the agent's thinking is directed onto this question and he or she understands the words in a certain way, that is, under certain concepts. In coming out with the answer 'Half-past four', the agent's consciousness is now directed onto a different object, producing a true answer to the question. None of this is applicable to the computer, which simply makes mechanical moves – with nothing in mind – according to the way it has been set up.

Searle's Chinese Room thought-experiment has itself not been criticism-free. One objection is as follows. The human being in the room is only a part of a larger system. She is not equivalent to a whole computer, only to a single component. Proponents of artificial intelligence do not claim that a transistor is capable of thought and understanding: these are ascribed to the system as a whole.

If we survey the various physicalist theories that have come to the fore in the last half-century – philosophical behaviourism, identity theory, functionalism, artificial intelligence – we can see them all as attempts to bring the mind within the ambit of physical science. Understanding how the mind works is, on this view, a matter of working from publicly observable data in the way that biologists and physicists do – rather than from the unobservable data of either a full-blooded Cartesian account or those accounts described earlier in this chapter emphasising intentionality and consciousness. More than this, since mental life on these accounts is effectively denuded of what would normally be taken to be the essential features of mentality, each of the projects mentioned can be seen as effectively ignoring the mental in favour of the physical.

In one of the more recent forms of physicalism, the attempt to by-pass the mental has been especially uncompromising. The suggestion is that the 'folk-psychological' terms we use in everyday life – 'belief', 'pain', 'thinking', 'trying', 'wanting', etc., used as they are with their usual implications of subjectivity, consciousness and (where appropriate) intentionality – fail to provide a reliable guide to reality and are best eliminated in favour of terms in a scientific psychology that do not carry these implications. The suggestion here is that it is likely that what we ordinarily take to be our mental states and experiences – deliberating, feeling grief, being in pain, wanting affection, etc. – simply do not exist: we have been misguided by language in thinking that they do.

The determination to bring mind under the laws of physical science has powered the main research programmes in philosophy of mind in the last few decades. Physicalism has now generated a large number of technical theories of increasing complexity. They should be distinguished – although they are often pursued together – from equally prolific work on the physiological bases of consciousness that has tried to identify those areas of human and non-human nervous systems causally responsible for mental phenomena. They should be distinguished, because those who hold that consciousness is something other than physical can also be interested in the physical causes of consciousness.

Although varieties of physicalism have dominated the field in the last half century, there have been many philosophers who have not accepted it. Among the most celebrated defences of an alternative position has been an essay by Thomas Nagel (1979) called 'What is it like to be a bat?' Nagel's topic is the feature of consciousness with which physicalist theories tend to have most trouble – its subjectivity. A bat senses the world differently from ourselves, by echo-location. This makes it difficult, perhaps impossible, for us to know what it is like, subjectively, for a bat to have such experiences. But although we perhaps can never know this – as distinct from imagining how *we* would be if inside a bat's body – it remains true that there is an aspect of being a creature capable of mental life – this subjective aspect – that physicalist ideas have not captured and perhaps can never capture.

John Searle of the Chinese Room argument is another philosopher who has stood out against the physicalist mainstream. In *The Rediscovery of Mind* (Searle 1992) and *Mind, Language and Society* (Searle 1999) he supports in more detail the claim that for all the attention physicalist theories have given to consciousness, they have not paid it its proper due (see Further reading below).

The debates continue. Whether they can in principle ever be settled is not clear. Will some new version of physicalism come up some day with conclusive evidence that the subjective point of view is illusory or that feeling a headache is identifiable with matter? Will supporters of the residual dualism that refuses to collapse the conscious into the non-conscious always be able to hold their own? Or should we believe that the mind–body problem is simply a mystery that will always remain so?

How much metaphysics do parents and teachers need?

I hope it has become clear why, in a book about philosophy of mind tailored to the interests of parents and teachers, I have relegated these debates about relations between the mental and the physical to an appendix. The reason lies in doubts about the educational relevance of these metaphysical discussions, intrinsically absorbing though they are. Whereas we can easily see how useful it may be to teachers and parents to gain a clearer understanding of what, after all, are the tools of their trade – the psychological concepts they use in their everyday work – it is not at all obvious what bearing the highly abstract and technical arguments for and against the still-burgeoning theories of mind might have on what they do.

Will controversies over current physicalist theories or their successors be shown one day to make a difference to practical matters of upbringing and schooling? Perhaps. But that day has not yet arrived. That is why I have included this present discussion in an appendix rather than in the main body of the text.

Summary and key points

The account of the mind in Chapter 1 has clear applications to the work of teachers and parents. There are also deeper issues about the mind and its relation to the body that tend to monopolise the attention of philosophers of mind, but whose relevance to education is less apparent. They are briefly sketched in this appendix.

Descartes' theory of two-way causal interaction between mind and body faces difficulties concerning the possibility of mental causation of physical events. Epiphenomenalism, as the one-way causation of mental events by physical, leaves the mental as a mere by-product of the physical. Dualist theories such as the two just mentioned have been opposed in the last half of the twentieth century by a variety of physicalist accounts of the mind. Philosophical behaviourism sees mental life as observable behaviour or in terms of dispositions to behave in an observable way. Problems in accounting for sensations like pains, which do not seem to fit a behavioural template, have generated physicalist theories of mind which identify pains with states of the brain.

The theoretical possibility of mental life in creatures without brains, differently constructed from human and other animals, has turned some philosophers' attention to functionalist theories, which see mental states in terms of causal relations between inputs and outputs, regardless of the kind of substance of which the system is composed. In one version of functionalism, artificial intelligence, minds are understood in terms of computer software as opposed to hardware, thus giving rise to questions about the possibility of thinking computers. There are many other recent variants of physicalism, including the view that folk-psychological terms are best eliminated in favour of the language of physical science. Although they have been dominant in the literature, physicalist theories have never lacked critics who have charged them with failing to pay proper regard to the subjectivity of experience.

To come back to educational matters. These controversies on relationships between the mental and the physical are both complex and deal with fundamental metaphysical issues. Their relevance to the work of parents and teachers is not at all clear.

Further reading

A brilliant, highly reliable cartoon survey of a range of recent positions on consciousness and its relation to the body is Papineau, D. and Selina, H., (2000) *Introducing Consciousness* Duxford: Icon Books. More conventional short treatments covering the same broad area are found in Scruton, R., (1994) *Modern Philosophy* London: Sinclair-Stevenson, ch. 16; McGinn C., (1982) *The Character of Mind* Oxford: Oxford University Press, ch. 2; as well as in the several entries on the mind and related topics in Honderich, T., (ed.) (1995) *The Oxford Companion to Philosophy* Oxford: Oxford University Press, pp. 569–580. A longer, book-length guided tour of the same topic is Heil, J., (1998) *Philosophy of Mind* London: Routledge. Guttenplan, S., (ed.) (1994) *A Companion to the Philosophy of Mind* Oxford: Blackwell contains a long introductory essay by the editor, relating the 'surface' features of the mind to 'the bedrock' underneath. Thomas Nagel's essay 'What is it like to be a bat? is included in his Nagel, T., (1979) *Mortal Questions* Cambridge: Cambridge University Press. John Searle is an admirably clear, readable author, accessible to the non-specialist. See Searle, J.R., (1984) *Minds, Brains and Science* London: British Broadcasting Corporation; Searle, J.R., (1992) *The Rediscovery of the Mind* Cambridge, Mass. MIT Press; Searle, J.R., (1999) *Mind, Language and Society* London: Phoenix.

Works referred to in the text

Clarke, F., (1923) *Essays in the Politics of Education* Oxford: Oxford University Press.

Descartes, R., (1641/1986) *Meditations on First Philosophy*, trans. John Cottingham, Cambridge: Cambridge University Press.

Donaldson, M., (1978) *Children's Minds* London: Fontana.

Goleman, D., (1996) *Emotional Intelligence: Why it Can Matter More Than IQ* London: Bloomsbury.

Herrnstein, R. and Murray, A., (1994) *The Bell Curve: Intelligence and Class Structure in American Life* London: Free Press.

Kenny, A., (1989) *The Metaphysics of Mind* Oxford: Oxford University Press.

McGinn, C., (1982) *The Character of Mind* Oxford: Oxford University Press.

MacIntyre, A.C., (1960) 'Purpose and intelligent action' *Proceedings of the Aristotelian Society* (Supplementary volume).

Nagel, T., (1979) 'The fragmentation of value' in his *Mortal Questions* Cambridge: Cambridge University Press.

Pinker, S., (1997) *How the Mind Works* London: Penguin.

Price, H.H., (1953) *Thinking and Experience* London: Hutchinson.

Ryle, G., (1949) *The Concept of Mind* London: Hutchinson.

Selleck, R.J.W., (1968) *The New Education: The English Background, 1870–1914* London: Pitman.

Service, R., (2000) *Lenin: a Biography* London: Macmillan.

White, J., (1998) *Do Howard Gardner's Multiple Intelligences Add Up?* London: Institute of Education.

Wiseman, S., (1967) (ed.) *Intelligence and Ability* Harmondsworth: Penguin Books.

Index